Kaplan Publishing are constantly finding new ways to make a difference to your studies and our exciting online resources really do offer something different to students looking for exam success.

This book comes with free MyKaplan online resources so that you can study anytime, anywhere

Having purchased this book, you have access to the following online study materials:

CONTENT	ACCA (including FFA,FAB,FMA)		AAT		FIA (excluding FFA,FAB,FMA)	
	Text	Kit	Text	Kit	Text	Kit
iPaper version of the book	✓	✓	✓	✓	✓	✓
Interactive electronic version of the book	✓					
Progress tests with instant answers	✓		✓			
Mock assessments online			✓	✓		
Material updates	✓	✓	✓	✓	✓	✓
Latest official ACCA exam questions		✓				
Extra question assistance using the signpost icon*		✓				
Timed questions with an online tutor debrief using the clock icon*		✓				
Interim assessment including questions and answers	✓					
Technical articles	✓	✓				

* Excludes F1, F2, F3, FFA, FAB, FMA

How to access your online resources

Kaplan Financial students will already have a MyKaplan account and these extra resources will be available to you online. You do not need to register again, as this process was completed when you enrolled. If you are having problems accessing online materials, please ask your course administrator.

If you are already a registered MyKaplan user go to www.MyKaplan.co.uk and log in. Select the 'add a book' feature and enter the ISBN number of this book and the unique pass key at the bottom of this card. Then click 'finished' or 'add another book'. You may add as many books as you have purchased from this screen.

If you purchased through Kaplan Flexible Learning or via the Kaplan Publishing website you will automatically receive an e-mail invitation to MyKaplan. Please register your details using this email to gain access to your content. If you do not receive the e-mail or book content, please contact Kaplan Flexible Learning.

If you are a new MyKaplan user register at www.MyKaplan.co.uk and click on the link contained in the email we sent you to activate your account. Then select the 'add a book' feature, enter the ISBN number of this book and the unique pass key at the bottom of this card. Then click 'finished' or 'add another book'.

Your Code and Information

This code can only be used once for the registration of one book online. This registration and your online content will expire when the final sittings for the examinations covered by this book have taken place. Please allow one hour from the time you submit your book details for us to process your request.

Please scratch the film to access your MyKaplan code.

Please be aware that this code is case-sensitive and you will need to include the dashes within the passcode, but not when entering the ISBN. For further technical support, please visit www.MyKaplan.co.uk

KAPLAN
PUBLISHING

ACCOUNTS PREPARATION

Qualifications and Credit Framework

AQ2013 Level 3 Diploma in Accounting

British Library Cataloguing-in-Publication Data

A catalogue record for this book is available from the British Library.

Published by
Kaplan Publishing UK
Unit 2, The Business Centre
Molly Millars Lane
Wokingham
Berkshire
RG41 2QZ

ISBN 978 0 85732 873 1

The text in this material and any others made available by any Kaplan Group company does not amount to advice on a particular matter and should not be taken as such. No reliance should be placed on the content as the basis for any investment or other decision or in connection with any advice given to third parties. Please consult your appropriate professional adviser as necessary. Kaplan Publishing Limited and all other Kaplan group companies expressly disclaim all liability to any person in respect of any losses or other claims, whether direct, indirect, incidental, consequential or otherwise arising in relation to the use of such materials.

Printed and bound in Great Britain

We are grateful to the Association of Accounting Technicians for permission to reproduce past assessment materials and example tasks based on the new syllabus. The solutions to past assessments and similar activities in the style of the new syllabus have been prepared by Kaplan Publishing.

CONTENTS

STUDY TEXT AND WORKBOOK

KAPLAN PUBLISHING

INTRODUCTION

HOW TO USE THESE MATERIALS

These Kaplan Publishing learning materials have been carefully designed to make your learning experience as easy as possible and to give you the best chance of success in your AAT assessments.

They contain a number of features to help you in the study process.

The sections on the Unit Guide, the Assessment and Study Skills should be read before you commence your studies.

They are designed to familiarise you with the nature and content of the assessment and to give you tips on how best to approach your studies.

STUDY TEXT

This study text has been specially prepared for the revised AAT qualification introduced in September 2013.

It is written in a practical and interactive style:

- key terms and concepts are clearly defined

- all topics are illustrated with practical examples with clearly worked solutions based on sample tasks provided by the AAT in the new examining style

- frequent activities throughout the chapters ensure that what you have learnt is regularly reinforced

- 'pitfalls' and 'examination tips' help you avoid commonly made mistakes and help you focus on what is required to perform well in your examination

- practice workbook activities can be completed at the end of each chapter.

WORKBOOK

The workbook comprises:

Practice activities at the end of each chapter with solutions at the end of the text, to reinforce the work covered in each chapter.

The questions are divided into their relevant chapters and students may either attempt these questions as they work through the textbook, or leave some or all of these until they have completed the textbook as a final revision of what they have studied

ICONS

The study chapters include the following icons throughout.

They are designed to assist you in your studies by identifying key definitions and the points at which you can test yourself on the knowledge gained.

 Definition

These sections explain important areas of Knowledge which must be understood and reproduced in an assessment

 Example

The illustrative examples can be used to help develop an understanding of topics before attempting the activity exercises

 Activity

These are exercises which give the opportunity to assess your understanding of all the assessment areas.

UNIT GUIDE

This is a Level 3 unit concerned with accounting principles and concepts, accounting for non-current assets and advanced bookkeeping to final adjusted trial balance stage.

It integrates with a number of other units in the qualification, all concerned with financial accounting. At Level 2, Processing Bookkeeping Transactions (PBKT) and Control Accounts, Journals and the Banking Systems (CJBS) introduce students to basic bookkeeping skills and the books of original entry. At Level 4, Financial Statements (FSTM) prepares students to produce financial statements for limited companies. The two Level 3 units, ACPR and Prepare Final Accounts for Sole Traders and Partnerships (FSTP) form a bridge between Level 2 basic bookkeeping and Level 4 higher level financial accounting skills. Together they cover the theoretical foundations of financial accounting, together with practical skills for the preparation of financial statements for unincorporated traders.

It is recommended that this unit is taken before FSTP. ACPR and FSTP are derived from the NOS FA-4, Prepare Accounts.

Purpose of the units

ACPR is the first of the two Level 3 financial accounting units. Covering accounting principles and concepts, accounting for non-current assets and advanced bookkeeping, it takes the student from Level 2 foundation knowledge and skills and prepares them for further development in FSTP where they will be preparing financial statements for sole traders and partnerships.

A business organisation employing a student who has been successful in these two units could expect to find a very useful member of the accounting team. Working with little supervision, this student could be expected to take bookkeeping to final trial balance and beyond, to prepare draft financial statements for unincorporated traders.

Terminology

Students should be familiar with IFRS terminology. Other terms are used in this document to match titles provided by the QCF.

Learning objectives

After completion of this unit, the student will have a good understanding of the accounting principles and concepts underlying all financial accounting. Having developed a fuller understanding of the accounting equation, they will understand the nature and importance of the different categories of account and how the books and records relate to each other.

This will enable students to perform more advanced bookkeeping functions such as accounting for non-current assets and accounting for adjustments and they will recognise the importance of reconciling control accounts. Finally they will use the extended trial balance to account for adjustments and extract a profit or loss figure for the period.

Learning outcomes and Assessment criteria

The unit consists of eight learning outcomes, which are further broken down into Assessment criteria for Knowledge and Skills. These are set out in the following table with Learning Outcomes in bold type and Assessment criteria listed underneath each Learning Outcome. Reference is also made to the relevant chapter within the text.

The unit consists of eight learning outcomes. The learner will:

1   Understand generally accepted accounting principles and concepts

2   Understand the principles of double entry bookkeeping

3   Understand the accounting methods used to record non-current assets

4   Account for the purchase of non-current assets

5   Account for depreciation

6   Account for the disposal of non-current assets

7   Account for adjustments

8   Prepare and extend the trial balance

There are a number of assessment criteria linked to each learning outcome. Those referenced K relate to knowledge and those referenced S relate to skills.

Knowledge and Skills

To perform this unit effectively you will need to be able to do the following.

Chapter

1 Understand generally accepted accounting principles and concepts

1.1K Explain the accounting principles of going concern, accruals, prudence and consistency   7

- Recognise the definitions of the underlying assumptions of the accrual basis and the going concern basis.

- Recognise when the accruals basis of accounting has been applied, for example, provision for depreciation charges, allowance for doubtful debts, accruals and prepayments, closing inventory.

- Recognise circumstances when a business is no longer a going concern and understand the effect this has on the value of its assets.

- Recognise the terms consistency and prudence; however prudence will not be explicitly tested as it is not encouraged in the IFRS Framework.

1.2K Explain the purpose of maintaining financial records for internal and external use   7

- Internal control.

- Measuring business performance.

- Obtaining credit/financing.

- Statutory requirements.

- Understand the importance of keeping financial records physically secure.

- Understand when it is appropriate to restrict access to financial records, and why

- Students should be aware of the content and purpose of a statement of profit or loss and a statement of financial position, although the requirement to prepare these statements is in the level 4 unit Financial Statements.

		Chapter
1.3K	Describe the type of accounting records that a business should maintain and the main uses of each	1,3,8

- Non-current assets register.

- Books of prime entry: day books, cash book and journal.

- General ledger accounts.

- Subsidiary ledger accounts: purchases and sales.

- Inventory records.

1.4K	Describe the main requirements of accounting standards (IFRS) in relation to inventory and non-current asset valuations	3,8

IAS 2: Inventories

- Understand that inventory must be valued at the lower of cost and net realisable value, on an item by item basis.

- Understand how to calculate net realisable value and apply this to given data.

- Recognise that unit cost, FIFO and weighted average cost are acceptable valuation methods but LIFO is not. Calculations of valuations on these bases will not be required.

- Understand what can be included in the cost of inventory:

- cost of purchase, including delivery

- cost of conversion including direct labour.

- Understand what cannot be included in the cost of inventory:

- storage costs of finished goods

- selling costs.

- Recognise the link with the accruals basis, that is, the cost of inventory is recognised in the statement of profit or loss when the goods are sold.

KAPLAN PUBLISHING

Chapter

IAS 16: Property, plant and equipment

- Recognise the term property, plant and equipment.

- Understand the terms useful life, residual value, depreciable amount, carrying amount.

- Recognise the need for depreciation charges and have a basic understanding of the purpose of depreciation (including a link with the accruals basis).

1.5K   Explain the accounting characteristics of relevance, reliability, comparability, ease of understanding and materiality   7

- Scope is based on the IFRS framework.

- Recognise that in order to be useful, financial information should have two fundamental characteristics:

- relevance – understand that materiality is an aspect of relevance specific to individual organisations

- faithful representation.

- Recognise that the following characteristics support relevance and faithful representation:

- comparability

- verifiability

- timeliness

- understandability.

- Students will need to recognise the terms and have a basic understanding of their meaning. Detailed explanation or application of the terms will not be expected.

Chapter

1.6K Explain the differences between capital and revenue expenditure, classifying items as one or the other

3

- Understand the importance of materiality in deciding to capitalise.

- Understand the relevance of the useful life of the purchase in deciding to capitalise.

- Understand the relevance of the accruals basis; how and why the capital expenditure is charged to the statement of profit or loss over time rather than at the time of purchase.

- Discriminate between capital expenditure and revenue expenditure in the context of the organisation in question by correctly applying the given capitalisation policy.

2 Understand the principles of double entry bookkeeping

2.1K Explain the accounting equation

1

- Recognise its importance in an effective double-entry bookkeeping system.

- Recognise and explain how elements of the equation are affected by a range of accounting transactions.

2.2K Define assets, liabilities and equity in an accounting context

1

- Equity will be referred to as capital in the context of sole traders and partnerships.

- Understand and apply the meanings of assets, liabilities and capital, including:

- non-current assets and current assets

- tangible and intangible assets

- current liabilities and non-current liabilities

- Basic understandings of what an intangible asset is and recognise goodwill as an intangible asset. (IAS 38 is beyond the scope of this unit).

Chapter

2.3K	Explain the purpose and use of books of prime entry and ledger accounts	1

- Day-books, cash book, journal, general (main, nominal) ledger accounts.

- Recognise the books of prime entry.

- Describe the type of information that is recorded in each of the various records.

- Understand how the accounting records relate to each other.

2.4K	Explain the purpose of reconciling the sales and purchases ledgers, and the cash book	10,11

- As external verification of correct bank balance.

- To find errors, including omissions.

- Understand that reconciliations may not show all errors.

3   Understand the accounting methods used to record non-current assets

3.1K	Describe how the acquisition of non-current assets can be funded, including part exchange	3

- Cash purchase (this includes standard commercial credit terms, for example, 30 days).

- Part exchange.

- Borrowing (loans, hire purchase, finance lease), but detailed knowledge of accounting treatment of these is not required.

- Identify the suitability of particular funding methods in the context of a given simple business situation.

Chapter

3.2K   Explain the accounting treatment for recording   3,5
the acquisition and disposal of non-current assets

- Understand how to calculate depreciation charges for non-current assets acquired or disposed of during an accounting period in accordance with the policies of the organisation.

- Understand how to use the disposal account.

3.3K   Explain the need for, and methods of, providing   4,5
for depreciation on non-current assets

- Understand the purpose of depreciation and the relevance of the accruals basis, that is, to allocate the depreciable amount over the asset's useful life.

- Understand how to choose an appropriate method of depreciation, that is, straight line or diminishing balance, according to the pattern of usage expected over the asset type's useful life.

- Understand how to choose an appropriate rate of depreciation, that is, the percentage or fraction, according the length of the asset type's expected useful life.

3.4K   Describe the contents and use of the non-current   3,4,5
asset register

- As internal control, to include verification of physical assets and/or general ledger accounts.

- Identify data types that would be appropriately included or not included in the register.

KAPLAN PUBLISHING

Chapter

3.5S	Resolve any queries, unusual features or discrepancies relating to the accounting records for non-current assets or refer to an appropriate person	4,5

- Understand that non-current asset register, non-current asset accounts and/or physical check may not correspond.

- Identify a reasonable explanation for any differences.

4 Account for the purchase of non-current assets

4.1S	Calculate total capital expenditure including all associated costs	3

- Identify directly attributable costs that can be included in the cost of capital expenditure when non-current assets are acquired, in accordance with the relevant accounting standards (IAS16).

- Identify revenue expenses that should not be included in the cost of capital expenditure when non-current assets are acquired.

4.2S	Record prior authority for the capital expenditure	3

- Understand why authorisation is necessary for an organisation.

- Identify the appropriate person to provide authorisation within a given organisation.

4.3S	Record in the appropriate accounts the acquisition of a non-current asset including funded by part exchange	3,5

Accounts that may be tested:

- non-current asset at cost account – (for example, motor vehicles, machinery)

- bank/cash account

- loan account (finance costs will not be tested).

4.4S Record the acquisition in a non-current assets register — 3,5

- Make the appropriate entries in accordance with the organisation's given policies and procedures.

- Funding methods:

- cash purchase (including standard commercial credit terms, for example 30 days)

- part exchange

- loan

- HP and finance leases – awareness only, no accounting entries or technical knowledge required.

4.5S Close off or transfer the ledger account balances at the end of the financial period — 3,5

- Understand which accounts will have balances carried forward and which are closed off to the statement of profit or loss at the end of the financial period.

- Understand that revenue or expense accounts will carry a balance prior to the closing off to the statement of profit or loss at the end of the financial period.

5   Account for depreciation

5.1S Calculate the depreciation charges for a non-current asset using the — 4

- Straight line method.

- Reducing balance method.

- Reducing balance method to be referred to as diminishing balance method.

- Calculate depreciation in accordance with the given policies of the organisation.

KAPLAN PUBLISHING

Chapter

- Straight line method, using a percentage, fraction or over a period of time, including cases when there is expected to be a residual value. Pro-rata calculations for part of a year will be required only when the organisational policy stipulates.

- Diminishing balance method using a percentage. Pro-rata calculations for part of a year will not be required.

5.2S   Record the depreciation in the non-current assets register   4

- Make the appropriate entries in accordance with the organisation's given policies and procedures.

5.3S   Record depreciation in the appropriate ledger accounts   4

- Non-current asset accumulated depreciation account (for example, motor vehicles, Machinery).

- Depreciation charges account.

5.4S   Close off the ledger accounts at the end of the financial period, correctly identifying any transfers to the statement of profit or loss   4

- Understand which accounts will have balances carried forward and which are closed off to the statement of profit or loss at the end of the financial period.

- Understand that revenue or expense accounts will carry a balance prior to the closing off to the statement of profit or loss at the end of the financial period.

6   Account for the disposal of non-current assets

6.1S   Identify the correct asset, removing it from the non-current asset register   5

- Understand that the carrying amount of an asset that has been disposed of will be shown as zero.

Chapter

6.2S   Record the disposal of non-current assets in the   5
       appropriate accounts

- Non-current asset at cost account – (for example, motor vehicles, machinery).

- Non-current asset accumulated depreciation account – (for example, motor vehicles, machinery).

- Non-current asset disposals account (or just disposals account).

- Bank/cash account.

6.3S   Calculate any gain or loss arising from the   5
       disposal, closing off or transferring the account
       balance

7   Account for adjustments

7.1K   Explain the accounting treatment of accruals and   12
       prepayments to expenses and revenue

- Recognise a given account as an income or expense type.

- Understand the terms accrued expenses, accrued income, prepaid expenses, prepaid income.

- Understand the significance of these at the period beginning and end and the link to the accruals basis.

- Understand how opening and closing accruals and prepayments affect income and expense ledger accounts, including recognition of the reversal of a previous period adjustment.

- Know that adjustments may need to be calculated pro-rata.

- Know how to calculate the amount transferred to the statement of profit or loss at the end of the period, including recognition that this is not necessarily the amount paid/received in the period.

Chapter

7.2K	Explain the reasons for, and method of, accounting for irrecoverable debts and allowances for doubtful debts	9

- Recognise and explain the link to the accruals basis.

- Know how to account for bad debts written off, allowances for specific doubtful debts and general allowances for doubtful debts.

- Recognise the recovery of a debt previously written off as irrecoverable.

- Excluding VAT implications.

7.3S	Record the journal entries for closing inventory	8

- Calculate correct closing inventory figure in accordance with the relevant accounting standards (IAS2). This may include calculating the cost from selling price including VAT and / or an element of profit.

- Use closing inventory account – statement of profit or loss (SPL).

- Use closing inventory account – statement of financial position (SFP).

- Journal narratives may be required.

7.4S	Record the journal entries for accrued and prepaid expenses and income	12

- Calculate adjustments pro-rata using given information, including organisational policies.

- Prepare journal entries for these adjustments.

- Journal narratives may be required.

- Reversal journals will not be required.

- Journal postings may be tested by the use of ledger accounts showing accrued and prepaid expenses and income at the beginning and/or end of the period.

		Chapter

7.5S   Record the journal entries for provision for depreciation, irrecoverable debts and allowances for doubtful debts   9

- Calculate a new allowance for doubtful debts according to a given policy – specific and/or general.

- Calculate the adjustment to an existing allowance (increase or decrease) according to a given policy.

- Correctly use the following accounts:

- non-current asset accumulated depreciation account (SFP)

- depreciation charges account (SPL)

- irrecoverable debts account (SPL) / Sales ledger control account (SFP)

- allowance for doubtful debts account (SFP)

- allowance for doubtful debts adjustment account (SPL).

7.6S   Record the journal entries to close off revenue accounts in preparation for the transfer of balances to the final accounts   6, 14

- Account types may be income or expense.

- Journal narratives may be required.

8   Prepare and extend the trial balance

8.1S   Prepare ledger account balances, reconciling them, identifying any discrepancies and taking appropriate action   6,10,11, 13,14

- Sales ledger control account to sales ledger.

- Adjustments may be required to either or both balances.

- Purchases ledger control account to purchases ledger.

- Adjustments may be required to either or both balances.

Chapter

- Bank account to bank statement; including an understanding that a debit entry or balance in the ledger will be a credit on the statement, and vice versa. Familiarity with terms such as BACS, direct debit etc will be expected.

- Discriminate between items that affect the reconciliation and those that do not.

- Correct ledger accounts by journal or show adjustment in ETB.

8.2S	Prepare a trial balance	1,6,14

- Transfer balances from ledger accounts, a list of balances or written task data into correct debit or credit column of trial balance.

- May require simple adjustments for accruals/prepayments according to given data.

8.3S	Account for these adjustments	4,6,8,9, 12,14

- Closing inventory.

- Accruals and prepayments to expenses and income.

- Provisions for depreciation on non-current assets.

- Irrecoverable debts.

- Allowance for doubtful debts.

- Use the appropriate columns in the extended trial balance or produce journal entries.

8.4S	Prepare the trial balance after adjustments	6,14

- Accurately extend figures in the ledger balances and adjustments columns into the statement of profit or loss and statement of financial position columns of the extended trial balance.

- Recognise that the balancing figure represents the profit or loss for the period, make the entries and label appropriately.

Chapter

8.5S Check for errors and/or inaccuracies in the trial   6,13,14
balance, taking appropriate action

- Correct errors creating imbalance and clear
  the suspense account, including:

- one-sided entry

- entry duplicated on one side, nothing on the
  other

- unequal entries

- account balance incorrectly transferred to trial
  balance.

- Correct errors not revealed by trial balance,
  including:

- errors of principle

- errors of original entry

- errors of omission

- errors of commission

- reversal of entries

- Identification or explanation of the type of error
  will not need to be recalled.

- Correct the errors using the journal or the
  appropriate columns of the extended trial
  balance

THE ASSESSMENT

The format of the assessment

The assessment consists of six independent tasks in one section.

The assessment will cover:

Maintaining accounting records for non-current assets

Tasks will include accounting for acquisitions, disposals and depreciation:

- the non-current assets register
- ledger accounts relating to non-current asset transactions.

Accounting adjustments and reconciliations

Typically tasks will require accounting for period end adjustments and the correction of errors. This will include using:

- ledger accounts
- the extended trial balance
- the journal
- short answer questions
- reconciliation of control accounts (sales, purchases) with subsidiary accounts
- reconciliation of bank account (cash book) with bank statement.

Principles, concepts and records

Tasks will include:

- showing basic understanding of accounting framework and concepts
- showing understanding of the principles of double entry bookkeeping
- showing awareness of the different types of accounting records, and their purpose.

The trial balance and extended trial balance

Tasks will include:

- production of a trial balance (or partial trial balance) from ledger accounts
- completion of an adjusted extended trial balance.

Summary

Achievement at Level 3 reflects the ability to identify and use relevant understanding, methods and skills to complete tasks and address problems that, while well defined, have a measure of complexity. It includes taking responsibility for initiating and completing tasks and procedures as well as exercising autonomy and judgement within limited parameters. It also reflects awareness of different perspectives or approaches within an area of study or work.

Knowledge and understanding

- Use factual, procedural and theoretical understanding to complete tasks and address problems that, while well defined, may be complex and non-routine.

- Interpret and evaluate relevant information and ideas.

- Be aware of the nature of the area of study or work.

- Have awareness of different perspectives or approaches within the area of study or work.

Application and action

- Address problems that, while well defined, may be complex and non-routine.

- Identify, select and use appropriate skills, methods and procedures.

- Use appropriate investigation to inform actions.

- Review how effective methods and actions have been.

Autonomy and accountability

- Take responsibility for initiating and completing tasks and procedures, including, where relevant, responsibility for supervising or guiding others

- Exercise autonomy and judgement within limited parameters.

Tasks types will include:

- completion of ledger accounts

- completion of pro-forma tables

- non-current assets register

- journal

- trial balance
- extended trial balance
- calculations
- multiple choice or similar.

Learners will normally be assessed by computer based assessment (CBA), the competency level for the AAT assessment is set at 70%.

Time allowed

The time allowed for this assessment is **two hours.**

STUDY SKILLS

Preparing to study

Devise a study plan

Determine which times of the week you will study.

Split these times into sessions of at least one hour for study of new material. Any shorter periods could be used for revision or practice.

Put the times you plan to study onto a study plan for the weeks from now until the assessment and set yourself targets for each period of study – in your sessions make sure you cover the whole course, activities and the associated questions in the workbook at the back of the manual.

If you are studying more than one unit at a time, try to vary your subjects as this can help to keep you interested and see subjects as part of wider knowledge.

When working through your course, compare your progress with your plan and, if necessary, re-plan your work (perhaps including extra sessions) or, if you are ahead, do some extra revision/practice questions.

Effective studying

Active reading

You are not expected to learn the text by rote, rather, you must understand what you are reading and be able to use it to pass the assessment and develop good practice.

A good technique is to use SQ3Rs – Survey, Question, Read, Recall, Review:

1   **Survey the chapter**

    Look at the headings and read the introduction, knowledge, skills and content, so as to get an overview of what the chapter deals with.

2   **Question**

    Whilst undertaking the survey ask yourself the questions you hope the chapter will answer for you.

3 **Read**

Read through the chapter thoroughly working through the activities and, at the end, making sure that you can meet the learning objectives highlighted on the first page.

4 **Recall**

At the end of each section and at the end of the chapter, try to recall the main ideas of the section/chapter without referring to the text. This is best done after short break of a couple of minutes after the reading stage.

5 **Review**

Check that your recall notes are correct.

You may also find it helpful to re-read the chapter to try and see the topic(s) it deals with as a whole.

Note taking

Taking notes is a useful way of learning, but do not simply copy out the text.

The notes must:

- be in your own words
- be concise
- cover the key points
- well organised
- be modified as you study further chapters in this text or in related ones.

Trying to summarise a chapter without referring to the text can be a useful way of determining which areas you know and which you don't.

Three ways of taking notes

1 **Summarise the key points of a chapter**

2 **Make linear notes**

A list of headings, subdivided with sub-headings listing the key points.

If you use linear notes, you can use different colours to highlight key points and keep topic areas together.

Use plenty of space to make your notes easy to use.

3 **Try a diagrammatic form**

The most common of which is a mind map.

To make a mind map, put the main heading in the centre of the paper and put a circle around it.

Draw lines radiating from this to the main sub-headings which again have circles around them.

Continue the process from the sub-headings to sub-sub-headings.

Highlighting and underlining

You may find it useful to underline or highlight key points in your study text – but do be selective.

You may also wish to make notes in the margins.

Revision phase

Kaplan has produced material specifically designed for your final examination preparation for this unit.

These include pocket revision notes and a bank of revision questions specifically in the style of the new syllabus.

Further guidance on how to approach the final stage of your studies is given in these materials.

Further reading

In addition to this text, you should also read the "Student section" of the "Accounting Technician" magazine every month to keep abreast of any guidance from the examiners.

TERMINOLOGY IAS AND UK GAAP

As of 1 January 2012 AAT adopted exam terminology consistent with IFRS and no longer examines UK GAAP specific terminology.

The list shown gives the 'translation' between UK GAAP and IFRS. Although this is not a comprehensive list, it does cover the main terms that you will come across in your studies and assessments.

UK GAAP	IFRS
Final accounts	Financial statements
Trading and profit and loss account	Statement of profit or loss
Turnover or Sales	Revenue or Sales revenue
Interest payable	Finance costs
Bad debt expense	Irrecoverable debt expense
Operating profit	Profit from operations
Net profit/loss	Profit/Loss for the year/period
Balance sheet	Statement of financial position
Fixed assets	Non-current assets
Net book value	Carrying amount
Tangible assets	Property, plant and equipment
Reducing balance depreciation	Diminishing balance depreciation
Depreciation/Depreciation expense(s)	Depreciation charge(s)
Stocks	Inventories
Trade debtors or Debtors	Trade receivables or Receivables
Debtors ledger control account	Receivables ledger control account
Sales ledger control account	Sales ledger control account
Provision for doubtful debts	Allowance for doubtful debts
Debtors and prepayments	Trade and other receivables
Cash at bank and in hand	Cash and cash equivalents
Trade creditors or Creditors	Trade payables or Payables
Creditors ledger control account	Payables ledger control account
Purchase ledger control account	Purchase ledger control account
Creditors and accruals	Trade and other payables
Long-term liabilities	Non-current liabilities
Profit and loss balance	Retained earnings
VAT/Sales tax	VAT/Sales tax

Double entry bookkeeping

1

Introduction

A sound knowledge of double entry underpins many of the learning outcomes and skills required for Accounts Preparation (ACPR). A sound understanding of double entry bookkeeping is essential in order to pass this unit and candidates will be assessed on double entry bookkeeping in the examination and so this must be very familiar ground. Although much of the content of this chapter should be familiar, it is essential that it is covered in order to build upon this basic knowledge in later chapters and for Prepare Final Accounts for Sole Traders and Partnerships (FSTP).

KNOWLEDGE

Describe the type of accounting records that a business should maintain and the main uses of each (1.3)

Explain the accounting equation (2.1)

Define assets, liabilities and equity in an accounting context (2.2)

Explain the purpose and use of books of prime entry and ledger accounts (2.3)

SKILLS

Prepare ledger account balances, reconciling them, identifying any discrepancies and taking appropriate action (8.1)

Prepare a trial balance (8.2)

CONTENTS

1 Principles behind double entry bookkeeping
2 Assets, liabilities, equity, income and expenses
3 Double entry – cash transactions
4 Double entry – credit transactions
5 Balancing a ledger account
6 Ledger accounting and the trial balance

1 Principles behind double entry bookkeeping

1.1 Introduction

Double entry bookkeeping is based upon three basic principles:

- the dual effect principle
- the separate entity principle
- the accounting equation.

1.2 The dual effect

 Definition

> The principle of the dual effect is that each and **every** transaction that a business makes has **two** effects.

For example if a business buys goods for cash then the two effects are that cash has decreased and that the business now has some purchases. The principle of double entry bookkeeping is that each of these effects must be shown in the ledger accounts by a **debit entry** in one account and an equal **credit entry** in another account.

Each and every transaction that a business undertakes has **two equal and opposite effects.**

1.3 The separate entity concept

 Definition

> The separate entity concept is that the business is a completely separate accounting entity from the owner.

Therefore if the owner pays his personal money into a business bank account this becomes the capital of the business which is owed back to the owner. Similarly if the owner takes money out of the business in the form of drawings then the amount of capital owed to the owner is reduced.

The business itself is a completely separate entity in accounting terms from the owner of the business.

KAPLAN PUBLISHING

1.4 The accounting equation

At its simplest, the accounting equation simply says that:

Assets = Liabilities

If we treat the owner's capital as a special form of liability then the accounting equation is:

Assets = Liabilities + Capital

Or, rearranging:

Assets – Liabilities = Capital

Profit will increase the proprietor's capital and drawings will reduce it, so that we can write the equation as:

Assets – Liabilities = Capital + Profit – Drawings

1.5 Rules for double entry bookkeeping

There are a number of rules that can help to determine which two accounts are to be debited and credited for a transaction:

- When money is paid out by a business this is a credit entry in the cash or bank account.
- When money is received by a business this is a debit entry in the cash or bank account.
- An asset or an increase in an asset is always recorded on the debit side of its account.
- A liability or an increase in a liability is always recorded on the credit side of its account.
- An expense is recorded as a debit entry in the expense account.
- Income is recorded as a credit entry in the income account.

The Golden Rule

Every debit has an equal and opposite credit.

Ledger account

A debit entry represents	A credit entry represents
An increase to an asset	An increase to a liability
A decrease to a liability	A decrease to an asset
An item of expense	An item of income

For increases we can remember this as DEAD CLIC

Ledger account

Debits increase:	Credits increase:
Expenses	Liabilities
Assets	Income
Drawings	Capital

2 Assets, liabilities, equity, income and expenses

2.1 Definitions

Accounts preparation involves five elements:

Assets:

An asset is an item of value controlled by a business. Assets may be tangible physical items or intangible items with no physical form, that add value to the business. For example, a building that is owned and controlled by a business and that is being used as part of the business activities would be classed as an asset.

Liabilities:

A liability is an obligation to something of value (such as an asset) as a result of past transactions or events. For example, owing a balance to a credit supplier is a liability.

Equity:

This is the 'residual interest' in a business and represents what is left when the business is wound up, all the assets sold and all the outstanding liabilities paid. It is effectively what is paid back to the owners when the business ceases to trade.

Income:

This is the recognition of the inflow of economic benefit to the entity in the reporting period. This can be achieved, for example, by earning sales revenue.

Expenses:

This is the recognition of the outflow of economic benefit from an entity in the reporting period. This can be achieved, for example, by purchasing goods or services.

3 Double entry – cash transactions

3.1 Introduction

For this revision of double entry bookkeeping we will start with accounting for cash transactions – remember that money paid out is a credit entry in the cash account and money received is a debit entry in the cash account.

Cash/Bank account	
DEBIT	**CREDIT**
Money in	Money out

Example

Dan Baker decides to set up in business as a sole trader by paying £20,000 into a business bank account. The following transactions are then entered into:

(i)   purchase of a van for deliveries by writing a cheque for £5,500

(ii) purchase of goods for resale by a cheque for £2,000

(iii) payment of shop rental in cash, £500

(iv) sale of goods for cash of £2,500

(v)   Dan took £200 of cash for his own personal expenses.

Note that cash received or paid is normally deemed to pass through the bank account.

State the two effects of each of these transactions and record them in the relevant ledger accounts.

Solution

Money paid into the business bank account by Dan:

- increase in cash

- capital now owed back to Dan.

Double entry:

- a debit to the bank account as money is coming in
- a credit to the capital account

Bank account

	£		£
Capital	20,000		

Capital account

	£		£
			20,000

(i) Purchase of a van for deliveries by writing a cheque for £5,500;

- cash decreases
- the business has a non-current asset, the van

Double entry:

- a credit to the bank account as cash is being paid out
- a debit to an asset account, the van account

Bank account

	£		£
Capital	20,000	Van	5,500

Van account

	£		£
Bank	5,500		

(ii) Purchase of goods for resale by a cheque for £2,000

- decrease in cash
- increase in purchases

Double entry:

- a credit to the bank account as money is paid out
- a debit to the purchases account, an expense account

Purchases of inventory are always recorded in a purchases account and never in an inventory account. The inventory account is only dealt with at the end of each accounting period and this will be dealt with in a later chapter.

Bank account

	£		£
Capital	20,000	Van	5,500
		Purchases	2,000

Purchases account

	£		£
Bank	2,000		

(iii) Payment of shop rental in cash, £500

- decrease in cash
- expense incurred

Double entry:

- a credit to the bank account as money is paid out
- a debit to the rent account, an expense

Bank account

	£		£
Capital	20,000	Van	5,500
		Purchases	2,000
		Rent	500

Rent account

	£		£
Bank	500		

(iv) Sale of goods for cash of £2,500

- cash increases
- sales increase

Double entry:

- a debit to the bank account as money is coming in
- a credit to the sales account, income

Bank account

	£		£
Capital	20,000	Van	5,500
Sales	2,500	Purchases	2,000
		Rent	500

Sales account

	£		£
		Bank	2,500

(v)   Dan took £200 of cash for his own personal expenses

- cash decreases

- drawings increase (money taken out of the business by the owner)

Double entry:

- a credit to the bank account as money is paid out

- a debit to the drawings account

Bank account

	£		£
Capital	20,000	Van	5,500
Sales	2,500	Purchases	2,000
		Rent	500
		Drawings	200

Drawings account

	£		£
Bank	200		

4   Double entry – credit transactions

4.1   Introduction

We will now introduce sales on credit and purchases on credit and the receipt of money from receivables and payment of money to payables. For the sales and purchases on credit there is no cash increase or decrease therefore the cash account rule cannot be used. Remember though that increase in income is always a credit entry and an increase in an expense is a debit entry.

Example

Dan now makes some further transactions:

(i) purchases are made on credit for £3,000

(ii) sales are made on credit for £4,000

(iii) Dan pays £2,000 to the credit suppliers

(iv) £2,500 is received from the credit customers

(v) Dan returned goods costing £150 to a supplier

(vi) goods were returned by a customer which had cost £200.

State the two effects of each of these transactions and write them up in the appropriate ledger accounts.

Solution

(i) Purchases are made on credit for £3,000

- increase in purchases
- increase in payables (PLCA)

Double entry:

- a debit entry to the purchases account, an expense
- a credit to the payables account

Purchases account

	£		£
Bank	2,000		
Payables	3,000		

Payables account (PLCA)

	£		£
		Purchases	3,000

(ii) Sales are made on credit for £4,000

- increase in sales
- increase in receivables

Double entry:

- a credit entry to the sales account, income
- a debit entry to the receivables account

Sales account

	£			£
		Bank		2,500
		Receivables		4,000

Receivables account (SLCA)

	£		£
Sales	4,000		

(iii)   Dan pays £2,000 to the suppliers

- decrease in cash
- decrease in payables

Double entry:

- a credit entry to the bank account as money is paid out
- a debit entry to payables as the liability is reduced

Bank account

	£		£
Capital	20,000	Van	5,500
Sales	2,500	Purchases	2,000
		Rent	500
		Drawings	200
		Payables	2,000

Payables account (PLCA)

	£		£
Bank	2,000	Purchases	3,000

(iv)   £2,500 is received from the credit customers

- increase in cash
- decrease in receivables

Double entry:

- a debit entry in the bank account as money is received
- a credit entry to receivables as they are reduced

Bank account

	£		£
Capital	20,000	Van	5,500
Sales	2,500	Purchases	2,000
Receivables	2,500	Rent	500
		Drawings	200
		Payables	2,000

Receivables account (SLCA)

	£		£
Sales	4,000	Bank	2,500

(v) Dan returned goods costing £150 to a supplier

- purchases returns increase
- payables decrease

Double entry:

- a debit entry to the payables account as payables are now decreasing
- a credit entry to the purchases returns account (the easiest way to remember this entry is that it is the opposite of purchases which are a debit entry)

Payables account (PLCA)

	£		£
Bank	2,000	Purchases	3,000
Purchases returns	150		

Purchases returns account

	£		£
		Payables	150

(vi) Goods were returned by a customer which had cost £200

- sales returns increase
- receivables decrease

Double entry:

- a credit entry to the receivables account as receivables are now decreasing
- a debit entry to sales returns (the opposite to sales which is a credit entry)

Receivables account (SLCA)

	£		£
Sales	4,000	Bank	2,500
		Sales returns	200

Sales returns account

	£		£
Receivables	200		

5 Balancing a ledger account

5.1 Introduction

Once the transactions for a period have been recorded in the ledger accounts it is likely that the owner will want to know certain matters, such as how much cash there is in the bank account, or how much has been spent on purchases? This can be found by balancing the ledger accounts.

5.2 Procedure for balancing a ledger account

The following steps should be followed when balancing a ledger account:

Step 1

Total both the debit and credit columns to find the higher total – enter this figure as the total for both the debit and credit columns.

Step 2

For the side that does not add up to this total put in the figure that makes it add up and call it the balance carried down, or 'bal c/d.'

Step 3

Enter the balance brought ('bal b/d') down on the opposite side below the totals.

Example

We will now balance Dan's bank account

Bank account

	£		£
Capital	20,000	Van	5,500
Sales	2,500	Purchases	2,000
Receivables	2,500	Rent	500
		Drawings	200
		Payables	2,000

Bank account

	£		£
Capital	20,000	Van	5,500
Sales	2,500	Purchases	2,000
Receivables	2,500	Rent	500
		Drawings	200
		Payables	2,000
		Balance c/d **Step 2**	14,800
Step 1	25,000	**Step 1**	25,000
Balance b/d **Step 3**	14,800		

Activity 1

(a) Show by means of ledger accounts how the following transactions would be recorded in the books of Bertie Dooks, a seller of second-hand books:

   (i)   paid in cash £5,000 as capital ✓

   (ii) took the lease of a stall and paid six months' rent – the yearly rental was £300

   (iii) spent £140 cash on the purchase of books from W Smith

   (iv) purchased on credit from J Fox books at a cost of £275

   (v) paid an odd-job man £25 to paint the exterior of the stall and repair a broken lock

(vi) put an advertisement in the local paper at a cost of £2

(vii) sold three volumes containing The Complete Works of William Shakespeare to an American for £35 cash

(viii) sold a similar set on credit to a local schoolmaster for £3

(ix) paid J Fox £175 on account for the amount due to him

(x) received £1 from the schoolmaster

(xi) purchased cleaning materials at a cost of £2 and paid £3 to a cleaner

(xii) took £5 from the business to pay for his own groceries.

(b) Balance off the ledgers, clearly showing balance carried down (c/d) and balance brought down (b/d).

6 Ledger accounting and the trial balance

6.1 Introduction

 Definition

A trial balance is the list of the balances on all of the ledger accounts in an organisation's general (main, nominal) ledger.

6.2 Trial balance

The trial balance will appear as a list of debit balances and credit balances depending upon the type of account. If the double entry has been correctly carried out then the debit balance total should be equal to the credit balance total (this will be dealt with in more detail in a later chapter).

A trial balance lists all of the ledger account balances in the general ledger.

6.3 Preparing the trial balance

When all of the entries have been made in the ledger accounts for a period, the trial balance will then be prepared.

Step 1

Balance off each ledger account and bring down the closing balance.

Step 2

List each balance brought down as either a debit balance or a credit balance.

Step 3

Total the debit balances and the credit balances to see if they are equal.

Example

Given below are the initial transactions for Mr Smith, a sole trader. Enter the transactions in the ledger accounts using a separate account for each receivable and payable. Produce the trial balance for this sole trader at the end of 12 January 20X1.

On 1 Jan 20X1	Mr Smith put £12,500 into the business bank account.
On 2 Jan 20X1	He bought goods for resale costing £750 on credit from J Oliver. He also bought on the same basis £1,000 worth from K Hardy.
On 3 Jan 20X1	Sold goods for £800 to E Morecombe on credit.
On 5 Jan 20X1	Mr Smith returned £250 worth of goods bought from J Oliver, being substandard goods.
On 6 Jan 20X1	Sold goods on credit to A Wise for £1,000.
On 7 Jan 20X1	Mr Smith withdrew £100 from the bank for his personal use.
On 8 Jan 20X1	Bought a further £1,500 worth of goods from K Hardy, again on credit.
On 9 Jan 20X1	A Wise returned £200 worth of goods sold to him on the 6th
On 10 Jan 20X1	The business paid J Oliver £500 by cheque, and K Hardy £1,000 also by cheque.
On 12 Jan 20X1	Mr Smith banked a cheque for £800 received from E Morecombe.

Solution

Step 1

Enter the transactions into the ledger accounts and then balance off each ledger account. Use a separate ledger account for each receivable and payable. (Note that in most examinations you will be required to complete the double entry for receivables and payables in the receivables and payables ledger control accounts, but for practice we are using the separate accounts.)

Step 2

Balance off each of the ledger accounts.

Capital account

	£			£
		1 Jan	Bank	12,500

Sales account

		£			£
			3 Jan	E Morecombe	800
Balance c/d		1,800	6 Jan	A Wise	1,000
		─────			─────
		1,800			1,800
		─────			─────
				Balance b/d	1,800

Purchases account

		£			£
2 Jan	J Oliver	750			
2 Jan	K Hardy	1,000			
8 Jan	K Hardy	1,500		Balance c/d	3,250
		─────			─────
		3,250			3,250
		─────			─────
Balance b/d		3,250			

Purchases returns account

	£			£
		5 Jan	J Oliver	250

Sales returns account

		£			£
9 Jan	A Wise	200			

Drawings account

		£			£
7 Jan	Bank	100			

Bank account

		£			£
1 Jan	Capital	12,500	7 Jan	Drawings	100
12 Jan	E Morecombe	800	10 Jan	J Oliver	500
				K Hardy	1,000
				Balance c/d	11,700
		13,300			13,300
	Balance b/d	11,700			

E Morecombe account

		£			£
3 Jan	Sales	800	12 Jan	Bank	800

A Wise account

		£			£
6 Jan	Sales	1,000	9 Jan	Sales returns	200
				Balance c/d	800
		1,000			1,000
	Balance b/d	800			

J Oliver account

		£			£
5 Jan	Purchases returns	250	2 Jan	Purchases	750
10 Jan	Bank	500			
		750			750

K Hardy account

	£			£
10 Jan Bank	1,000	2 Jan	Purchases	1,000
Balance c/d	1,500	8 Jan	Purchases	1,500
	2,500			2,500
			Balance b/d	1,500

Note that accounts with only one entry do not need to be balanced as this entry is the final balance on the account.

Step 3

Produce the trial balance by listing each balance brought down as either a debit balance or a credit balance.

Make sure that you use the balance brought down below the total line as the balance to list in the trial balance.

Step 4

Total the debit and credit columns to check that they are equal.

Trial balance as at 12 January 20X1

	Debits £	Credits £
Capital		12,500
Sales		1,800
Purchases	3,250	
Purchases returns		250
Sales returns	200	
Drawings	100	
Bank	11,700	
A Wise	800	
K Hardy		1,500
	16,050	16,050

NB: E Morecombe has a nil balance so has not appeared in the trial balance.

6.4   Purpose of the trial balance

One of the main purposes of a trial balance is to serve as a check on the double entry. If the trial balance does not balance, i.e. the debit and credit totals are not equal then some errors have been made in the double entry (this will be covered in more detail in a later chapter).

The trial balance can also serve as the basis for preparing an extended trial balance (see later in this text) and finally the financial statements of the organisation.

 Activity 2

Enter the following details of transactions for the month of May 20X6 into the appropriate books of account. You should also extract a trial balance as at 1 June 20X6. Open a separate ledger account for each receivable and payable, and also keep separate 'cash' and 'bank' ledger accounts. Balance off each account and prepare a trial balance.

20X6

1 May	Started in business by paying £6,800 into the bank.
3 May	Bought goods on credit from the following: J Johnson £400; D Nixon £300 and J Agnew £250.
5 May	Cash sales £300.
6 May	Paid rates by cheque £100.
8 May	Paid wages £50 in cash.
9 May	Sold goods on credit: K Homes £300; J Homes £300; B Hood £100.
10 May	Bought goods on credit: J Johnson £800; D Nixon £700.
11 May	Returned goods to J Johnson £150.
15 May	Bought office fixtures £600 by cheque.
18 May	Bought a motor vehicle £3,500 by cheque.
22 May	Goods returned by J Homes £100.
25 May	Paid J Johnson £1,000; D Nixon £500, both by cheque.
26 May	Paid wages £150 by cheque

6.5   Debit or credit balance?

When you are balancing a ledger account it is easy to see which side, debit or credit, the balance brought down is on. However if you were given a list of balances rather than the account itself then it is sometimes difficult to decide which side the balance should be shown in the trial balance, the debit or the credit?

There are some rules to help here:

- assets are debit balances

- expenses are debit balances

- liabilities are credit balances

- income is a credit balance.

This can be remembered using the 'DEAD CLIC' mnemonic.

6.6   Debit or credit balance?

Another common problem area is determining whether settlement discounts allowed and received are debits or credits.

The double entry for a discount allowed to a customer is:

- debit to the discounts allowed account (an expense account)

- credit to the receivables account (reducing the amount owed by the customer).

Therefore the balance on the discounts allowed account is a debit balance. This is an expense of the business as it is the cost to the business of getting the money due into their bank account earlier.

The double entry for a discount received from a supplier is:

- debit to the payables account (reducing the amount owed to the supplier)

- credit to the discounts received account (a form of sundry income).

Therefore the balance on the discounts received account is a credit balance. This is income as it means that the business has paid less for the goods than originally envisaged although the payment was made earlier.

Activity 3

The following balances have been extracted from the books of Fitzroy at 31 December 20X2:

Prepare a trial balance at 31 December 20X2.

	£	Debit	Credit
Capital on 1 January 20X2	106,149		✓
Freehold factory at cost	360,000		
Motor vehicles at cost	126,000	✓	
Inventories at 1 January 20X2	37,500	✓	
Receivables	15,600	✓	
Cash in hand	225	✓	
Bank overdraft	82,386		✓
Payables	78,900		✓
Sales	318,000		✓
Purchases	165,000	✓	
Rent and rates	35,400	✓	
Discounts allowed	6,600		✓
Insurance	2,850	✓	
Sales returns	10,500	✓	
Purchase returns	6,300		✓
Loan from bank	240,000	✓	
Sundry expenses	45,960		✓
Drawings	26,100	✓	✓
TOTALS		659175	638 625

Activity 4

(1) The bank account for January is as follows:

Bank account

	£		£
Balance b/d	1,900	Payables	7,000
Receivables	2,500		
Cash sales	500		

At the end of the month there is a **debit/credit** balance of **£7,000/4,900/2,100.**

Circle the correct answer

(2) True or false, to increase a liability a debit entry is made.

       True
       False

  Tick the correct answer for task 2

  Circle the correct answer for task 3, 4, 5,6 and 7

(3) When a sole trader uses goods for resale for his own personal use the drawings account is **Debited / Credited** and the purchases account is **Debited / Credited**

(4) When a supplier is paid the bank account is **Debited / Credited** and the supplier account is **Debited / Credited**

(5) When goods are sold to a receivable, the sales account is **Debited / Credited** and the receivable account is **Debited / Credited**

(6) A bank overdraft is a **Debit / Credit** account in the trial balance

(7) Discounts received are a **Debit / Credit** balance in the trial balance.

7 Summary

In this opening chapter the basic principles of double entry bookkeeping have been revised from your basic accounting studies.

The basic principles of double entry are of great importance for this unit and in particular all students should be able to determine whether a particular balance on an account is a debit or a credit balance in the trial balance.

Answers to chapter activities

Activity 1

Ledger accounts

Cash account

	£		£
Capital account (i)	5,000	Rent (six months) (ii)	150
Sales (vii)	35	Purchases (iii)	140
Receivables (x)	1	Repairs (v)	25
		Advertising (vi)	2
		Payables (ix)	175
		Cleaning (xi)	5
		Drawings (xii)	5
		Balance c/d	4,534
	———		———
	5,036		5,036
	———		———
Balance b/d	4,534		

Payable account (J Fox)

	£		£
Cash (ix)	175	Purchases (iv)	275
Balance c/d	100		
	———		———
	275		275
	———		———
		Balance b/d	100

Receivable account (School master)

	£		£
Sales (viii)	3	Cash (x)	1
		Balance c/d	2
	———		———
	3		3
	———		———
Balance b/d	2		

Capital account

	£		£
Balance c/d	5,000	Cash (i)	5,000
	5,000		5,000
		Balance b/d	5,000

Sales account

	£		£
		Cash (vii)	35
Balance c/d	38	Receivables (Schoolmaster) (viii)	3
	38		38
		Balance b/d	38

Purchases account

	£		£
Cash (iii)	140	Balance c/d	415
Payable (J Fox) (iv)	275		
	415		415
Balance b/d	415		

Rent account

	£		£
Cash (ii)	150	Balance c/d	150
	150		150
Balance b/d	150		

Repairs account

	£		£
Cash (v)	25	Balance c/d	25
	25		25
Balance b/d	25		

Advertising account

	£		£
Cash (vi)	2	Balance c/d	2
	——		——
	2		2
	——		——
Balance b/d	2		

Cleaning account

	£		£
Cash (xi)	5	Balance c/d	5
	——		——
	5		5
	——		——
Balance b/d	5		

Drawings account

	£		£
Cash (xii)	5	Balance c/d	5
	——		——
	5		5
	——		——
Balance b/d	5		

Activity 2

Cash account

		£			£
5 May	Sales	300	8 May	Wages	50
			31 May	Balance c/d	250
		——			——
		300			300
		——			——
1 June	Balance b/d	250			

Bank account

	£			£
1 May Capital	6,800	6 May	Rates	100
		15 May	Office fixtures	600
		18 May	Motor vehicle	3,500
		25 May	J Johnson	1,000
			D Nixon	500
		26 May	Wages	150
		31 May	Balance c/d	950
	6,800			6,800
1 June Balance b/d	950			

J Johnson account

	£			£
11 May Purchase returns	150	3 May	Purchases	400
25 May Bank	1,000	10 May	Purchases	800
31 May Balance c/d	50			
	1,200			1,200
		1 June	Balance b/d	50

D Nixon account

	£			£
25 May Bank	500	3 May	Purchases	300
31 May Balance c/d	500	10 May	Purchases	700
	1,000			1,000
		1 June	Balance b/d	500

J Agnew account

	£			£
31 May Balance c/d	250	3 May	Purchases	250
		1 June	Balance b/d	250

K Homes account

		£			£
9 May	Sales	300	31 May	Balance c/d	300
		300			300
1 June	Balance b/d	300			

J Homes account

		£			£
9 May	Sales	300	22 May	Sales returns	100
			31 May	Balance c/d	200
		300			300
1 June	Balance b/d	200			

B Hood account

		£			£
9 May	Sales	100	31 May	Balance c/d	100
1 June	Balance b/d	100			

Capital account

		£			£
31 May	Balance c/d	6,800	1 May	Bank	6,800
			1 June	Balance b/d	6,800

Purchases account

		£			£
3 May	J Johnson	400			
	D Nixon	300			
	J Agnew	250			
10 May	J Johnson	800			
	D Nixon	700	31 May	Balance c/d	2,450
		2,450			2,450
1 June	Balance b/d	2,450			

Sales account

	£			£
		5 May	Cash	300
		9 May	K Homes	300
			J Homes	300
31 May Balance c/d	1,000		B Hood	100
	1,000			1,000
		1 June	Balance b/d	1,000

Rates account

	£		£
6 May Bank	100	31 May Balance c/d	100
1 June Balance b/d	100		

Wages account

	£		£
8 May Cash	50		
26 May Bank	150	31 May Balance c/d	200
	200		200
1 June Balance b/d	200		

Purchase returns account

	£		£
31 May Balance c/d	150	11 May J Johnson	150
		1 June Balance b/d	150

Office fixtures account

	£		£
15 May Bank	600	31 May Balance c/d	600
1 June Balance b/d	600		

Motor vehicle account

	£		£
18 May Bank	3,500	31 May Balance c/d	3,500
1 June Balance b/d	3,500		

Sales returns account

	£		£
22 May J Homes	100	31 May Balance c/d	100
1 June Balance b/d	100		

Trial balance as at 30 May 20X6

	Dr £	Cr £
Cash	250	
Bank	950	
J Johnson		50
D Nixon		500
J Agnew		250
K Homes	300	
J Homes	200	
B Hood	100	
Capital		6,800
Purchases	2,450	
Sales		1,000
Rates	100	
Wages	200	
Purchase returns		150
Office fixtures	600	
Motor vehicles	3,500	
Sales returns	100	
	8,750	8,750

Activity 3

Trial balance at 31 December 20X2

	Dr £	Cr £
Capital on 1 January 20X2		106,149
Freehold factory at cost	360,000	
Motor vehicles at cost	126,000	
Inventories at 1 January 20X2	37,500	
Receivables	15,600	
Cash in hand	225	
Bank overdraft		82,386
Payables		78,900
Sales		318,000
Purchases	165,000	
Rent and rates	35,400	
Discounts allowed	6,600	
Insurance	2,850	
Sales returns	10,500	
Purchase returns		6,300
Loan from bank		240,000
Sundry expenses	45,960	
Drawings	26,100	
	831,735	831,735

Activity 4

(1)   The bank account for January is as follows:

Bank account

	£		£
Balance b/d	1,900	Payables	7,000
Receivables	2,500		
Cash sales	500		
Balance c/d	**2,100**		
	─────		─────
	7,000		7,000
	─────		─────
		Balance b/d	**2,100**

The correct answer is **CREDIT** of **£2,100**

(2)   False

(3)   When a sole trader uses goods for resale for his own personal use the drawings account is **Debited** and the purchases account is **Credited**

(4)   When a supplier is paid the bank account is **Credited** and the supplier account is **Debited**

(5)   When goods are sold to a receivable, the sales account is **Credited** and the receivable account is **Debited**

(6)   A bank overdraft is a **Credit** balance in the trial balance

(7)   Discounts received are a **Credit** balance in the trial balance.

KAPLAN PUBLISHING

8 Test your knowledge

Workbook Activity 5

Musgrave starts in business with capital of £20,000, in the form of cash £15,000 and non-current assets of £5,000.

In the first three days of trading he has the following transactions:

- Purchases inventory £4,000 on credit terms, supplier allows one month's credit.

- Sells some inventory costing £1,500 for £2,000 and allows the customer a fortnight's credit.

- Purchases a motor vehicle for £6,000 and pays by cheque.

The accounting equation at the start would be:

Assets less Liabilities	=	Ownership interest
£20,000 – £0	=	£20,000

Required:

Re-state in values the accounting equation after all the transactions had taken place.

Workbook Activity 6

Heather Simpson notices an amount of £36,000 on the trial balance of her business in an account called 'Capital'. She does not understand what this account represents.

Briefly explain what a capital account represents.

Workbook Activity 7

Tony

Tony started a business selling tapes and CDs. In the first year of trading he entered into the following transactions:

(a) Paid £20,000 into a business bank account.

(b) Made purchases from Debbs for £1,000 cash.

(c) Purchased goods costing £3,000 from Gary for cash.

(d) Paid £200 for insurance.

(e) Bought storage units for £700 cash from Debbs.

(f) Paid £150 cash for advertising.

(g) Sold goods to Dorothy for £1,500 cash.

(h) Paid the telephone bill of £120 in cash.

(i) Sold further goods to Dorothy for £4,000 cash.

(j) Bought stationery for £80 cash.

(k) Withdrew £500 cash for himself.

Required:

Show how these transactions would be written up in Tony's ledger accounts.

Workbook Activity 8

Dave

Dave had the following transactions during January 20X3:

1 Introduced £500 cash as capital.

2 Purchased goods on credit from A Ltd worth £200.

3 Paid rent for one month, £20.

4 Paid electricity for one month, £50.

5 Purchased a car for cash, £100.

6 Sold half of the goods on credit to X Ltd for £175.

7 Drew £30 for his own expenses.

8 Sold the remainder of the goods for cash, £210.

Required:

Write up the relevant ledger accounts necessary to record the above transactions.

KAPLAN PUBLISHING

Workbook Activity 9

Audrey Line

Audrey Line started in business on 1 March, opening a toy shop and paying £6,000 into a business bank account. She made the following transactions during her first six months of trading:

	£
Payment of six months' rent	500
Purchase of shop fittings	600
Purchase of toys on credit	2,000
Payments to toy supplier	1,200
Wages of shop assistant	600
Electricity	250
Telephone	110
Cash sales	3,700
Drawings	1,600

All payments were made by cheque and all inventories had been sold by the end of August.

Required:

Record these transactions in the relevant accounts.

Accounting for VAT (sales tax)

Introduction

When dealing with the accounts of sole traders and partnerships it is highly likely that they will be registered for sales tax (called VAT in the UK) unless they are a very small sole trader. Therefore at this stage it is important to consider the accounting for VAT (sales tax) and the rules that apply.

KNOWLEDGE	CONTENTS
Describe the type of accounting records that a business should maintain and the main uses of each (1.3)	1 The operation of VAT (sales tax)

1 The operation of VAT (sales tax)

1.1 Introduction

This chapter will begin with just a brief reminder of how the VAT (sales tax) system operates. VAT is studied in much further depth in the indirect tax unit.

1.2 What is VAT (sales tax)?

VAT is:

- an indirect tax
- charged on most goods and services supplied within the UK,
- is borne by the final consumer, and
- collected by businesses on behalf of HM Revenue and Customs.

VAT is an indirect tax because it is paid indirectly when you buy most goods and services, rather than being collected directly from the taxpayer as a proportion of their income or gains.

VAT is charged by **taxable persons** when they make **taxable supplies** in the course of their business. VAT is not generally charged on non business transactions.

1.3 Taxable persons

Definition

Taxable persons are businesses which are (or should be) registered for VAT (sales tax).

1.4 Registration and non-registration for VAT (sales tax)

When a business reaches a set annual turnover level, currently £79,000, then it must register for VAT (sales tax). If turnover is below this limit, the business can, if it wishes, register voluntarily. If a business is registered it must:

- charge VAT (sales tax) on its sales or services to its customers
- recover the VAT (sales tax) charged on its purchases and expenses rather than having to bear these costs as part of the business.

In such cases, as the VAT (sales tax) charged and incurred is neither revenue nor expense, the revenues and costs of the business are entered in books at their net of VAT (sales tax) value, and the VAT (sales tax) is entered in the VAT (sales tax) account.

If the business is not registered for VAT (sales tax) then the cost of purchases and expenses must include the VAT (sales tax) as these amounts are said to be irrecoverable. Thus, the costs of the business are entered in the books at their gross, VAT (sales tax) inclusive, value and there is no VAT (sales tax) account.

A person can be an individual or a legal person such as a company.

1.5 Taxable supplies

Taxable supplies or outputs, are most sales made by a taxable person. Taxable supplies can also include gifts and goods taken from the business for personal use.

1.6 Output VAT (sales tax)

 Definition

The VAT (sales tax) charged on sales or taxable supplies is called **output VAT (sales tax).**

1.7 Input VAT (sales tax)

When a business buys goods or pays expenses (inputs), then it will also be paying VAT (sales tax) on those purchases or expenses.

 Definition

VAT paid by a business on purchases or expenses is called **input VAT (sales tax).**

Businesses are allowed to reclaim their input tax. They do this by deducting the input tax they have paid from the output tax which they owe, and paying over the net amount only. If the input tax exceeds the output tax, then the balance is recoverable from HMRC.

1.8 Rates of VAT (sales tax)

VAT is currently charged at two main rates, the standard rate of 20% and the zero rate 0%. The zero rate of VAT (sales tax) applies to items such as food, drink, books, newspapers, children's clothes and most transport.

1.9 Standard rated activities

Any taxable supply which is not charged at the zero or reduced rates is charged at the standard rate.

This is calculated by taking the VAT (sales tax) exclusive amount and multiplying by 20%.

If you are given the VAT (sales tax) inclusive rate then calculate the VAT (sales tax) amount by **20/120**.

The following VAT (sales tax) structure can also be used to calculate VAT (sales tax), VAT (sales tax) inclusive or VAT (sales tax) exclusive figures.

	£
VAT inclusive	120
VAT	20
VAT exclusive	100

🔆 Example

Suppose that a business makes sales on credit of £1,000 and purchases on credit of £400 (both amounts exclusive of any VAT (sales tax)). How would these be accounted for in the ledger accounts.

Solution

The sales and purchases must be shown net and the VAT (sales tax) entered in the VAT (sales tax) account. As the sales and purchases were on credit the full double entry would be as follows:

DR	Receivables account	£1,200
CR	Sales account	£1,000
CR	VAT control account	£200

DR	Purchases account	£400
DR	VAT control account	£80
CR	Payables account	£480

Sales account

	£			£
			Receivables	1,000

Receivables account

	£		£
Sales and VAT (sales tax)	1,200		

Purchases account

	£		£
Payables	400		

Payables account

	£		£
		Purchases	480

VAT control account

	£		£
Payables	80	Receivables	200
Balance c/d	120		
	———		———
	200		200
	———		———
		Balance b/d	120

The amount due to HM Revenue and Customs is the balance on the VAT (sales tax) account, £120.

If a business is not registered for VAT (sales tax) then it will not charge VAT (sales tax) on its sales, and its expenses must be recorded at the gross amount (inclusive of VAT (sales tax)).

If a business is registered for VAT (sales tax) then it will charge VAT (sales tax) on its sales, although they will be recorded as sales at their net amount, and its expenses will also be recorded at the net amount. The output and input VAT (sales tax) is recorded in the VAT (sales tax) account and the difference paid over to HM Revenue and Customs.

1.10 Zero-rated activities

If a business is registered for VAT (sales tax) and sells zero-rated products or services then it charges no VAT (sales tax) on the sales but can still reclaim the input VAT (sales tax) on its purchases and expenses. Such a business will normally be owed VAT (sales tax) by HM Revenue and Customs each quarter.

Example

Suppose that a business makes sales on credit of £1,000 plus VAT (sales tax) @ 20% and purchases on credit of £400 plus VAT (sales tax) @ 20%. How would these be accounted for if the rate of VAT (sales tax) on the sales was zero, whereas the purchases were standard rated?

Solution

DR	Receivables	£1,000
CR	Sales	£1,000
DR	Purchases	£400
DR	VAT (400 × 20%)	£80
CR	Payables	£480

This would leave a debit balance on the VAT (sales tax) account which is the amount that can be claimed back from HM Revenue and Customs by the business.

1.11 Exempt activities

Certain supplies are exempt from VAT (sales tax) such as financial and postal services.

If a business sells such services then not only is no VAT (sales tax) charged on the sales of the business but also no input VAT (sales tax) can be reclaimed on purchases and expenses.

 Example

Suppose that a business makes sales on credit of £1,000 plus VAT (sales tax) and purchases on credit of £400 plus VAT (sales tax). How would these be accounted for if the sales are exempt activities, whereas the purchases were standard-rated?

Solution

DR	Receivables	£1,000
CR	Sales	£1,000
DR	Purchases	£480
CR	Payables	£480

There is no VAT (sales tax) on sales due to HM Revenue and Customs and the business cannot claim the £80 from HM Revenue and Customs. However, the seller of the purchases should pay the £80 of VAT (sales tax) over to HM Revenue and Customs.

Activity 1

A business that is registered for VAT (sales tax) makes credit sales of £110,000 in the period and credit purchases of £75,000. Each of these figures is net of VAT (sales tax) at the standard rate of 20%.

Show how these transactions should be entered into the ledger accounts and state how much VAT (sales tax) is due to HM Revenue and Customs.

1.12 Differences between zero rated and exempt supplies

You must be careful to distinguish between traders making zero rated and exempt supplies.

	Exempt	Zero rated
Can register for VAT (sales tax)?	No	Yes
Charge output VAT (sales tax) to customers?	No	Yes at 0%
Can recover input tax?	No	Yes

 Activity 2

Robbie's business bank account shows administrative expenses of £27,216 which is inclusive of VAT (sales tax) at the standard rate 20%.

1   Calculate the administrative expenses to be included in the trial balance.

2   Calculate the VAT (sales tax) figure on administrative expenses for inclusion in the VAT (sales tax) control account.

3   Update the VAT (sales tax) control account below and find the closing balance figure for VAT (sales tax).

VAT control account

	£		£
VAT on purchases	35,000	Balance b/d	5,000
Paid to HMRC	5,000	VAT on sales	26,250
	——		——
	——		——

2 Summary

For this unit in most cases you will be dealing with VAT (sales tax) registered businesses and therefore you will need to be able to account for VAT (sales tax) and deal with the amount of VAT (sales tax) that is due either to or from HM Revenue and Customs.

In particular you must understand what is meant by the balance on the VAT (sales tax) control account in the trial balance.

Answers to chapter activities

Activity 1

Sales account

	£		£
		SLCA	110,000

Sales ledger control account

	£		£
Sales + VAT 110,000 + 22,000	132,000		

Purchases account

	£		£
PLCA	75,000		

VAT control account

	£		£
PLCA 75,000 × 20/100	15,000	SLCA 110,000 × 20/100	22,000
Balance c/d	7,000		
	22,000		22,000
		Balance b/d	7,000

Purchases ledger control account

	£		£
		Purchases + VAT 75,000 + 15,000	90,000

The amount due to HM Revenue and Customs is the balance on the VAT control account, £7,000.

Activity 2

1　The amount that should be included in the trial balance is the NET amount. As £27,216 is the VAT inclusive amount, the NET is calculated as follows:

27,216 × 100/120 = 22,680 (or 27,216/1.2)

2　The VAT can be calculated using the gross figure £27,216 × 20/120 = £4,536

3　The VAT control would be completed as follows:

VAT control account

	£		£
VAT on purchases	35,000	Balance b/d	5,000
Paid to HMRC	5,000	VAT on sales	26,250
VAT on expenses	4,536	**Balance c/d**	**13,286**
	44,536		44,536
Balance b/d	**13,286**		

A debit balance represents a refund due from HMRC.

3 Test your knowledge

Workbook Activity 3

A business that is registered for VAT has the following record relating to sales, purchases and expenses.

Sales for the quarter ending 31 March 20X4 of £236,175 (including VAT)

Purchases and expenses of £143,600 (excluding VAT).

At 1 January 20X4 there was an amount of £8,455 owing to HM Revenue and Customs and this was paid on 28 January 20X4.

Required:

Write up the VAT control account for the quarter ending 31 March 20X4. (VAT rate is 20%)

VAT control account

	£		£
	———		———
	———		———

Explain what the balance on the account represents.

Capital and revenue expenditure

Introduction

A large proportion of the Accounts Preparation syllabus is accounting for non-current assets. The ACPR assessment covers all areas of accounting for non-current assets including acquisition, depreciation and disposal.

In this chapter we will start to look at the details of authorising and accounting for capital expenditure.

KNOWLEDGE	CONTENTS
Describe the type of accounting records that a business should maintain and the main uses of each, including non-current asset register (1.3)	1 Capital and revenue expenditure
	2 Recording the purchase of non-current assets
Explain the differences between capital and revenue expenditure, classifying items as one or the other (1.6)	3 Types of non-current assets
	4 Non-current asset register
Describe how the acquisition of non-current assets can be funded, including part exchange (3.1)	
Explain the accounting treatment for recording the acquisition and disposal of non-current assets (3.2)	
Describe the contents and use of the non-current asset register (3.4)	

SKILLS

Calculate total capital expenditure including all associated costs (4.1)

Record prior authority for the capital expenditure (4.2)

Record in the appropriate accounts the acquisition of a non-current asset including funded by part exchange (4.3)

Record the acquisition in a non-current assets register (4.4)

Close off or transfer the ledger account balances at the end of the financial period (4.5)

1 Capital and revenue expenditure

1.1 Introduction

In the statement of financial position, assets are split between non-current assets and current assets.

1.2 Non-current assets

 Definition

The non-current assets of a business are the assets that were purchased with the intention of long term-use within the business.

Examples of non-current assets include buildings, machinery, motor vehicles, office fixtures and fittings and computer equipment.

1.3 Capital expenditure

 Definition

Capital expenditure is expenditure on the purchase or improvement of non-current assets.

The purchase of non-current assets is known as capital expenditure. This means that the cost of the non-current asset is initially taken to the statement of financial position rather than the statement of profit or loss. We will see in a later chapter how this cost is then charged to the statement of profit or loss over the life of the non-current asset by the process of depreciation.

1.4 Revenue expenditure

 Definition

Revenue expenditure is all other expenditure incurred by the business other than capital expenditure.

Revenue expenditure is charged as an expense to the statement of profit or loss in the period that it is incurred.

Capital expenditure is shown as a non-current asset in the statement of financial position.

Revenue expenditure is shown as an expense in the statement of profit or loss.

1.5 Authorising capital expenditure

Many types of non-current asset are relatively expensive. Most non-current assets will be used to generate income for the business for several years into the future. Therefore they are important purchases. Timing may also be critical. It may be necessary to arrange a bank overdraft or a loan, or alternatively capital expenditure may have to be delayed in order to avoid a bank overdraft.

For these reasons, most organisations have procedures whereby capital expenditure must be authorised by a responsible person. In small organisations, most non-current asset purchases are likely to be authorised by the owner of the business. In large organisations, there is normally a system whereby several people have the authority to approve capital expenditure up to a certain limit which depends on the person's level of seniority.

The method of recording the authorisation is also likely to vary according to the nature and size of the organisation, and according to the type of non-current asset expenditure it normally undertakes. In a small business, there may be no formal record other than a signature on a cheque.

In a large company, the directors may record their approval of significant expenditure in the minutes of a board meeting. Other possibilities include the use of requisition forms and signing of the invoice.

In most organisations, disposals of non-current assets must also be authorised in writing.

Where standard forms are used, these will vary from organisation to organisation, but the details for acquisition of an asset are likely to include:

- date
- description of asset
- reason for purchase
- supplier
- cost/quotation

- details of quotation (if applicable)

- details of lease agreement (if applicable)

- authorisation (number of signatures required will vary according to the organisation's procedures)

- method of financing.

 Activity 1

When authorising the purchase of a new machine, choose the most suitable policy.

New machinery purchases should be authorised by:

(a) The office assistant

(b) The accounting technician

(c) The machine operator

(d) A partner of the business

2 Recording the purchase of non-current assets

2.1 Introduction

We have seen that the cost of a non-current asset will appear in the statement of financial position as capitalised expenditure. Therefore it is important that the correct figure for cost is included in the correct ledger account.

2.2 Cost

The cost figure that will be used to record the non-current asset is the full purchase price of the asset. Care should be taken when considering the cost of some assets, in particular motor cars, as the invoice may show that the total amount paid includes some revenue expenditure, for example petrol and road fund licences. These elements of revenue expenditure must be written off to the statement of profit or loss and only the capital expenditure included as the cost of the non-current asset.

> ### Definition
>
> Cost should include the cost of the asset and the cost of getting the asset to its current location and into working condition. Therefore cost is:
>
> **Purchase price + additional costs which may include freight costs, installation costs and test runs**.

> ### Activity 2
>
> When a company purchases disks for the new computer, the amount of the purchase is debited to computer equipment (cost) account.
>
> (a) Is this treatment correct?
>
> (b) If so, why; if not, why not?

2.3 Ledger accounts

If a non-current asset is paid for by cheque then the double entry is:

DR Non-current asset account

CR Bank account

If the non-current asset was bought on credit the double entry is:

DR Non-current asset account

CR Payables/loan account

In practice most organisations will have different non-current asset accounts for the different types of non-current assets, for example: ·

- land and buildings account
- plant and machinery account
- motor vehicles account
- office fixtures and fittings account
- computer equipment account.

2.4 Purchase of non-current assets and VAT

When most non-current assets are purchased VAT will be added and this can normally be recovered from HMRC as input VAT. Therefore the cost of the non-current asset is the amount net of VAT.

 Activity 3

A piece of machinery has been purchased on credit from a supplier for £4,200 plus VAT.

How will this purchase be recorded?

	Account name	Amount £
DR	Machinery/Building/Fixtures	4,200/5,040
DR	Machinery/VAT/Payables	5,040/840
CR	Bank /Payables/VAT	4,200/5,040

Circle the correct account name and the amount.

2.5 Purchase of cars and VAT

When new cars are purchased the business is not allowed to reclaim the VAT. Therefore the cost to be capitalised for the car must include the VAT.

 Example

Raymond has just purchased a new car for his business by cheque and an extract from the invoice shows the following:

	£
Cost of car	18,000
Road fund licence	155
	18,155
VAT on cost of car	3,600
Total cost	21,755

Record this cost in the ledger accounts of the business.

Motor cars account

	£		£
Bank (18,000 + 3,600)	21,600		

Motor expenses account

	£		£
Bank	155		

Bank account

	£		£
		Motor vehicle + expenses	21,755

Note that only the motor cars account balance would appear in the statement of financial position, i.e. be capitalised, while the motor expenses account balance would appear in the statement of profit or loss as an expense for the period.

2.6 Transfer journal

Non-current asset acquisitions do not normally take place frequently in organisations and many organisations will tend to record the acquisition in the transfer journal.

 Definition

The transfer journal is a primary record which is used for transactions that do not appear in the other primary records of the business.

The transfer journal will tend to take the form of an instruction to the bookkeeper as to which accounts to debit and credit and what this transaction is for.

An example of a transfer journal for the purchase of a non-current asset is given below.

Journal entry			No: 02714	
Date	**20 May 20X1**			
Prepared by	C Jones			
Authorised by	F Peters			
Account	Code	Debit £	Credit £	
Computers: Cost	0120	5,000		
VAT	0138	1,000		
Bank	0163		6,000	
Totals		6,000	6,000	

A transfer journal is used for entries to the ledger accounts that do not come from any other primary records.

 Activity 4

Below is an invoice for the purchase of a motor car purchased on the 1 June 20X1. The payment was made by cheque.

The business's year end is 31 December 20X1

	£
Cost of car	20,000
Road fund licence	165
	20,165
VAT (20,000 × 20%)	4,000
	24,165

Note that in the assessment you may be given different forms to fill in for journal entries, and may be told to ignore any reference columns for the entry. Complete the journal entries to record the purchase of the asset.

Ref	Account name	Dr (£)	CR (£)

2.7 Non-current assets produced internally

In some instances a business may make its own non-current assets. For example a construction company may construct a new head office for the organisation.

Where non-current assets are produced internally then the amount that should be capitalised as the cost is the production cost of the asset.

 Definition

Production cost is the direct cost of production (materials, labour and expenses) plus an appropriate amount of the normal production overheads relating to production of this asset.

2.8 Capitalising subsequent expenditure

It is frequently the case that there will be further expenditure on a non-current asset during its life in the business. In most cases this will be classed as revenue expenditure and will therefore be charged to the statement of profit or loss. However in some cases the expenditure may be so major that it should also be capitalised as an addition to the cost of the non-current asset.

IAS 16 Property, Plant and Equipment states that subsequent expenditure should only be capitalised in three circumstances:

- where it enhances the value of the asset
- where a major component of the asset is replaced or restored
- where it is a major inspection or overhaul of the asset.

2.9 Financing non-current asset acquisitions

Non-current assets generally cost a lot of money and are purchased with the intention that they be used over a period of years. For most businesses the full purchase cost cannot be funded from cash available in the business, and so other financing methods must be found, including the following:

Borrowing – a bank or other lender lends the business cash to pay for the asset, at a negotiated interest rate. Often the loan will be secured on the asset, so that it can be sold directly for the benefit of the bank or lender in the event of non-payment or liquidation.

Hire purchase – the business makes regular payments to the finance company (comprising capital amounts plus interest) but the asset remains the finance company's property until the last regular payment is made, when the business can elect to take over the asset's full ownership.

Leasing – the business makes regular payments to the finance company and makes full use of the asset, but never actually becomes the asset's owner.

Part exchange – part of the purchase price of the asset is satisfied by transferring ownership of another asset to the seller. This is frequently seen in the case of motor vehicles, and represents a disposal of the old asset and a purchase of the new asset at the same time. (This will be covered in chapter 5.)

3 Types of non-current assets

3.1 Introduction

We have seen how the non-current assets of a business will be classified between the various types, e.g. buildings, plant and machinery, etc. However there is a further distinction in the classification of non-current assets that must be considered. This is the distinction between tangible non-current assets and intangible non-current assets.

3.2 Tangible non-current assets

 Definition

Tangible non-current assets are assets which have a tangible, physical form.

Tangible non-current assets therefore are all of the types of assets that we have been considering so far such as machinery, cars, computers, etc.

3.3 Intangible non-current assets

 Definition

Intangible non-current assets are assets for long-term use in the business that have no physical form e.g. patents, licences and goodwill.

3.4 Goodwill

Many businesses will have a particular intangible non-current asset known as goodwill. Goodwill is the asset arising from the fact that a going concern business is worth more in total than the value of its tangible net assets in total. The reasons for this additional asset are many and varied but include factors such as good reputation, good location, quality products and quality after sales service.

3.5 Accounting treatment of goodwill

Although it is recognised that goodwill exists in many businesses, it is generally not included as a non-current asset on the statement of financial position. This is for a number of reasons including the difficulty in valuation of goodwill and also its innate volatility. Consider a restaurant with an excellent reputation which suddenly causes a bout of food poisoning. The asset, goodwill, could literally be wiped out overnight.

Even though goodwill will not generally be included in the statement of financial position, you need to be aware of its existence for this unit and to be able to deal with it when accounting for partnerships in Prepare Final Accounts for Sole Traders and Partnership (FSTP).

4 Non-current asset register

4.1 Introduction

The non-current assets of a business will tend to be expensive items that the organisation will wish to have good control over. In particular the organisation will wish to keep control over which assets are kept where and check on a regular basis that they are still there.

Therefore most organisations that own a significant number of non-current assets will tend to maintain a non-current asset register as well as the ledger accounts that record the purchase of the non-current assets. The non-current asset register forms a record from which control can be maintained through physical verifications and reconciliations with the ledger accounts.

4.2 Layout of a non-current asset register

The purpose of a non-current asset register is to record all relevant details of all of the non-current assets of the organisation. The format of the register will depend on the organisation, but the information to be recorded for each non-current asset of the business will probably include the following:

- asset description
- asset identification code/barcode
- asset location/member of staff the asset has been issued to
- date of purchase
- purchase price
- supplier name and address
- invoice number
- any additional enhancement expenditure
- depreciation method
- estimated useful life
- estimated residual value
- accumulated depreciation to date
- carrying value
- disposal details.

A typical format for a non-current asset register is shown below.

4.3 Example of a non-current asset register

Date of purchase	Invoice number	Serial number	Item	Cost	Accum'd depreciation b/f at 1.1.X8	Date of disposal	Depreciation charge in 20X8	Accum'd depreciation c/f	Disposal proceeds	Loss/ gain on disposal
				£	£		£	£	£	£
3.2.X5	345	3488	Chair	340						
6.4.X6	466	–	Bookcase	258						
10.7.X7	587	278	Chair	160						
				——						
				758						
				——						

There may also be a further column or detail which shows exactly where the particular asset is located within the business. This will facilitate checks that should be regularly carried out to ensure that all of the assets the business owns are still on the premises.

Activity 5

Record the cost of the motor car in the non-current asset register below for the previous Activity 4.

Date of purchase	Invoice number	Serial number	Item	Cost	Accum'd depreciation b/f at 1.1.X8	Date of disposal	Depreciation charge in 20X8	Accum'd depreciation c/f	Disposal proceeds	Loss/gain on disposal
				£	£		£	£	£	£
				——						
				——						

 Activity 6

1   Purchase of a motor van is classified as **revenue / capital** expenditure?

2   Decorating the office is an example of **revenue / capital** expenditure

3   Other than its actual purchase price, what additional costs can be capitalised as part of the cost of the non-current asset?

4   What are the three occasions where subsequent expenditure on a non-current asset can be capitalised according to IAS 16?

5   Goodwill is an example of **a tangible asset / a current asset / an intangible asset**?

5   Summary

In this chapter we have considered the acquisition of non-current assets. The acquisition of a non-current asset must be properly authorised and the most appropriate method of funding used. The correct cost figure must be used when capitalising the non-current asset and care should be taken with VAT and the exclusion of any revenue expenditure in the total cost. The details of the acquisition of the asset should also be included in the non-current asset register.

Answers to chapter activities

Activity 1

The answer is D

Activity 2

(a) No.

(b) Although, by definition, the computer disks may be considered as non-current assets, their treatment would come within the remit of the concept of materiality and would probably be treated as office expenses – revenue expenditure.

Activity 3

	Account name	Amount £
DR	Machinery	4,200
DR	VAT	840
CR	Payables	5,040

Activity 4

Ref	Account name	Dr (£)	CR (£)
	Motor car	24,000	
	Motor expenses	165	
	Bank		24,165

Activity 5

Date of purchase	Invoice number	Serial number	Item	Cost	Accum'd depreciation b/f at 1.1.X8	Date of disposal	Depreciation charge in 20X8	Accum'd depreciation c/f	Disposal proceeds	Loss/gain on disposal
				£	£		£	£	£	£
1 Jun X1			Motor car	24,000						
				——						
				24,000						
				——						

 Activity 6

1   Capital expenditure.

2   Revenue expenditure.

3   The full purchase price of the asset plus the cost of getting the asset to its location and into working condition.

4   Where the expenditure enhances the economic benefits of the asset.

   Where the expenditure is on a major component which is being replaced or restored.

   Where the expenditure is on a major inspection or overhaul of the asset.

5   Intangible asset.

KAPLAN PUBLISHING

6 Test your knowledge

Workbook Activity 7

Stapling machine

When a company purchases a new stapler so that accounts clerks can staple together relevant pieces of paper, the amount of the purchase is debited to the fittings and equipment (cost) account.

(a)   Is this treatment correct?

(b)   If so, why; if not; why not

Workbook Activity 8

Office equipment

A company bought a small item of computer software costing £32.50. This had been treated as office equipment. Do you agree with this treatment?

Give brief reasons.

Workbook Activity 9

Engine

If an airline replaces one of its plane's engines, which are depreciated at a different rate to the rest of the plane's components, at a cost of £1,800,000 would this represent capital or revenue expenditure? Give brief reasons.

Depreciation

Introduction

Depreciation features prominently within the assessment of Accounts Preparation.

You need to be able to understand the purpose of depreciation, calculate the annual depreciation charge using one of two standard methods, account correctly for the annual depreciation charge and treat the depreciation accounts correctly in the extended trial balance.

KNOWLEDGE	CONTENTS
Explain the need for, and methods of, providing for depreciation on non-current assets (3.3)	1 The purpose of depreciation
	2 Calculating depreciation
Describe the contents and use of the non-current asset register (3.4)	3 Accounting for depreciation
	4 Assets acquired during an accounting period
	5 Depreciation in the non-current asset register

SKILLS

Calculate the depreciation charges for a non-current asset using (5.1)

Straight line method

Diminishing (reducing) balance method

Record the depreciation in the non-current assets register(5.2)

Record depreciation in the appropriate ledger accounts (5.3)

Close off the ledger accounts at the end of the financial period, correctly identifying any transfers to the statement of profit or loss (5.4)

Resolve any queries, unusual features or discrepancies relating to the accounting records for non-current assets or refer to an appropriate person (3.5)

1 The purpose of depreciation

1.1 Introduction

We have already seen that non-current assets are capitalised in the accounting records which means that they are treated as capital expenditure and their cost is initially recorded in the statement of financial position and not charged to the statement of profit or loss. However this is not the end of the story and this cost figure must eventually go through the statement of profit or loss by means of the annual depreciation charge.

1.2 Accruals concept

The accruals concept states that the costs incurred in a period should be matched with the income produced in the same period. When a non-current asset is used it is contributing to the production of the income of the business. Therefore in accordance with the accruals concept some of the cost of the non-current asset should be charged to the statement of profit or loss each year that the asset is used.

1.3 What is depreciation?

 Definition

Depreciation is the measure of the cost of the economic benefits of the tangible non-current assets that have been consumed during the period. Consumption includes the wearing out, using up or other reduction in the useful economic life of a tangible non-current asset whether arising from use, effluxion of time or obsolescence through either changes in technology or demand for the goods and services produced by the asset. (IAS 16 Property, Plant and Equipment.)

This demonstrates the purpose of depreciation is to charge the statement of profit or loss with the amount of the cost of the non-current asset that has been used up during the accounting period.

1.4 How does depreciation work?

The basic principle of depreciation is that a proportion of the cost of the non-current asset is charged to the statement of profit or loss each period and deducted from the cost of the non-current asset in the statement of financial position. Therefore as the non-current asset gets older its value in the statement of financial position reduces and each year the statement of profit or loss is charged with this proportion of the initial cost.

Definition

Carrying value is the cost of the non-current asset less the accumulated depreciation to date.

	£
Cost	X
Less: Accumulated depreciation	(X)
Carrying value	X

The aim of depreciation of non-current assets is to show the cost of the asset that has been consumed during the year. It is not to show the true or market value of the asset. So this carrying value will probably have little relation to the actual market value of the asset at each statement of financial position date. The important aspect of depreciation is that it is a charge to the statement of profit or loss of the amount of the non-current asset consumed during the year.

2 Calculating depreciation

2.1 Introduction

The calculation of depreciation can be done by a variety of methods, although there are two principal methods, the straight line method and the diminishing (reducing) balance method (see later in the chapter). The principles behind each method are the same.

2.2 Factors affecting depreciation

There are three factors that affect the depreciation of a non-current asset:

- the cost of the asset (dealt with in Chapter 3 Capital and Revenue Expenditure)

- the length of the useful economic life of the asset

- the estimated residual value of the asset.

2.3 Useful economic life

Definition

The useful economic life of an asset is the estimated life of the asset for the current owner.

This is the estimated number of years that the business will be using this asset and therefore the number of years over which the cost of the asset must be spread via the depreciation charge.

One particular point to note here is that land is viewed as having an infinite life and therefore no depreciation charge is required for land. However, any buildings on the land should be depreciated.

2.4 Estimated residual value

Many assets will be sold for a form of scrap value at the end of their useful economic lives.

Definition

The estimated residual value of a non-current asset is the amount that it is estimated the asset will be sold for when it is no longer of use to the business.

The aim of depreciation is to write off the cost of the non-current asset less the estimated residual value over the useful economic life of the asset.

2.5 The straight line method of depreciation

Definition

The straight line method calculates a consistent amount of depreciation over the life of the asset.

The method of calculating depreciation under this method is:

$$\text{Annual depreciation charge} = \frac{\text{Cost} - \text{estimated residual value}}{\text{Useful economic life}}$$

It should be noted that it is possible to multiply the depreciable amount by a percentage, e.g. instead of dividing by four years you can multiply by 25%; instead of dividing by five years you can multiply by 20%.

Example

An asset has been purchased by an organisation for £400,000 and is expected to be used in the organisation for 6 years. At the end of the six -year period it is currently estimated that the asset will be sold for £40,000.

What is the annual depreciation charge on the straight line basis?

Solution

$$\text{Annual depreciation charge} \quad = \quad \frac{400,000 - 40,000}{6}$$

$$= \quad £60,000$$

2.6 The diminishing (reducing) balance method

 Definition

The diminishing balance method of depreciation allows a higher amount of depreciation to be charged in the early years of an asset's life compared to the later years. This reflects the increased levels of usage of such assets in the earlier periods of their lives.

The depreciation is calculated using this method by multiplying the carrying value of the asset at the start of the year by a fixed percentage.

 Example

A non-current asset has a cost of £100,000.

It is to be depreciated using the diminishing balance method at 30% over its useful economic life of four years, after which it will have an estimated residual value of approximately £24,000.

Show the amount of depreciation charged for each of the four years of the asset's life.

Solution

	£
Cost	100,000
Year 1 depreciation 30% × 100,000	(30,000)
Carrying value at the end of year 1	70,000
Year 2 depreciation 30% × 70,000	(21,000)
Carrying value at the end of year 2	49,000
Year 3 depreciation 30% × 49,000	(14,700)
Carrying value at the end of year 3	34,300
Year 4 depreciation 30% × 34,300	(10,290)
Carrying value at the end of year 4	24,010

 Activity 1

A business buys a motor van for £20,000 and depreciates it at 10% per annum by the diminishing balance method.

Calculate:

- The depreciation charge for the second year of the motor van's use.

- Calculate the carrying value at the end of the second year.

Solution

	£
Cost	
Year 1 depreciation	
Carrying value at the end of year 1	
Year 2 depreciation	
Carrying value at the end of year 2	

2.7 Choice of method

Whether a business chooses the straight line method of depreciation or the diminishing balance method (or indeed any of the other methods which are outside the scope of this syllabus) is the choice of the management.

The straight line method is the simplest method to use. Often however the diminishing balance method is chosen for assets which do in fact reduce in value more in the early years of their life than the later years. This is often the case with cars and computers and the diminishing balance method is often used for these assets.

Once the method of depreciation has been chosen for a particular class of non-current assets then this same method should be used each year in order to satisfy the accounting objective of comparability. The management of a business can change the method of depreciation used for a class of non-current assets but this should only be done if the new method shows a truer picture of the consumption of the cost of the asset than the previous method.

 Activity 2

Give one reason why a business might choose diminishing balance as the method for depreciating its delivery vans?

(a) It is an easy method to apply.

(b) It is the method applied for non-current assets that lose more value in their early years.

(c) It is the method that is most consistent.

3 Accounting for depreciation

3.1 Introduction

Now we have seen how to calculate depreciation we must next learn how to account for it in the ledger accounts of the business.

3.2 Dual effect of depreciation

The two effects of the charge for depreciation each year are:

- there is an expense to the statement of profit or loss and therefore a debit entry to a depreciation expense account

- therefore we create a provision for accumulated depreciation account and there is a credit entry to this account.

Definition

The provision for accumulated depreciation account is used to reduce the value of the non-current asset in the statement of financial position.

 Example

An asset has been purchased by an organisation for £400,000 and is expected to be used in the organisation for six years.

At the end of the six year period it is currently estimated that the residual value will be £40,000.

The asset is to be depreciated on the straight line basis.

Show the entries in the ledger accounts for the first two years of the asset's life and how this asset would appear in the statement of financial position at the end of each of the first two years.

Solution

Step 1

Record the purchase of the asset in the non-current asset account.

Non-current asset account

	£		£
Year 1 Bank	400,000		

Step 2

Record the depreciation expense for Year 1.

$$\text{Depreciation charge} = \frac{£400,000 - £40,000}{6}$$

$$= £60,000 \text{ per year}$$

Dr   Depreciation expense account

Cr   Accumulated depreciation account

Depreciation expense account

	£		£
Year 1	60,000		
Accumulated depreciation			

Accumulated depreciation account

	£		£
		Expense account	60,000

Note the statement of financial position will show the cost of the asset and the accumulated depreciation is then deducted to arrive at the carrying value of the asset.

Step 3.

Show the entries for the year 2 depreciation charge

Depreciation expense account

	£		£
Year 2	60,000		
Accumulated depreciation			

Accumulated depreciation account

	£		£
		Balance b/d	60,000
		Expense account	60,000

Note that the expense account has no opening balance as this was transferred to the statement of profit or loss at the end of year 1.

However the accumulated depreciation account being a statement of financial position account is a continuing account and does have an opening balance being the depreciation charged so far on this asset.

Step 4

Balance off the accumulated depreciation account and show how the non-current asset would appear in the statement of financial position at the end of year 2.

Accumulated depreciation account

	£		£
		Balance b/d	60,000
Balance c/d	120,000	Expense account	60,000
	———		———
	120,000		120,000
	———		———
		Balance b/d	120,000

Statement of financial position extract

	Cost £	Accumulated depreciation £	Carrying value £
Non-current asset	400,000	120,000	280,000

Activity 3

The following task is about recording non-current asset information in the general ledger.

A new asset has been acquired. Sales tax can be reclaimed on this asset.

- The cost of the asset excluding VAT is £85,000 and this was paid for by cheque.

- The residual value is expected to be £5,000 excluding VAT

- The asset is to be depreciated using the straight line basis and the assets useful economic life is 5 years.

Make entries to account for:

(a) The purchase of the new asset

(b) The depreciation on the new asset

Asset at cost account

£		£
——		——
——		——

Accumulated depreciation

£		£
——		——
——		——

Depreciation expense

£		£
——		——
——		——

Activity 4

At 31 March 20X3, a business owned a motor vehicle which had a cost of £12,100 and accumulated depreciation of £9,075.

Complete the statement of financial position extract below.

	Cost	Accumulated Depreciation	Carrying Value
Motor vehicle			

3.3 Carrying value

As you have seen from the statement of financial position extract the non-current assets are shown at their carrying value. As previously stated, the carrying value is made up of the cost of the asset less the accumulated depreciation on that asset or class of assets.

The carrying value is purely an accounting value for the non-current asset. It is not an attempt to place a market value or current value on the asset and it in fact often bears little relation to the actual value of the asset.

3.4 Ledger entries with diminishing balance depreciation

No matter what method of depreciation is used the ledger entries are always the same. So here is another example to work through.

 Example

On 1 April 20X2 a machine was purchased for £12,000 with an estimated useful life of 4 years and estimated scrap value of £4,920. The machine is to be depreciated at 20% diminishing balance.

The ledger accounts for the years ended 31 March 20X3, 31 March 20X4 and 31 March 20X5 are to be written up.

Show how the non-current asset would appear in the statement of financial position at each of these dates.

Solution

Step 1

Calculate the depreciation charge.

Cost			£
			12,000
Year-end March 20X3 – depreciation	12,000 × 20%	=	2,400
			9,600
Year-end March 20X4 – depreciation	9,600 × 20%	=	1,920
			7,680
Year-end March 20X5 – depreciation	7,680 × 20%	=	1,536
			6,144

Step 2

Enter each year's figures in the ledger accounts bringing down a balance on the machinery account and accumulated depreciation account but clearing out the entry in the expense account to the statement of profit or loss.

Machinery account

	£		£
April 20X2 Bank	12,000	Mar 20X3 Balance c/d	12,000
April 20X3 Balance b/d	12,000	Mar 20X4 Balance c/d	12,000
April 20X4 Balance b/d	12,000	Mar 20X5 Balance c/d	12,000
April 20X5 Balance b/d	12,000		

Depreciation expense account

	£		£
Mar 20X3 Accumulated dep'n a/c	2,400	Mar 20X3 SPL	2,400
Mar 20X4 Accumulated dep'n a/c	1,920	Mar 20X4 SPL	1,920
Mar 20X5 Accumulated dep'n a/c	1,536	Mar 20X5 SPL	1,536

Machinery: accumulated depreciation account

	£		£
Mar 20X3 Balance c/d	2,400	Mar 20X3 Depreciation expense	2,400
		Apr 20X3 Balance b/d	2,400
Mar 20X4 Balance c/d	4,320	Mar 20X4 Depreciation expense	1,920
	4,320		4,320
		Apr 20X4 Balance b/d	4,320
Mar 20X5 Balance c/d	5,856	Mar 20X5 Depreciation expense	1,536
	5,856		5,856
		Apr 20X5 Balance b/d	5,856

Statement of financial position extract

Non-current assets		Cost £	Accumulated depreciation £	Carrying value £
At 31 Mar 20X3	Machinery	12,000	2,400	9,600
At 31 Mar 20X4	Machinery	12,000	4,320	7,680
At 31 Mar 20X5	Machinery	12,000	5,856	6,144

Make sure that you remember to carry down the accumulated depreciation at the end of each period as the opening balance at the start of the next period.

 Activity 5

ABC Co owns the following assets as at 31 December 20X6:

	£
Plant and machinery	5,000
Office furniture	800

Depreciation is to be provided as follows:

(a)   plant and machinery, 20% reducing-balance method

(b)   office furniture, 25% on cost per year, straight-line method.

The plant and machinery was purchased on 1 January 20X4 and the office furniture on 1 January 20X5.

Required:

Show the ledger accounts for the year ended 31 December 20X6 necessary to record the transactions.

4 Assets acquired during an accounting period

4.1 Introduction

So far in our calculations of the depreciation charge for the year we have ignored precisely when in the year the non-current asset was purchased. Pro rata calculations for the straight line method of depreciation will be required only when the organisational policy stipulates. Pro rata calculations for part of a year will not be required for the diminishing balance method.

There are two main methods of expressing a depreciation policy and both of these will now be considered.

4.2 Calculations on a monthly basis

The policy may state that depreciation is to be charged on a monthly basis. This means that the annual charge will be calculated using the depreciation method given and then pro-rated for the number of months in the year that the asset has been owned.

 Example

A piece of machinery is purchased on 1 June 20X1 for £20,000. It has a useful life of 5 years and zero scrap value. The organisation's accounting year ends on 31 December.

What is the depreciation charge for 20X1? Depreciation is charged on a monthly basis using the straight line method.

Solution

$$\text{Annual charge} = \frac{£20,000}{5} = £4,000$$

Charge for 20X1: £4,000 × 7/12 (i.e. June to Dec) = £2,333

Activity 6

A business buys a machine for £40,000 on 1 January 20X3 and another one on 1 July 20X3 for £48,000.

Depreciation is charged at 10% per annum on cost, and calculated on a monthly basis.

What is the total depreciation charge for the two machines for the year ended 31 December 20X3?

4.3 Acquisition and disposal policy

The second method of dealing with depreciation in the year of acquisition is to have a depreciation policy as follows:

'A full year's depreciation is charged in the year of acquisition and none in the year of disposal.'

Ensure that you read the instructions in any question carefully as in the exam you will always be given the depreciation policy of the business.

 Activity 7

A business purchased a motor van on 7 August 20X3 at a cost of £12,640.

It is depreciated on a straight-line basis using an expected useful economic life of five years and estimated residual value of zero.

Depreciation is charged with a full year's depreciation in the year of purchase and none in the year of sale.

The business has a year end of 30 November.

What is the carrying value of the motor van at 30 November 20X4?

What does this amount represent?

5 Depreciation in the non-current asset register

5.1 Introduction

In the previous chapter we considered how the cost of non-current assets and their acquisition details should be recorded in the non-current asset register.

5.2 Recording depreciation in the non-current asset register

Let us now look at recording depreciation in the non-current asset register.

Example

Date of purchase	Invoice number	Serial number	Item	Cost	Accum'd depreciation b/f at 1.1.X8	Date of disposal	Depreciation charge in 20X8	Accum'd deprec- iation c/f	Disposal proceeds	Loss/ gain on disposal
				£	£		£	£	£	£
3.2.X5	345	3488	Chair	340						
6.4.X6	466	–	Bookcase	258						
10.7.X7	587	278	Chair	160						
				758						

Using the example from the previous chapter, reproduced above, we have now decided that fixtures and fittings (including office furniture) should be depreciated at 10% per annum using the straight-line method.

A full year's depreciation is charged in the year of purchase and none in the year of disposal.

The current year is the year to 31 December 20X8.

The chair acquired on 10.7.X7 was sold on 12.7.X8. A new table was purchased for £86 on 30.8.X8.

Do not worry at this stage about the disposal proceeds. We will look at disposals in the next chapter.

Solution

Date of purchase	Invoice number	Serial number	Item	Cost	Accum'd depreciation b/f at 1.1.X8	Date of disposal	Depreciation charge in 20X8	Accum'd deprec- iation c/f	Disposal proceeds	Loss/ gain on disposal
				£	£		£	£	£	£
3.2.X5	345	3488	Chair	340	102 (W1)		34	136		
6.4.X6	466	–	Bookcase	258	52 (W2)		26	78		
10.7.X7	587	278	Chair	160	16 (W3)	12.7.X8	– (W4)			
30.8.X8	634	1,228	Table	86			9	9		
				844	170			69	223	

Workings:

(W1) 3 years' depreciation – £340 × 10% × 3 = £102

(W2) 2 years' depreciation – £258 × 10% × 2 = £52

(W3) 1 year's depreciation – £160 × 10% = £16

(W4) No depreciation in year of sale

Note how the depreciation charge is calculated for each asset except the one disposed of in the year as the accounting policy is to charge no depreciation in the year of sale. If the policy was to charge depreciation even in the year of disposal, then the charge would be calculated and included in the total.

The total accumulated depreciation should agree with the balance carried forward on the accumulated depreciation ledger account in the general ledger.

 Activity 8

A business called Stig Trading has asked your advice on improving their accounting system. They would like your advice on how to improve the records of non-current assets.

The business produces fashion clothing. They have the following information on the sewing machines in the business.

Machine number	Cost
	£
SEW 789367	15,500
ING 401388	25,000
MAC 402765	21,500

(a) Which accounting record would you suggest that the business should keep to record the details of these machines?

(b) Name three additional items that you would suggest to the business that they should keep a record of, regarding the machines?

(c) Name one advantage of recording the machines in the record that you have suggested in part (a).

6 Summary

This chapter considered the manner in which the cost of non-current assets is charged to the statement of profit or loss over the life of the non-current assets, known as depreciation.

There are a variety of different methods of depreciation though only the straight-line method and diminishing balance method are required for Accounts Preparation.

The accounting entries in the general ledger are the same regardless of the method of depreciation selected. The statement of profit or loss is charged with the depreciation expense and the accumulated depreciation account shows the accumulated depreciation over the life of the asset to date.

The accumulated balance is netted off against the cost of the non-current asset in the statement of financial position in order to show the non-current asset at its carrying value.

Finally the depreciation must also be entered into the non-current asset register each year.

Answers to chapter activities

Activity 1

	£
Cost	20,000
Year 1 depreciation	(2,000)
	———
Carrying value at the end of year 1	18,000
Year 2 depreciation	(1,800)
	———
Carrying value at the end of year 2	16,200
	———

Activity 2

The answer is B

The diminishing balance method is used to equalise the combined costs of depreciation and maintenance over the vehicle's life (i.e. in early years, depreciation is high, maintenance low; in later years, depreciation is low, maintenance is high).

The diminishing balance method is also used for non-current assets that are likely to lose more value in their early years than their later years such as cars or vans.

Activity 3

Annual depreciation charge $= \dfrac{85{,}000 - 5{,}000}{5}$

$= £16{,}000$

Asset at cost account

	£		£
Bank	85,000	Balance c/d	85,000
	85,000		**85,000**

Accumulated depreciation

	£		£
Balance c/d	16,000	Depreciation expense	16,000
	16,000		**16,000**

Depreciation expense

	£		£
Accumulated depreciation	16,000	Statement of profit or loss	16,000
	16,000		**16,000**

Activity 4

Statement of financial position extract below.

	Cost	Accumulated depreciation	Carrying Value
Motor Vehicle	12,100	9,075	3,025

Activity 5

Plant and machinery account

Date		£	Date		£
1.1.X6	Balance b/d	5,000	31.12.X6	Balance c/d	5,000
1.1.X7	Balance b/d	5,000			

Office furniture account

Date		£	Date		£
1.1.X6	Balance b/d	800	31.12.X6	Balance c/d	800
1.1.X7	Balance b/d	800			

Depreciation expense account

Date		£	Date		£
31.12.X6	Accumulated dep'n a/c – plant and machinery	640	31.12.X6	SPL	840
31.12.X6	Accumulated dep'n a/c – office furniture	200			
		840			840

Accumulated depreciation account – Plant and machinery

Date		£	Date		£
31.12.X6	Balance c/d	2,440	1.1.X6	Balance b/d	1,800
			31.12.X6	Dep'n expense	640
		2,440			2,440
			1.1.X7	Balance b/d	2,440

Accumulated depreciation account – Office furniture

Date		£	Date		£
31.12.X6	Balance c/d	400	1.1.X6	Balance b/d	200
			31.12.X6	Dep'n expense	200
		———			———
		400			400
		———			———
			1.1.X7	Balance b/d	400

The opening balance on the accumulated depreciation account is calculated as follows:

	Plant and machinery	Office furniture
	£	£
20X4 20% × £5,000	1,000	–
20X5 20% × £(5,000 – 1,000)	800	
25% × £800		200
	———	———
Opening balance 1.1.X6	1,800	200
	———	———

The depreciation charge for the year 20X6 is calculated as follows:

	Plant and machinery	Office furniture	Total
	£	£	£
20% × (5,000 – 1,800)	640		
25% × £800		200	840
	———	———	

Activity 6

		£
Machine 1	£40,000 × 10%	4,000
Machine 2	£48,000 × 10% × 6/12	2,400
		———
		6,400
		———

Activity 7

Annual depreciation $= \dfrac{£12,640}{5} = £2,528$

CV $= £12,640 - (2 \times £2,528) = £7,584$

This is the cost of the van less the accumulated depreciation to date. It is the amount remaining to be depreciated in the future. It is not a market value.

 Activity 8

1   Non-current asset register

2   Any of the following:

       Asset description

       Asset identification code

       Asset location

       Date of purchase

       Purchase price

       Supplier name and address

       Invoice number

       Any additional enhancement expenditure

       Estimated useful life

       Estimated residual value

       Accumulated depreciation to date

       Carrying value

       Disposal details

3   It would be easy to locate the machine.

7 Test your knowledge

Workbook Activity 9

Mead is a sole trader with a 31 December year end. He purchased a car on 1 January 20X3 at a cost of £12,000. He estimates that its useful life is four years, after which he will trade it in for £2,400. The annual depreciation charge is to be calculated using the straight line method.

Task

Write up the motor car cost and accumulated depreciation accounts and the depreciation expense account for the first three years, bringing down a balance on each account at the end of each year.

Workbook Activity 10

S Telford purchases a machine for £6,000. He estimates that the machine will last eight years and its scrap value then will be £1,000.

Tasks

(1) Prepare the machine cost and accumulated depreciation accounts for the first three years of the machine's life, and show the statement of financial position extract at the end of each of these years charging depreciation on the straight line method.

(2) What would be the carrying value of the machine at the end of the third year if depreciation was charged at 20% on the diminishing balance method?

KAPLAN PUBLISHING

Workbook Activity 11

Hillton

(a) Hillton started a veggie food manufacturing business on 1 January 20X6. During the first three years of trading he bought machinery as follows:

January	20X6	Chopper	Cost	£4,000
April	20X7	Mincer	Cost	£6,000
June	20X8	Stuffer	Cost	£8,000

Each machine was bought for cash.

Hillton's policy for machinery is to charge depreciation on the straight line basis at 25% per annum. A full year's depreciation is charged in the year of purchase, irrespective of the actual date of purchase.

Required:

For the three years from 1 January 20X6 to 31 December 20X8 prepare the following ledger accounts:

(i) Machinery account

(ii) Accumulated depreciation account (machinery)

(iii) Depreciation expense account (machinery)

Bring down the balance on each account at 31 December each year.

Tip – *Use a table to calculate the depreciation charge for each year.*

(b) Over the same three year period Hillton bought the following motor vehicles for his business:

January 20X6	Metro van	Cost £3,200
July 20X7	Transit van	Cost £6,000
October 20X8	Astra van	Cost £4,200

Each vehicle was bought for cash.

Hillton's policy for motor vehicles is to charge depreciation on the diminishing balance basis at 40% per annum. A full year's depreciation is charged in the year of purchase, irrespective of the actual date of purchase.

Required:

For the three years from 1 January 20X6 to 31 December 20X8 prepare the following ledger accounts:

(i)   Motor vehicles account

(ii)   Accumulated depreciation account (motor vehicles)

(iii)   Depreciation expense account (motor vehicles)

Bring down the balance on each account at 31 December each year.

Tip – *Use another depreciation table.*

 Workbook Activity 12

On 1 December 20X2 Infortec Computers owned motor vehicles costing £28,400. During the year ended 30 November 20X3 the following changes to the motor vehicles took place:

		£
1 March 20X3	Sold vehicle – original cost	18,000
1 June 20X3	Purchased new vehicle – cost	10,000
1 September 20X3	Purchased new vehicle – cost	12,000

Depreciation on motor vehicles is calculated on a monthly basis at 20% per annum on cost.

Complete the table below to calculate the total depreciation charge to profits for the year ended 30 November 20X3.

	£
Depreciation for vehicle sold 1 March 20X3	
Depreciation for vehicle purchased 1 June 20X3	
Depreciation for vehicle purchased 1 September 20X3	
Depreciation for other vehicles owned during the year	
Total depreciation for the year ended 30 November 20X3	

Disposal of capital assets

5

Introduction

When a capital asset or non-current asset is disposed of there are a variety of accounting calculations and entries that need to be made.

Firstly, the asset being disposed of must be removed from the accounting records as it is no longer controlled. In most cases the asset will be disposed of for either more or less than its carrying value leading to a profit or a loss on disposal which must be accounted for.

Finally, the fact that the asset has been disposed of must be recorded in the non-current register.

In most examinations you will be required to put through the accounting entries for the disposal of a capital asset (i.e. a non-current asset) and to record the disposal in the non-current register.

This is a favourite area in examinations and must be fully understood. In particular the method of acquiring a new non-current, with an old asset as a part-exchange is a favourite topic, which will be covered in detail in this chapter.

Finally in this chapter we must consider the purpose of the non-current register and how it can be used to regularly check that all of the non-currents owned by the business are in place.

KNOWLEDGE	CONTENTS
Describe how the acquisition of non-current assets can be funded including part exchange (3.1)	1 Accounting for the disposal of capital assets
Explain the accounting treatment for recording the acquisition and disposal of non-currents (3.2)	2 Part-exchange of assets
Explain the need for, and methods of, providing for depreciation on non-current assets (3.3)	3 Authorising disposals 4 Disposals and the non-current register
Describe the contents and use of the non-current register (3.4)	5 Reconciliation of physical assets to the non-current register

SKILLS

Resolve any queries, unusual features or discrepancies relating to the accounting records for non-current assets or refer to an appropriate person (3.5)

Record in the appropriate accounts the acquisition of a non-current asset including funded by part exchange (4.3)

Record the acquisition in a non-current assets register (4.4)

Close off or transfer the ledger account balances at the end of the financial period (4.5)

Identify the correct asset, removing it from the non-current asset register (6.1)

Record the disposal of non-current assets in the appropriate accounts (6.2)

Calculate any gain or loss arising from the disposal, closing off or transferring the account balance (6.3)

1 Accounting for the disposal of capital assets

1.1 Introduction

When a capital or non-current is sold then there are two main aspects to the accounting for this disposal:

Firstly the existing entries in the ledger accounts for the asset being disposed of must be removed as the asset is no longer controlled.

Secondly there is likely to be a profit or loss on disposal and this must be calculated and accounted for.

1.2 Removal of existing ledger account balances

When an asset is sold, the balances in the ledger accounts that relate to that asset must be removed. There are two such balances:

(a) the original cost of the asset in the non-current cost account

(b) the depreciation to date on the asset in the non-current accumulated depreciation account.

In order to remove these two balances we must do the following:

Step 1

Open a disposal account.

Step 2

Transfer the two amounts to the disposal account.

Step 3

Enter any proceeds from the sale of the asset in the disposal account.

 Definition

The disposal account is the account which is used to make all of the entries relating to the sale of the asset and also determines the profit or loss on disposal.

1.3 Profit or loss on disposal

The value that the non-current is recorded at in the books of the organisation is the carrying value, i.e. cost less accumulated depreciation. However this is unlikely to be exactly equal to the amount for which the asset is actually sold. The difference between these two is the profit or loss on disposal.

	£
Cost of asset	X
Less: accumulated depreciation	(X)
Carrying value	X
Disposal proceeds	(X)
(Profit)/loss on disposal	X

If the disposal proceeds are greater than the carrying value a profit has been made, if the proceeds are less than the carrying value a loss has been made.

Example

A non-current cost £14,000

The accumulated depreciation is £9,600.

This asset has just been sold for £3,800.

(a) What is the profit or loss on disposal?

(b) Write up the relevant ledger accounts to record this disposal.

Solution

(a)

	£
Cost	14,000
Accumulated depreciation	(9,600)
Carrying value	4,400
Proceeds	(3,800)
Loss on disposal	600

(b) **Step 1**

Determine the cost and accumulated depreciation ledger account balances for this asset.

Non-current asset

	£		£
Balance b/d	14,000		

Accumulated depreciation

	£		£
		Balance b/d	9,600

Step 2

Open the disposal account and transfer balances on the above two accounts.

Cost

Debit	Disposal account	£14,000
Credit	Non-currents account	£14,000

Accumulated depreciation

Debit	Accumulated depreciation	£9,600
Credit	Disposal account	£9,600

Non-current asset

	£		£
Balance b/d	14,000	Disposal	14,000
	_____		_____
	14,000		14,000
	_____		_____

Accumulated depreciation

	£		£
Disposal	9,600	Balance b/d	9,600
	_____		_____
	9,600		9,600
	_____		_____

Disposal

	£		£
Cost	14,000	Accumulated dep'n	9,600

Step 3

Enter the proceeds in the disposal account and balance the disposal account with the profit/loss on disposal.

Disposal

	£		£
Cost	14,000	Accumulated dep'n	9,600
		Cash	3,800
		Loss – SPL	600
	14,000		14,000

Note 1: The loss of £600 is credited to the disposal account to balance the account. The corresponding debit is in the income statement and represents the loss on the disposal.

Note 2: The profit or loss on disposal can actually be calculated as the balancing figure in the disposal account:

- if there is a debit entry to balance the account then this is a profit on disposal which is credited to the income statement as income

- if there is a credit entry to balance the account then this is a loss on disposal which is debited to the income statement as an additional expense.

 Activity 1

A business buys a car for £20,000 and expects it to have a useful life of five years.

It depreciates the car at 50% reducing balance and sells it after three years for £10,000.

Record the ledger entries for the three years.

Clearly show the profit or loss on disposal.

Car account

	£		£
	___		___
	___		___

Accumulated depreciation

	£		£
	___		___
	___		___

Disposal account

	£		£
	─────		─────
	─────		─────

1.4 Journal entries

We have already seen that journal entries are an instruction to the bookkeeper to put through double entry in the ledger accounts where the transaction is not necessarily recorded in any of the books of prime entry.

The disposal of a non-current is a typical area where journal entries will need to be drafted and this is a favourite topic in examinations.

 Example

Nigel sells his van for £700.

It originally cost £2,000 and so far depreciation has amounted to £1,500.

Record this transaction in the disposals account

Show the journal entries required to account for this disposal.

Solution

Disposal account

	£		£
Motor van (step 1)	2,000	Accumulated depreciation (step 2)	1,500
Income statement – profit on disposal (step 4)	200	Cash (step 3)	700
	─────		─────
	2,200		2,200
	─────		─────

Now for each of the journal entries:

Step 1

To remove the motor van cost from the books of the business.

| Dr | Disposals | 2,000 | |
| Cr | Motor van | | 2,000 |

Step 2

To remove the associated depreciation from the books of the business.

Dr	Accumulated depreciation	1,500
Cr	Disposals	1,500

Note: These two entries together effectively remove the carrying value of the van to the disposals account.

Step 3

To record the cash proceeds.

Dr	Cash	700
Cr	Disposals	700

Step 4

Balance the disposal account

The resulting balance is the profit on sale which is transferred to the statement of profit or loss.

Dr	Disposals	200
Cr	Statement of profit or loss	200

1.5 Journal

As with the acquisition of non-currents, the journal or journal voucher is used as the book of prime entry. The journal voucher for this entire disposal is shown as follows:

Journal entry			No: 234	
Date	4 July 20X8			
Prepared by	J Allen			
Authorised by	A Smith			
Account	**Code**	**Debit £**		**Credit £**
Disposals	0240	2,000		
Motor vehicles cost	0130			2,000
Motor vehicles acc. dep'n	0140	1,500		
Disposals	0240			1,500
Cash at bank (receipts)	0163	700		
Disposals	0240			700
Totals		4,200		4,200

Activity 2

Complete the journal voucher below for the following information:

A company buys a car for £20,000.

The depreciation charged to date is £7,500.

The car is sold for £10,000 at the end of three years.

Using the information above and the following account names and codes, complete the journal voucher below:

0130 Motor vehicles at cost

0140 Motor vehicles accumulated depreciation

0163 Cash at bank (receipts)

0240 Disposals

Journal entry No 235

Date	13 June 20X8		
Prepared by	A Tech		
Authorised by	B Jones		
Account	**Code**	**Debit** **£**	**Credit** **£**

2 Part-exchange of assets

2.1 Introduction

There is an alternative to selling a non-current for cash, particularly if a new asset is to be purchased to replace the one being sold. This is often the case with cars or vans where the old asset may be taken by the seller of the new asset as part of the purchase price of the new asset. This is known as a part-exchange deal.

2.2 Part-exchange deal value

When a part exchange deal takes place the seller of the new asset will place a value on the old asset and this will be its part-exchange value.

 Example

A new car is being purchased for a list price of £18,000. An old car of the business has been accepted in part-exchange and the cheque required for the new car is £14,700.

What is the part-exchange value of the old car?

Solution

	£
List price	18,000
Cheque required	14,700
	————
Part-exchange value	3,300
	————

2.3 Accounting for the part-exchange value

The part-exchange value has two effects on the accounting records:

(a) it is effectively the sale proceeds of the old asset

(b) it is part of the full cost of the new asset together with the cash/cheque paid.

The double entry for the part exchange value is:

- credit the disposal account as these are the effective proceeds of the old asset

- debit the new asset cost account as this value is part of the total cost of the new asset.

Example

Suppose Nigel (from the earlier example) had part exchanged his van for a new one.

The old van had cost £2,000 and depreciation amounted to £1,500.

The garage gave him an allowance of £700 against the price of the new van which was £5,000. He paid the balance by cheque.

Show all the accounting entries for the disposal of the old van and the acquisition of the new van.

Solution

Step 1

Transfer balances from van and accumulated depreciation accounts to the disposal account.

Old van

	£		£
Balance b/d	2,000	Disposal	2,000
	___		___
	2,000		2,000
	___		___

Accumulated depreciation

	£		£
Disposal	1,500	Balance b/d	1,500
	___		___
	1,500		1,500
	___		___

Disposal

	£		£
Old van	2,000	Depreciation	1,500

Note: We have closed off the van and depreciation account to make the entries clearer.

Step 2

Open a new van account and enter in it:

(a) the part exchange value (£700) from the disposal account; and

(b) the balance of the cost of the new van (£4,300).

The £700 part exchange value is also credited to the disposal account as the effective proceeds of the old van.

Disposal

	£		£
Old van	2,000	Depreciation	1,500
		New van	700

New van

	£		£
Disposal	700		
Bank	4,300		

Step 3

Balance the accounts

(a) Close the disposal account to the income statement with a profit of £200 being recorded.

(b) Bring down the total cost (£5,000) of the new van.

Disposal

	£		£
Old van	2,000	Depreciation	1,500
I/S – profit on disposal – old van	200	New van	700
	———		———
	2,200		2,200
	———		———

New van

	£		£
Disposal	700	C/d	5,000
Bank	4,300		
	———		———
	5,000		5,000
	———		———
B/d	5,000		

Note 1: You could put all the entries in the one van account. It would look like this.

Motor van

	£		£
Balance b/d	2,000	Disposal	2,000
Disposal	700	Balance c/d	5,000
Bank	4,300		
	———		———
	7,000		7,000
	———		———
Balance b/d	5,000		

Example

A business is purchasing a new van and the invoice for this van has just been received showing the following details:

	£
Registration number GU44 HFF – list price	18,000.00
VAT at 20%	3,600.00
	—————
Carrying value	21,600.00
Vehicle excise duty	140.00
	—————
Total due	21,740.00
Less: part-exchange value Y624 UFD	(4,000.00)
	—————
Balance to pay	17,740.00
	—————

The old van taken in part exchange originally cost £11,000 and at the time of disposal had accumulated depreciation charged to it of £8,340.

From the invoice you can find the total cost of the new van, £18,000, and the part-exchange value of the old van, £4,000.

Write up the van account, accumulated depreciation on vans account and the disposal account to reflect this transaction.

KAPLAN PUBLISHING

Solution

Van account

	£		£
Old van – cost	11,000	Disposal account	11,000
New van (17,740 – 140 – 3,600)	14,000		
Disposal account – exchange value	4,000	Balance c/d	18,000
	29,000		29,000
Balance b/d	18,000		

Remember that the vehicle excise duty is revenue expenditure and is therefore not part of the cost of the new van and that VAT on the purchase of vans (rather than cars) is recoverable. Therefore the VAT is debited to the VAT control account rather than the van account. The balance b/d on the van account after all of these transactions is simply the full cost of the van of £18,000.

Accumulated depreciation accounts – van

	£		£
Disposal account	8,340	Balance b/d	8,340

Disposal account

	£		£
Van at cost	11,000	Acc. Depreciation	8,340
Profit on disposal	1,340	Van account – part exchange value	4,000
	12,340		12,340

2.4 Original documentation

In an exam question you will be required to put through the accounting entries for a part-exchange but you may also be required to find some of the information necessary from the sales invoice for the new asset.

Activity 3

On 31 December 20X3 a business part-exchanges a van which it bought on 1 January 20X0 for £6,000 and has depreciated each year at 25% pa by the straight-line method (assuming nil residual value). The business charges a full year's charge in the year of acquisition and none in the year of disposal.

It trades this van in for a new one costing £10,000 and pays the supplier £9,200 by cheque.

1 Record the entries in ledger accounts for the disposal of the OLD van.

2 Record the entries in ledger accounts for the addition of the NEW van.

3 Complete the disposal account and calculate the profit/loss on disposal.

3 Authorising disposals

3.1 Introduction

It is important that disposals of non-currents are properly controlled. For most organisations, this means that there must be some form of written authorisation before a disposal can take place. In some ways, authorisation is even more important for disposals than for additions.

3.2 Importance of authorisation

Disposals can easily be made without the knowledge of management and are difficult to detect from the accounting records alone. Sales of assets are often for relatively small amounts of cash and they may not be supported by an invoice (for example, if they are to an employee of the business). Although the transaction itself may not be significant, failure to detect and record the disposal correctly in the accounting records may result in the overstatement of non-currents in the accounts.

3.3 Requirements of valid authorisation

Possibilities for written authorisation include board minutes (for material disposals), memos or authorisation forms. The following information is needed:

- date of purchase
- date of disposal
- description of asset
- reason for disposal
- original cost
- accumulated depreciation
- sale proceeds
- authorisation (number of signatures required will depend upon the organisation's procedures).

4 Disposals and the non-current register

4.1 Introduction

When a non-current is disposed of then this must be recorded not only in the ledger accounts but also in the non-current register.

 Example

Date of purchase	Invoice number	Serial number	Item	Cost	Accum'd depreciation b/f at 1.1.X8	Date of disposal	Depreciation charge in 20X8	Accum'd depreciation c/f	Disposal proceeds	Loss/ gain on disposal
				£	£		£	£	£	£
3.2.X5	345	3488	Chair	340	102		34	136		
6.4.X6	466	–	Bookcase	258	52		26	78		
10.7.X7	587	278	Chair	160	16	12.7.X8	–			
30.8.X8	634	1228	Table	86			9	9		
				—	—		—	—		
				844	170		69	223		
				—	—		—	—		

Using the non-current register example from the previous two chapters (reproduced above) we will now complete the entries for the chair (serial number 278) being disposed of.

The disposal proceeds are £15.

The profit or loss must also be entered into the non-current register and the total of all of the profits or losses should equal the amount transferred to the income statement for the period.

Solution

(W1)	£
Cost	160
Cumulative dep'n	(16)
CV	144
Proceeds	(15)
Loss	129

Date of purchase	Invoice number	Serial number	Item	Cost	Accum'd depreciation b/d at 1.1.X8	Date of disposal	Depreciation charge in 20X8	Accum'd depreciation c/d	Disposal proceeds	Loss/gain on disposal
				£	£		£	£	£	£
3.2.X5	345	3488	Chair	340	102		34	136		
6.4.X6	466	–	Bookcase	258	52		26	78		
10.7.X7	587	278	Chair	160	16	12.7.X8	–		15	(129)(W1)
30.8.X8	634	1228	Table	86			9	9		
				—	—					
				844	170					
12.7.X8		278	Chair	(160)	(16)					
				—	—		—	—		—
				684	154		69	223		(129)
				—	—		—	—		—

5.1 Introduction

One of the purposes of the non-current register is to allow control over the non-currents of a business. Obviously many of the non-currents are extremely valuable and some are also easily moved, especially assets such as personal computers and cars. Therefore on a regular basis the organisation should carry out random checks to ensure that the non-currents recorded in the non-current register are actually on the premises.

5.2 Details in the non-current register

The non-current register will show the purchase cost, depreciation and disposal details of the non-currents that the business owns and have recently disposed of.

The non-current register should also normally show the location of the assets. This will either be by an additional column in the non-current register or by grouping assets in each department or area of the business together. This enables periodic checks to be carried out to ensure that the physical assets in each department agree to the non-current register.

5.3 Discrepancies

A variety of possible discrepancies might appear between the physical assets and the book records.

- An asset recorded in the non-current register is not physically present – this might be due to the asset being disposed of but not recorded in the non-current register, the asset having been moved to another location or the asset having been stolen or removed without authorisation.

- An asset existing that is not recorded in the non-current register – this might be due to the non-current register not being up to date or the asset having been moved from another location.

Whatever type of discrepancy is discovered it must be either resolved or reported to the appropriate person in the organisation so that it can be resolved.

5.4 Agreement of accounting records to non-current register

The ledger accounts for the non-currents should also be agreed on a regular basis to the non-current register.

The cost total with any disposals deducted should agree to the non-currents at cost accounts totals.

The accumulated depreciation column total for each class of assets should also agree to the accumulated depreciation account balance for each class of asset.

Any total in the loss or gain on disposals column should also agree to the amount charged or credited to the income statement.

On a regular basis the non-current register details should be agreed to the physical assets held and to the ledger accounts.

6 Summary

The two main aspects to accounting for disposals of non-currents are to remove all accounting entries for the asset disposed of and to account for any profit or loss on disposal. This can all be done by using a disposal account.

Some assets will not be sold outright but will be transferred as a part-exchange deal when purchasing a new asset. The part-exchange value is not only equivalent to the proceeds of sale but is also part of the cost of the new asset being purchased.

Control over the disposal of non-currents is extremely important and as such authorisation of a disposal and whether it is as a sale or a part-exchange is key to this. Allied to this is the control feature of the non-current register.

All purchases and disposals of non-currents should be recorded in the non-current register and the actual physical presence of the non-currents should be checked on a regular basis to the non-current register details.

Answers to chapter activities

Activity 1

	£	Depreciation
Cost	20,000	
Year 1 depreciation	(10,000)	10,000
(20,000 × 50%)	————	
	10,000	
Year 2 dep'n	(5,000)	5,000
(10,000 × 50%)	————	
	5,000	
Year 3 depreciation	(2,500)	2,500
(5,000 × 50%)		————
		17,500
		————

Car account

	£		£
Yr 1 Bank	20,000	Yr 1 Balance c/d	20,000
	————		————
	20,000		20,000
	————		————
Yr 2 Balance b/d	20,000	Yr 2 Balance c/d	20,000
	————		————
	20,000		20,000
	————		————
Yr 3 Balance b/d	20,000	Yr 3 Disposal account	20,000
	————		————
	20,000		20,000
	————		————

Accumulated depreciation

	£		£
Yr 1 Balance c/d	10,000	Yr 1 Depreciation exps	10,000
	10,000		10,000
Yr 2 Balance c/d	15,000	Yr 2 Balance b/d	10,000
		Yr 2 Depreciation exps	5,000
	15,000		15,000
Yr 3 Disposal account	17,500	Yr 3 Balance b/d	15,000
		Yr 3 Depreciation exps	2,500
	17,500		17,500

Disposal account

	£		£
Yr 3 Van cost	20,000	Yr 3 Accumulated dep'n	17,500
Yr 3 Profit on disposal	7,500	Yr 3 Proceeds	10,000
	27,500		27,500

Activity 2

Journal entry No 235

Date	13 June 20X8		
Prepared by	A Tech		
Authorised by	B Jones		

Account	Code	Debit £	Credit £
Disposals	0240	20,000	
Motor vehicles	0130		20,000
Accum dep'n	0140	7,500	
Disposals	0240		7,500
Cash at bank	0163	10,000	
Disposals	0240		10,000

Activity 3

Van account

	£		£
Cost b/d	6,000	Disposals account	6,000
Disposal account	800		
Bank	9,200	Balance c/d	10,000
	16,000		16,000
Balance b/d	10,000		

Accumulated depreciation

	£		£
Disposal account	4,500	Balance b/d £6,000 × 25% × 3	4,500
Balance c/d	2,500	Depreciation charge £10,000 × 25%	2,500
	7,000		7,000
		Balance b/d	2,500

Disposal account

	£		£
Van	6,000	Accumulated depreciation	4,500
		Part exchange allowance	800
		Loss on disposal	700
	6,000		6,000

7 Test your knowledge

 ## Workbook Activity 4

Spanners Ltd has a car it wishes to dispose of. The car cost £12,000 and has accumulated depreciation of £5,000. The car is sold for £4,000.

Tasks

(a) Clearly state whether there is a profit or a loss on disposal.

(b) Show the entries in the motor car account, accumulated depreciation account and disposal account.

 ## Workbook Activity 5

Baldrick's venture

On 1 April 20X6, Baldrick started a business growing turnips and selling them to wholesalers. On 1 September 20X6 he purchased a turnip-digging machine for £2,700. He sold the machine on 1 March 20X9 for £1,300.

Baldrick's policy for machinery is to charge depreciation on the reducing balance method at 25% per annum. A full year's charge is made in the year of purchase and none in the year of sale.

Required:

For the three years from 1 April 20X6 to 31 March 20X9 prepare the following ledger accounts:

(a) Machinery account

(b) Accumulated depreciation account (machinery)

(c) Depreciation expense account (machinery)

(d) Disposals account

Bring down the balance on each account at 31 March each year.

Workbook Activity 6

Keith

The following transactions relate to Keith Manufacturing Co Ltd's plant and machinery:

1 January 20X7	Lathe machine purchased for £10,000. It is to be depreciated on a straight line basis with no expected scrap value after four years.
1 April 20X7	Cutting machine purchased for £12,000. It is estimated that after a five-year working life it will have a scrap value of £1,000.
1 June 20X8	Laser machine purchased for £28,000. This is estimated to have a seven year life and a scrap value of £2,800.
1 March 20X9	The cutting machine purchased on 1 April 20X7 was given in part exchange for a new micro-cutter with a purchase price of £20,000. A part-exchange allowance of £3,000 was given and the balance paid by cheque. It is estimated that the new machine will last for five years with a scrap value of £3,000. It will cost £1,500 to install.

The accounting year-end is 31 December. The company depreciates its machines on a straight line basis, charging a full year in the year of purchase and none in the year of sale.

At 31 December 20X6 the plant register had shown the following:

Date of purchase	Machine	Cost £	Anticipated residual value £	Rate of depreciation
1 June 20X5	Piece machine	10,000	Nil	Straight line over 5 years
1 January 20X6	Acrylic machine	5,000	1,000	Straight line over 5 years
1 June 20X6	Heat seal machine	6,000	Nil	Straight line over 5 years

Required:

Write up the plant and machinery account, the accumulated depreciation account and the disposal accounts for 20X7, 20X8 and 20X9. Show the relevant extracts from the financial statements.

Workbook Activity 7

A motor vehicle which had originally been purchased on 31 October 20X1 for £12,000 was part exchanged for a new vehicle on 31 May 20X3. The new vehicle cost £15,000 and was paid for using the old vehicle and a cheque for £5,000.

Prepare a disposals account for the old vehicle showing clearly the transfer to the income statement. (Depreciation for motor vehicles is calculated on a monthly basis at 20% per annum straight line method assuming no residual value.)

Disposals account

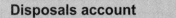

Workbook Activity 8

A business is purchasing a new van for deliveries from Grammoth Garages. It has just received the following invoice from Grammoth Garages:

GRAMMOTH GARAGES
Park Road • Valedon • HE4 8NB
SALES INVOICE

Delivery of Ford Transit Van Registration GS55 OPP

	£
List price	21,000.00
VAT	4,200.00
	25,200.00
Less: part exchange value Ford Transit Van Reg X234 JDF	(5,500.00)
Amount due	19,700.00

The van that is being part-exchanged originally cost £16,400 and has been depreciated on a straight-line basis for four years at 15% per annum.

Required:

Write up the motor vans at cost account, accumulated depreciation and the disposal account to reflect the purchase of the new van and the part-exchange of the old van.

The extended trial balance – an introduction

Introduction

The examination will contain an exercise involving preparation or completion of an extended trial balance. You need to be familiar with the technique for entering adjustments to the initial trial balance and extending the figures into the statement of financial position and statement of profit or loss columns.

The relevant adjustments you may be required to make are accruals, prepayments, depreciation charges, disposals of non-current assets, irrecoverable and doubtful debts, errors and closing inventory), will be covered in the chapters that follow.

In this chapter we introduce the purpose and layout of the extended trial balance. The skills that are detailed below will be achieved once all the adjustments have been reviewed and once the extended trial balance in action has been studied.

SKILLS	CONTENTS
Record the journal entries to close off revenue accounts in preparation for the transfer of balances to the final accounts (7.6)	1 From trial balance to extended trial balance
Prepare ledger account balances, reconciling them, identifying any discrepancies and taking appropriate action (8.1)	
Prepare a trial balance (8.2)	
Account for these adjustments (8.3)	
Closing inventory	
Accruals and prepayments to expenses and income	
Provisions for depreciation on non-current assets	
Irrecoverable debts	
Allowance for doubtful debts	

Use the appropriate columns in the extended trial balance or produce journal entries

Prepare the trial balance after adjustments (8.4)

Check for errors and/or inaccuracies in the trial balance, taking appropriate action (8.5)

1   From trial balance to extended trial balance

1.1   Introduction

In an earlier chapter we have seen how a trial balance is prepared regularly in order to provide a check on the double entry bookkeeping in the accounting system.

The other purpose of the trial balance is as a starting point for the preparation of final accounts. This is often done by using an extended trial balance.

1.2   The purpose of the extended trial balance

 Definition

An extended trial balance is a working paper which allows the initial trial balance to be converted into all of the figures required for preparation of the final accounts.

The extended trial balance brings together the balances on all of the main ledger accounts and includes all of the adjustments that are required in order to prepare the final accounts.

1.3   Layout of a typical extended trial balance

A typical extended trial balance (ETB) will have eight columns for each ledger account as follows:

Account name (e.g.)	Trial balance		Adjustments		Statement of profit or loss		Statement of fin. pos.	
	Dr £	Cr £	Dr £	Cr £	Dr £	Cr £	Dr £	Cr £
SLCA								
Non-current asset cost								

1.4 Procedure for preparing an extended trial balance

Step 1

Each ledger account name and its balance is initially entered in the trial balance columns.

Total the debit and credit columns to ensure they equal; i.e. that all balances have been transferred across. Any difference should be put to a suspense account.

Step 2

The adjustments required are then entered into the adjustments column. The typical adjustments required are:

- correction of any errors
- depreciation charges for the period
- write off any irrecoverable debts
- increase or decrease in allowance for doubtful debts
- accruals or prepayments
- accrued income or deferred income
- closing inventory

Note: it is always important to ensure that all adjustments have an equal and opposite debit and credit. Never enter a one sided journal.

Step 3

Total the adjustments columns to ensure that the double entry has been correctly made in these columns.

Step 4

All the entries on the line of each account are then cross-cast and the total is entered into the correct column in either the Statement of profit or loss columns or statement of financial position columns.

Step 5

The statement of profit or loss column totals are totalled in order to determine the profit (or loss) for the period. This profit (or loss) is entered in the statement of profit or loss columns as the balancing figure. See example below for further clarification on the adjustment required.

Step 6

The profit (or loss) for the period calculated in step 5 is entered in the statement of financial position columns and the statement of financial position columns are then totalled.

2 Summary

This chapter has introduced the purpose and layout of the extended trial balance. The chapters that follow will review the different accounting adjustments you may need to make. These adjustments will be closing inventory, depreciation, disposals, irrecoverable and doubtful debts, accruals and prepayments. These can all be conveniently put through on the extended trial balance. NB depreciation and disposals were considered in chapters 4 and 5.

Once the adjustments have been reviewed, chapter 14 looks in detail at the extended trial balance in action.

Financial statements and accounting concepts

7

Introduction

Financial statements are prepared under a number of well established and generally accepted accounting concepts or principles and you need to be able to define these concepts and apply them to particular situations.

KNOWLEDGE	CONTENTS
Explain the accounting principles of going concern, accruals, prudence and consistency (1.1) Explain the purpose and importance of maintaining financial records for internal and external use (1.2) Describe the type of accounting records that a business should maintain and the main uses of each (1.3) Explain the accounting characteristics of relevance, reliability, comparability, ease of understanding and materiality (1.5)	1 Introduction 2 Financial statements 3 Accounting concepts and policies

1 Introduction

1.1 What are financial statements?

Periodically all organisations will produce financial statements in order to show how the business has performed and what assets and liabilities it has.

The two main financial statements are the statement of profit or loss and the statement of financial position.

2 Financial statements

2.1 Statement of profit or loss

Definition

The statement of profit or loss summarises the transactions of a business over a period and determines whether the business has made a profit or a loss for the period.

A typical statement of profit or loss is shown below.

Statement of profit or loss of Stanley for the year ended 31 December 20X2

	£	£
Revenue		X
Less: Cost of sales		
Inventory, at cost on 1 January (opening inventory)	X	
Add: Purchases of goods	X	
	X	
Less: Inventory, at cost on 31 December (closing inventory)	(X)	
		(X)
Gross profit		X
Sundry income:		
Discounts received	X	
Commission received	X	
Rent received	X	
		X
		X
Less: Expenses:		
Rent	X	
Rates	X	
Lighting and heating	X	
Telephone	X	
Postage	X	
Insurance	X	
Stationery	X	
Payroll expenses	X	
Depreciation	X	
Accountancy and audit fees	X	
Bank charges and interest	X	
Irrecoverable debts	X	
Allowance for doubtful debts adjustment	X	
Delivery costs	X	
Van running expenses	X	
Selling expenses	X	
Discounts allowed	X	
		(X)
Net profit		X

The trading account section is the comparison of sales to the cost of the goods sold. This gives the gross profit.

Take careful note of the types of items that appear in the statement of profit or loss. For Prepare Final Accounts for Sole Traders and Partnerships (FSTP) you will have to prepare a statement of profit or loss for a sole trader or partnership.

2.2 Statement of financial position

 Definition

The statement of financial position is a list of all of the assets and liabilities of the business on the last day of the accounting period.

An example of a typical sole trader's statement of financial position is given below:

Statement of financial position of Stanley at 31 December 20X2

	Cost £	Depreciation £	£
Non-current assets			
Freehold factory	X	X	X
Machinery	X	X	X
Motor vehicles	X	X	X
	X	X	X
	X	X	X
Current assets			
Inventories		X	
Receivables	X		
Less: allowance for doubtful debts	(X)		
		X	
Other receivables		X	
Cash at bank		X	
Cash in hand		X	
		X	
Current liabilities			
Trade payables	X		
Other payables	X		
		(X)	

Net current assets	X
	—
Total assets less current liabilities	X
Non-current liabilities	
12% loan	(X)
	—
Net assets	X
	—
Capital at 1 January	X
Net profit for the year	X
	—
	X
Less: drawings	(X)
	—
Proprietor's funds	X
	—

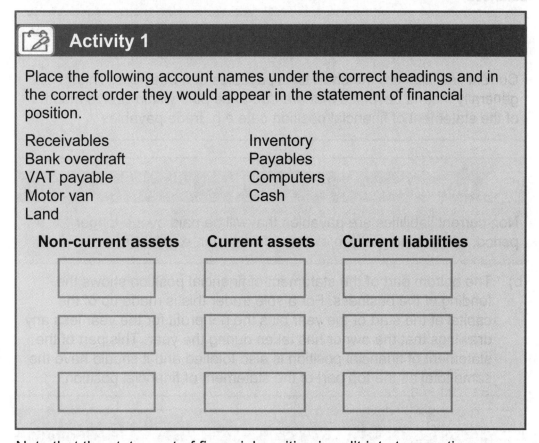

Activity 1

Place the following account names under the correct headings and in the correct order they would appear in the statement of financial position.

Receivables   Inventory
Bank overdraft   Payables
VAT payable   Computers
Motor van   Cash
Land

Non-current assets	Current assets	Current liabilities

Note that the statement of financial position is split into two sections.

(a) The top part of the statement of financial position lists all of the assets and liabilities of the organisation. This is then totalled by adding together all of the asset values and deducting the liabilities.

The assets are split into non-current assets and current assets.

Definition

Non-current assets are those that will be used within the business over a long period (usually greater than one year), e.g. land and buildings

 Definition

Current assets are those that are expected to be realised within the business in the normal course of trading (usually a period less than one year) e.g. inventory.

Current assets are always listed in the reverse order of liquidity, which means how easily they are converted into their liquid, or cash, form. To this end inventory is shown first, then receivables and then bank and cash balances.

 Definition

Current liabilities are the short term payables of a business. This generally means payables that are due to be paid within twelve months of the statement of financial position date e.g. trade payables

 Definition

Non-current liabilities are payables that will be paid over a longer period, which is normally in excess of one year, e.g. loans

(b) The bottom part of the statement of financial position shows the funding of the business. For a sole trader this is made up of the capital at the start of the year plus the net profit for the year less any drawings that the owner has taken during the year. This part of the statement of financial position is also totalled and it should have the same total as the top part of the statement of financial position.

 Definition

The accounting equation represents the statement of financial position as follows:

ASSETS – LIABILITIES = CAPITAL + PROFIT – DRAWINGS

As with the statement of profit or loss, for this unit you need to be able to understand how to prepare a statement of financial position for a sole trader or a partnership but the skills to prepare the accounts will be applied in FSTP.

Activity 2

1   The final figure calculated in the trading account known as?

    Assets   Net profit   Gross profit   Cost of sales

    Circle the correct answer

2   What is the accounting equation?

Activity 3

Trial balance at 31 December 20X2

	Dr £	Cr £
Capital on 1 January 20X2		106,149
Freehold factory at cost	360,000	
Motor vehicles at cost	126,000	
Inventories at 1 January 20X2	37,500	
Receivables	15,600	
Cash in hand	225	
Bank overdraft		82,386
Payables		78,900
Revenue		307,500
Purchases	158,700	
Wages and salaries	39,060	
Rent and rates	35,400	
Postage	400	
Discounts allowed	6,600	
Insurance	2,850	
Motor expenses	5,500	
Loan from bank		240,000
Sundry expenses	1,000	
Drawings	26,100	
	814,935	814,935

Prepare a statement of profit or loss and statement of financial position.

3 Accounting concepts and policies

3.1 Introduction

There are many transactions and events that must be reflected in a set of accounts and it is not always obvious how they should be recorded. For example: a sale of goods for £100 cash is quite simple to record; you record the sale of £100 and an increase in cash of £100. A more complex transaction might be the agreement of a three year cleaning contract for a fixed monthly charge, with discounts available for prompt payment and a refund available at the end of year three if the client has always paid on time. Another point to consider is how do you value an asset, such as land and buildings? Do you record it at cost or at market value? If the asset falls in value should this be reflected and, on a similar note, what should you do if the value rises?

Hopefully you can appreciate that accounting is not one dimensional and what may work for one business may not work for another. Therefore accountants need guidance to allow them to appropriately reflect transactions and events in the financial statements and to reduce the risk of manipulation of financial statements to deceive users (fraud).

For this reason companies have to comply with financial reporting standards. Whilst this guidance is not necessarily relevant for sole traders and partnerships (as they do not have to comply with company regulations) it is considered best practice.

3.2 Accounting concepts

Over the years a number of accounting concepts have been judged to be fundamental to the preparation of financial statements. There are, however, two main concepts that underpin modern financial accounting; the going concern concept and the accruals concept. These are defined in the Conceptual Framework for Financial Reporting 2010 ('the Framework'). The Framework provides the basis upon which all IFRS are created.

3.3 Going concern concept

Going concern is an assumption that a business will continue to trade into the foreseeable future. Financial statements should be prepared on this assumption unless the business has ceased to trade or has no realistic alternative other than to cease.

This concept affects the valuation of assets shown in the statement of financial position in particular. If the business is a going concern then assets will continue to be shown in the statement of financial position at their appropriate carrying value. If the business were not a going concern then assets would be revalued to their immediate settlement value (i.e. how much they could be sold for).

3.4   Accruals concept

The accruals basis of accounting requires that transactions should be reflected in the financial statements for the period in which they occur. This means that the amount of income should be recognised as it is earned and expenses when they are incurred. They should not be recognised when cash is received or paid.

For example, consider credit sales and credit purchases. When a sale is made on credit it is still recorded even though it may be a considerable time before the cash is actually received from the receivable. We will come across further examples of applying the accruals basis of accounting when we deal with accruals and prepayments in Chapter 12.

3.5   Objectives in selecting accounting policies

As well as the two underlying concepts the Framework also requires that financial statements adopt two fundamental qualitative characteristics and four enhancing qualitative characteristics.

3.6   The two fundamental qualitative characteristics

Relevance: financial information is regarded as relevant if it is capable of influencing the decisions of users.

Faithful representation: this means that financial information must be complete, neutral and free from error.

3.7   The four enhancing qualitative characteristics

Comparability: it should be possible to compare an entity over time and with similar information about other entities.

Verifiability: if information can be verified (e.g. through an audit) this provides assurance to the users that it is both credible and reliable.

Timeliness: information should be provided to users within a timescale suitable for their decision making purposes.

Understandability: information should be understandable to those that might want to review and use it. This can be facilitated through appropriate classification, characterisation and presentation of information.

3.8 IAS 8 Accounting Policies, Changes in Accounting Estimates and Errors

IAS 8 states that when preparing financial statements a company must comply with IFRS, or other IASB pronouncements. If a transaction or event is so unusual that it falls outside of this guidance management must use judgement in determining the policy that is most appropriate to the business. In so doing management must consider the current guidance available in both IFRS's and the Framework.

The policies chosen must be applied consistently for all similar transactions and events and should only be changed if a new IFRS (or other IASB pronouncement) requires it or if it makes the financial statements more relevant to the users.

3.9 Materiality

One further important accounting concept is that of materiality.

 Definition

An item is deemed to be material if its omission or misstatement will influence the economic decisions of the users of the accounts taken on the basis of the financial statements.

Accounting standards do not apply to immaterial items and judgement is required when determining whether or not an item is material.

An example might be the purchase of a stapler for use in the office. Technically this should be treated as a non-current asset as it is presumably for fairly long term use in the business. However rather than including it on the statement of financial position and then depreciating it, it is more likely that on the basis of it being an immaterial item it would be written off as an expense in the statement of profit or loss.

 Activity 4

1   What is meant by the going concern concept?

2   What is meant by the accruals concept?

3   What are the two fundamental qualitative characteristics of financial statements?

4   What is materiality?

4 Summary

For Accounts Preparation you need to have a sound knowledge of the items that appear in the financial statements of a sole trader or a partnership in good form. In this chapter we introduced the statement of profit or loss and statement of financial position formats. At this stage you need to be familiar with the pro-forma for a statement of profit or loss and a statement of financial position however you are not examined on the preparation of the financial statements until Prepare Final Accounts for Sole Traders and Partnerships (FSTP).

You also need to appreciate that accounting is not an exact science and that when dealing with transactions and events the accountant is faced with many choices regarding accounting treatment. The accounting methods chosen are known as the organisation's accounting policies and, according to IAS 8, these should be chosen on the basis of IFRS and the Framework.

Answers to chapter activities

Activity 1

Non-current assets	Current assets	Current liabilities
Land	Inventory	Bank overdraft
Motor Van	Receivables	VAT payable to HMRC
Computers	Cash	Payables

Activity 2

1 Gross profit

2 Assets – Liabilities = Capital + Profit – Drawings

Activity 3

Statement of profit or loss for the year ended 31 December 20X2

	£	£
Revenue		307,500
Less: Cost of sales		
Opening inventory	37,500	
Purchases	158,700	
	196,200	
Less: Closing inventory	0	
		(196,200)
Gross profit		111,300
Less: Expenses		
Rent and rates	35,400	
Insurance	2,850	
Motor expenses	5,500	
Wages and salaries	39,060	
Postage	400	
Sundry expenses	1,000	
Discounts allowed	6,600	
		(90,810)
Profit for the year		20,490

Statement of financial position as at 31 December 20X2

	£	£	£
Non-current assets:			
Freehold factory	360,000	0	360,000
Motor vehicles	126,000	0	126,000
	486,000	0	486,000
Current assets:			
Inventory			0
Receivables		15,600	
Cash in hand		225	
		15,825	
Current liabilities:			
Payables		78,900	
Bank overdraft		82,386	
		161,286	
Net current assets/(liabilities)			(145,461)
Total assets less current liabilities			340,539
Loan from bank			(240,000)
Net assets			**100,539**
Owner's capital			
Capital at 1.1.X2			106,149
Net profit for the year			20,490
Less: drawings			(26,100)
Proprietors funds			**100,539**

Activity 4

1   The going concern concept is that the financial statements are prepared on the basis that the business will continue for the foreseeable future.

2   The accruals concept is that transactions are accounted for in the period in which they take place rather than the period in which the cash is received or paid.

3   Relevance and faithful representation.

4   Materiality is an underlying concept which states that accounting policies and standards need only apply to material items. A material item is one which has the ability to influence the economic decisions of users of the financial statements.

5 Test your knowledge

Workbook Activity 5

Lara

The following transactions took place in July 20X6:

1 July	Lara started a business selling cricket boots and put £200 in the bank.
2 July	Marlar lent him £1,000.
3 July	Bought goods from Greig Ltd on credit for £296.
4 July	Bought motor van for £250 cash.
7 July	Made cash sales amounting to £105.
8 July	Paid motor expenses £15.
9 July	Paid wages £18.
10 July	Bought goods on credit from Knott Ltd, £85.
14 July	Paid insurance premium £22.
25 July	Received £15 commission as a result of successful sales promotion of MCC cricket boots.
31 July	Paid electricity bill £17.

Required:

(a) Write up the necessary ledger accounts in the books of Lara.

(b) Extract a trial balance at 31 July.

Workbook Activity 6

Peter

From the following list of balances you are required to draw up a trial balance for Peter at 31 December 20X8:

	£
Fixtures and fittings	6,430
Delivery vans	5,790
Cash at bank (in funds)	3,720
General expenses	1,450
Receivables	2,760
Payables	3,250
Purchases	10,670
Sales	25,340
Wages	4,550
Drawings	5,000
Lighting and heating	1,250
Rent, rates and insurance	2,070
Capital	15,100

Workbook Activity 7

Peter Wall

Peter Wall started business on 1 January 20X8 printing and selling astrology books. He put up £10,000 capital and was given a loan of £10,000 by Oswald. The following is a list of his transactions for the three months to 31 March 20X8:

1   Purchased printing equipment for £7,000 cash.

2   Purchased a delivery van for £400 on credit from Arnold.

3   Bought paper for £100 on credit from Butcher.

4   Bought ink for £10 cash.

5   Paid £25 for one quarter's rent and rates.

6   Paid £40 for one year's insurance premium.

7   Sold £200 of books for cash and £100 on credit to Constantine.

8   Paid Oswald £450 representing the following:

    (i)   Part repayment of principal.

    (ii)   Interest calculated at an annual rate of 2% per annum for three months.

9   Received £60 from Constantine.

10   Paid £200 towards the delivery van and £50 towards the paper.

11   Having forgotten his part payment for the paper he then paid Butcher a further £100.

Required:

(a)   Write up all necessary ledger accounts, including cash.

(b)   Extract a trial balance at 31 March 20X8 (before period-end accruals).

Accounting for inventory

Introduction

In this chapter we will consider the accounting for opening and closing inventory and the issues that surround valuing and recording closing inventory.

As well as being able to enter a valuation for closing inventory correctly in the extended trial balance and financial statements, candidates can also expect to be assessed on other aspects of inventory valuation from IAS 2.

This will include:

- valuing inventory at the lower of cost and net realisable value

- determining the cost of inventory and its net realisable value

- various methods of costing inventory units and

- a closing inventory reconciliation.

KNOWLEDGE	CONTENTS
Describe the main requirements of accounting standards (IFRS) in relation to inventory and non-current asset valuations (1.4)	1 Closing inventory in the financial statements 2 Closing inventory reconciliation 3 Valuation of closing inventory 4 Methods of costing 5 Accounting for closing inventory
SKILLS	
Record the journal entries for closing inventory (7.3) Account for these adjustments, including closing inventory (8.3)	

1 Closing inventory in the financial statements

1.1 Introduction

Most businesses will have a variety of different types of inventory. In a retail business this will be the goods that are in inventory and held for resale. In a manufacturing business there are likely to be raw material inventories (that are used to make the business's products), partly finished products (known as work in progress) and completed goods ready for sale (known as finished goods).

These inventories are assets of the business and therefore must be included in the financial statements as current assets.

1.2 Counting closing inventory

At the end of the accounting period a inventory count will normally take place where the quantity of each line of inventory is counted and recorded. The organisation will then know the number of units of each type of inventory that it has at the year end. The next stage is to value the inventory. Both of these areas will be dealt with in detail later in the chapter.

1.3 Closing inventory and the financial statements

Once the inventory has been counted and valued it must then be included in the financial statements. The detailed accounting for this will be considered later in the chapter.

At this stage we will just look at an overview of how the closing inventory will appear in the financial statements.

1.4 Statement of financial position

The closing inventory is an asset of the business and as such will appear on the statement of financial position. It is a current asset and will normally be shown as the first item in the list of current assets, as it is the least liquid of the current assets.

KAPLAN PUBLISHING

1.5 Statement of profit or loss

The layout of the statement of profit or loss was considered in detail in an earlier chapter. Below is a reminder of how inventory appears as part of the cost of sales in the statement of profit or loss:

	£	£
Revenue		X
Less: cost of sales		
Opening inventory	X	
Plus: purchases	X	
	—	
	X	
Less: closing inventory	(X)	
	—	(X)
		—
Gross profit		X
		—

As you will see the 'cost of sales' figure is made up of the opening inventory, plus the purchases of the business for the period, less the closing inventory.

The opening inventory is the figure included in the accounts as last year's closing inventory.

The purchases figure is the balance on the purchases account.

From this the closing inventory is deducted in order to determine the cost of the goods actually sold in the period, as this inventory has clearly not yet been sold. This is part of the matching concept, and matches the cost of the goods sold with the revenue generated from the sales.

Closing inventory therefore appears in both the statement of financial position and the statement of profit or loss.

2 Closing inventory reconciliation

2.1 Introduction

Before the inventory of a business can be valued, the physical amount of inventory held must be counted and the amounts physically on hand checked to the stores records. Any discrepancies must be investigated. This is known as a closing inventory reconciliation.

2.2 Stores records

For each line of inventory the stores department should keep a bin card or inventory card which shows the following:

- the quantity of inventory received from suppliers (sourced from delivery notes or goods received notes). This should be netted off by any goods returned to the suppliers (sourced from credit notes or despatch notes)

- the quantity issued for sale or use in manufacture (sourced from store requisitions)

- any amounts returned to the stores department (sourced from goods returned notes), and

- the amount/balance that should be on hand at that time.

At any point in time the balance on the stores record should agree with the number of items of that line of inventory physically held by the stores department.

2.3 Possible reasons for differences

If there is a difference between the quantity physically counted and the stores records this could be for a variety of reasons:

- Goods may have been delivered and therefore have been physically counted but the stores records have not yet been updated to reflect the delivery.

- Goods may have been returned to suppliers and therefore will not have been counted but again the stores records have not yet been updated.

- Goods may have been issued for sales or for use in manufacturing, therefore they are not in the stores department but the stores records do not yet reflect this issue.

- Some items may have been stolen so are no longer physically in inventory.

- Errors may have been made, either in counting the number of items held, or in writing up the stores records.

KAPLAN PUBLISHING

Example

At 30 June 20X4 a sole trader carried out an inventory count and compared the quantity of each line of inventory to the inventory records. In most cases the actual inventory quantity counted agreed with the stores records but, for three lines of inventory, the sole trader found differences.

	Inventory code		
	FR153	JE363	PT321
Quantity counted	116	210	94
Inventory record quantity	144	150	80

The inventory records and documentation were thoroughly checked for these inventory lines and the following was discovered:

- On 28 June, 28 units of FR153 had been returned to the supplier as they were damaged. A credit note has not yet been received and the despatch note had not been recorded in the inventory records.

- On 29 June, a goods received note showed that 100 units of JE363 had arrived from a supplier but this had not yet been entered in the inventory records.

- Also on 29 June, 14 units of PT321 had been recorded as an issue to sales; however they were not physically dispatched to the customer until after the inventory was counted.

- On 28 June, the sole trader had taken 40 units of JE363 out of inventory in order to process a rush order for a customer and had forgotten to update the inventory record.

The closing inventory reconciliation must now be performed and the actual quantities for each line of inventory that are to be valued must be determined.

Solution

Closing inventory reconciliation – 30 June 20X4

FR153	Quantity
Inventory record	144
Less: Returned to supplier	(28)
Counted	116

When valuing the FR153 inventory line, the actual quantity counted of 116 should be used. There should also be a journal entry to reflect the purchase return:

Debit   Purchases ledger control account

Credit   Purchases returns

JE363	*Quantity*
Inventory record	150
Add: GRN not recorded	100
Less: Sales requisition	(40)
Counted	210

The quantity to be valued should be the quantity counted of 210 units. If the sale has not been recorded then an adjustment will be required for the value of the sales invoice:

Debit   Sales ledger control account

Credit   Sales account

In addition, if the purchase has not been recorded then an adjustment will be required for the value of the purchase invoice:

Debit   Purchases

Credit   Purchase ledger control account

PT321	*Quantity*
Inventory record	80
Add: Subsequent sale	14
Counted	94

In this case the amount to be valued is the inventory record amount of 80 units and if the sale has not been recorded then an adjustment must be made at the selling price of the 14 units, (note that this is done as the inventory was sold on 30th June, pre period end, but after the inventory count):

Debit   Sales ledger control account

Credit   Sales account

3 Valuation of closing inventory

3.1 Introduction

Now that we know how many units of inventory we have from the inventory count, we will consider how the units of inventory are valued.

3.2 IAS 2

IAS 2 *Inventory* is the accounting standard that deals with the way in which inventories should be valued for inclusion in the financial statements. The basic rule from IAS 2 is that inventories should be valued at: 'the lower of cost and net realisable value'.

 Definition

Cost is defined in IAS 2 as 'that expenditure which has been incurred in the normal course of business in bringing the product or service to its present location and condition. This expenditure should include, in addition to cost of purchase, such costs of conversion as are appropriate to that location and condition'.

3.3 Cost

Purchase cost is defined as:

'including import duties, transport and handling costs and any other directly attributable costs, less trade discounts, rebates and subsidies'.

Costs of conversion includes:

- direct production costs
- production overheads, and
- other overheads attributable to bringing the product to its present location and condition.

This means the following:

- Only **production overheads** – not those for marketing, selling and distribution – should be included in cost.

- Exceptional spoilage, idle capacity and other abnormal costs are not part of the cost of inventories.

- General management and non-production related administration costs should not be included in inventory cost.

So far, then, we can summarise that the **cost of inventory** is:

- the amount it was bought for from the supplier, less any trade discounts

- any extra costs (delivery costs) to get it to its current location, and

- the production cost of any work performed on it since it was bought.

This means that different items of the same inventory in different locations may have different costs.

 Activity 1

A company had to pay a special delivery charge of £84 on a delivery of urgently required games software it had purchased for resale. This amount had been debited to Office Expenses account.

(a) This treatment is incorrect. Which account should have been debited? (Tick)

Purchases account ☐

Inventory account ☐

Returns Inwards account ☐

(b) Give the journal entry to correct the error.

3.4 Net realisable value

Definition

IAS 2 defines net realisable value (NRV) as 'the actual or estimated selling price (net of trade but before settlement discounts) less all further costs to completion and all costs to be incurred in marketing, selling and distributing'.

NRV can be summarised as the actual or estimated selling price less any future costs that will be incurred before the product can be sold.

Example

Jenny manufactures widgets. Details of the basic version are given below:

	Cost £	Selling price £	Selling cost £
Basic widgets	5	10	2

What value should be attributed to each widget in inventory?

Solution

Inventory valuation	£
Cost	5
Net realisable value (£10 – £2)	8

Therefore inventory should be valued at £5 per widget, the lower of cost and NRV.

It is wrong to add the selling cost of £2 to the production cost of £5 and value the inventory at £7 because it is not a production cost.

3.5 Justification of the IAS 2 rule

The valuation rule from IAS 2 that inventory must be valued at the lower of cost and net realisable value is an example of an old accounting concept known as 'prudence.' It is still relevant with regard to inventory today but it is now seen as a simple application of the accruals concept and revenue recognition rules.

Normally inventories are likely to sell for a high enough price that NRV is higher than cost (i.e. they are sold for a profit). If inventories were valued at NRV then the accounts would include the profit before they were sold. This is not allowed and so the inventory should be valued at cost.

In some circumstances it is possible that the selling price of the goods has fallen so that NRV is now lower than the original cost of the goods (i.e. they will be sold at a loss). In these circumstances the business should take a prudent approach and record the loss immediately. Therefore these goods should be valued at net realisable value.

3.6 Separate items or groups of inventory

IAS 2 also makes it quite clear that when determining whether the inventory should be valued at cost or net realisable value EACH item of inventory or groups of similar items should be considered separately.

Example

A business has three lines of inventory A, B and C. The details of cost and NRV for each line is given below:

	Cost £	NRV £
A	1,200	2,000
B	1,000	800
C	1,500	2,500
	3,700	5,300

What is the value of the closing inventory of the business?

Solution

It is incorrect to value the inventory at £3,700, the total cost, although it is clearly lower than the total NRV. Each line of inventory must be considered separately.

	Cost £	NRV £	Inventory Value £
A	1,200	2,000	1,200
B	1,000	800	800
C	1,500	2,500	1,500
	3,700	5,300	3,500

You will see that the NRV of B is lower than its cost and therefore the NRV is the value that must be included for B.

Make sure that you look at each inventory line separately and do not just take the total cost of £3,700 as the inventory value.

Activity 2

Karen sells three products: A, B and C. At the company's year-end, the inventories held are as follows:

	Cost £	Selling price £
A	1,200	1,500
B	6,200	6,100
C	920	930

At sale a 5% commission is payable by the company to its agent.

What is the total value of these inventories in the company's accounts?

(Complete the following table)

	Cost £	Selling price £	NRV £
A			
B			
C			

Total inventory valuation =

3.7   Adjustment to closing inventory value

If closing inventory has been valued at cost and it is subsequently determined that some items of have a net realisable value which is lower than cost, then the valuation of the closing inventory must be reduced.

 4 Methods of costing

4.1   Introduction

In order to determine the valuation of closing inventory the cost must be compared to the net realisable value. We have seen how cost is defined and the major element of cost will be the purchase price of the goods.

In many cases organisations buy goods at different times and at different prices, as such it is difficult to determine the exact purchase price of the goods that are left in inventory at the end of the accounting period. Therefore assumptions have to be made about the movement of inventory in and out of the warehouse.

You need to be aware of two methods of determining the purchase price of the goods – first in first out and weighted average cost. The last-in-first-out method, which used to be common, is not permitted by IAS 2.

4.2 First in, first out

The first in, first out (FIFO) method of costing inventory makes the assumption that the goods going out of the warehouse are the earliest purchases. Therefore the inventory items left are the most recent purchases.

4.3 Weighted average cost

The weighted average cost method values inventory at the weighted average of the purchase prices each time inventory is issued. This means that the total purchase price of the inventory is divided by the number of units of inventory, but this calculation must be carried out before every issue out of the warehouse.

4.4 IAS 2 and costing methods

In practice, as already stated, a business is unlikely to know exactly how much a particular item of inventory originally cost. A standard policy for valuation is therefore adopted and the most common is FIFO. You should, however, make sure that you are clear about the other methods as well.

This is covered further in the cost and revenues unit.

5 Accounting for closing inventory

5.1 Introduction

You will need to be able to enter closing inventory in the statement of profit or loss and statement of financial position; and to correctly enter the figure for closing inventory in the extended trial balance. Therefore in this section the actual accounting for inventory will be considered.

5.2 Opening inventory

In some of the trial balances that you have come across in this text you may have noticed a figure for opening inventory. This is the balance on the inventory account that appeared in last year's statement of financial position as the closing inventory figure. This inventory account then has no further entries put through it until the year end which is why it still appears in the trial balance.

Remember that all purchases of goods are accounted for in the purchases account, they should never be entered into the inventory account.

5.3 Year end procedure

At the year end there is a set of adjustments that must be made in order to correctly account for inventories in the statement of profit or loss and the statement of financial position.

Step 1

The opening inventory balance in the inventory account (debit balance as this was a current asset at the end of last year) is transferred to the statement of profit or loss as part of cost of sales.

The double entry for this is:

Dr **Statement of profit or loss** (opening inventory in cost of sales)

Cr **Inventory account**

This opening inventory balance has now been removed.

Step 2

The closing inventory, at its agreed valuation, is entered into the ledger accounts with the following double entry:

Dr **Closing inventory (asset on the statement of financial position)**

Cr **Closing inventory (in cost of sales)**

We will study this double entry with an example.

Example

John prepares accounts to 31 December 20X4.

His opening inventory on 1 January 20X4 is £20,000. During the year he purchases goods which cost £200,000. At 31 December 20X4 his closing inventory is valued at £30,000.

You are required to enter these amounts into the ledger accounts and transfer the amounts as appropriate to the statement of profit or loss.

(You should open a statement of profit or loss account in the ledger and treat it as part of the double entry as this will help you to understand the double entry).

Solution

Step 1

Open the required accounts and enter the opening inventory and purchases into the accounts.

Opening inventory

	£		£
1.1.X4 Balance b/d	20,000		

Purchases

	£		£
1.1.X4 PDB	200,000		

Statement of profit or loss

	£		£

Step 2

Write off the opening inventory and purchases to the statement of profit or loss.

Opening inventory

	£		£
1.1.X4 Balance b/d	20,000	31.12.X4 SPL	20,000

Purchases

	£		£
PDB	200,000	31.12.X4 SPL	200,000
	200,000		200,000

Statement of profit or loss

	£		£
31.12.X4 Opening inventory	20,000		
31.12.X4 Purchases	200,000		

Note

(a)   The opening inventory of £20,000 was brought down as an asset at the end of December 20X3, and has remained in the ledger account for the whole year without being touched.

At 31 December 20X4 it is finally written off to the debit of the statement of profit or loss as part of the cost of sales.

(b)   Purchases of goods made during the year are accumulated in the purchases account. At the end of the year (31 December 20X4) the entire year's purchases are written off to the debit of the statement of profit or loss as the next element of cost of sales. The purchases account now balances and we have closed it off. Next year will start with a nil balance on the purchases account.

Step 3

Enter the closing inventory £30,000 into the inventory account.

Closing inventory statement of profit or loss			
	£		£
		31.12.X4 Closing inventory	30,000

Closing inventory statement of financial position		
	£	
31.12.X4 Closing inventory	30,000	

Note

The double entry for closing inventory is therefore:

Debit   Closing inventory statement of financial position

Credit Closing inventory statement of profit or loss

(a)   On the closing inventory statement of financial position account, we are just left with a debit entry of £30,000. This is the closing inventory at 31 December 20X4 and is the opening inventory at 1 January 20X5. This £30,000 will be entered on the statement of financial position and it will remain untouched in the inventory account until 31 December 20X5.

(b)   The statement of profit or loss has a balance of £190,000. This is the cost of sales for the year. If we write this out in its normal form, you will see what we have done.

Step 4

Transfer the credit entry for closing inventory to the statement of profit or loss and bring down the balances on the inventory and the statement of profit or loss.

Closing inventory statement of profit or loss			
	£		£
31.12.X4 SPL	30,000	31.12.X4 Closing inventory	30,000
	30,000		30,000

Statement of profit or loss

	£		£
31.12.X4 Op. inventory	20,000	31.12.X4 Closing inventory	30,000
31.12.X4 Purchases	200,000	31.12.X4 Balance c/d	190,000
	220,000		220,000
31.12.X4 Balance b/d (Cost of sales)	190,000		

Statement of profit or loss at 31.12.X4

	£	£
Revenue (not known)		X
Cost of sales		
Opening inventory (1.1.X4)	20,000	
Add: purchases	200,000	
	220,000	
Less: closing inventory (31.12.X4)	(30,000)	
		190,000

For the purposes of the exam you need to remember the following:

Opening Inventory is recorded as part of **cost of sales** (as above) in the **statement of profit or loss.**

Closing inventory is recorded as part of **cost of sales** (as above) and as **current assets** in the **statement of financial position.**

Example

A business has a figure for opening inventory in its trial balance of £10,000. The closing inventory has been counted and valued at £12,000.

Show the entries in the ledger accounts to record this.

Solution

Opening inventory statement of profit or loss

	£		£
Balance b/d – opening inventory	10,000	SPL	10,000
	10,000		10,000

Closing inventory statement of profit or loss

SPL	12,000	Closing inventory (SFP)	12,000
	12,000		12,000

Closing inventory statement of financial position

Closing inventory (SPL)	12,000	Balance c/d	12,000
	12,000		12,000
Balance b/d	12,000		

Statement of profit or loss

	£		£
Opening inventory	10,000	Closing inventory	12,000

Activity 3

1 Where will the closing inventory appear in the statement of financial position? (Tick)

Non-current assets ☐

Current assets ☐

2 Where will the closing inventory appear in the statement of profit or loss? (Tick)

Expenses ☐

Cost of sales ☐

3 A line of inventory has been counted and the inventory count shows that there are 50 units more in the inventory room than is recorded on the inventory card. What possible reasons might there be for this difference?

_____

_____

_____

_____

4   Complete the following sentence.

Inventory should be valued at the _____ of_____ and _____

5   The closing inventory of a sole trader has been valued at cost of £5,800 and recorded in the trial balance. However, one item of inventory which cost £680 has a net realisable value of £580. What is the journal entry required for this adjustment? (Tick)

Debit	Credit	
Closing inventory SoFP	Closing inventory SPL	☐
Closing inventory SPL	Closing inventory SoFP	☐

Answers to chapter activities

Activity 1

(a) Purchases account

		£	£
(b)	Dr Purchases a/c	84	
	Cr Office expenses a/c		84

Activity 2

Inventory is valued at the lower of cost and net realisable value (costs to be incurred 5% in selling inventory are deducted from selling price in computing NRV).

	Cost	Selling price	NRV
	£	£	£
A	1,200	1,500	1,425
B	6,200	6,100	5,795
C	920	930	884

Total inventory values (1,200 + 5,795 + 884) = **£7,879**

Activity 3

1 As a current asset.

2 As a reduction to cost of sales.

3 • A delivery has not yet been recorded on the inventory card.

   • A return of goods from a customer has not yet been recorded on the inventory card.

   • An issue to sales has been recorded on the inventory card but not yet despatched.

   • A return to a supplier has been recorded on the inventory card but not yet despatched.

4 Inventory should be valued at the lower of cost and NRV (net realisable value).

5 Debit   Closing inventory – SPL   £100

     Credit   Closing inventory – SoFP   £100

6 Test your knowledge

 ## Workbook Activity 4

Phil Townsend is the proprietor of Infortec and he sends you the following note:

'I have been looking at the inventory valuation for the year end and I have some concerns about the Mica40z PCs.

We have ten of these in inventory, each of which cost £500 and are priced to sell to customers at £580. Unfortunately they all have faulty hard drives which will need to be replaced before they can be sold. The cost is £100 for each machine.

However, as you know, the Mica40z is now out of date and having spoken to some computer retailers I am fairly certain that we are going to have to scrap them or give them away for spares. Perhaps for now we should include them in the closing inventory figure at cost. Can you please let me have your views.'

Required:

Write a memo in reply to Phil Townsend's note. Your memo should refer to alternative inventory valuations and to appropriate accounting standards.

Workbook Activity 5

Melanie Langton trades as 'Explosives'.

You have received the following note from Melanie Langton:

'I have been looking at the draft financial statements you have produced. In the valuation of the closing inventory you have included some of the jeans at less than cost price. The figure you used is net realisable value and this has effectively reduced the profit for the period.

The closing inventory will be sold in the next financial period and my understanding of the accruals concept is that the revenue from selling the inventory should be matched against the cost of that inventory.

This is not now possible since part of the cost of the inventory has been written off in reducing the closing inventory valuation from cost price to net realisable value.'

Required:

Write a suitable response to Melanie Langton in the form of a memorandum.

Your answer should include references to relevant accounting concepts and to IAS 2.

Irrecoverable and doubtful debts

Introduction

When producing a trial balance or extended trial balance, and eventually a set of final accounts, a number of adjustments are often required to the initial trial balance figures.

One of these adjustments may be to the receivables balance in order to either write off any irrecoverable debts or to provide for any allowance for doubtful debts.

KNOWLEDGE
Explain the reasons for, and method of, accounting for irrecoverable debts and allowances for doubtful debts (7.2)

SKILLS
Record accurately the journal entries for irrecoverable debts and allowances for doubtful debts. (7.5)
Account for these adjustments, including; (8.3)
Irrecoverable debts
Allowance for doubtful debts

CONTENTS

1 Problems with receivable accounts
2 Irrecoverable debts
3 Doubtful debts
4 Types of allowances for doubtful debts
5 Writing off a debt already provided for
6 Money received from irrecoverable and doubtful debts

1 Problems with receivable accounts

1.1 Introduction

When sales are made to credit customers the double entry is to debit the sales ledger control account and credit the sales account. Therefore the sale is recorded in the accounts as soon as the invoice is sent out to the customer on the basis that the customer will pay for these goods.

1.2 Conditions of uncertainty

It was mentioned in an earlier chapter that part of the accounting objective of reliability means that in conditions of uncertainty more evidence is needed of the existence of an asset than is needed for the existence of a liability.

This has been known in the past as the **concept of prudence**. Therefore if there is any evidence of significant uncertainty about the receipt of cash from a receivable then it may be that this asset, the receivable, should not be recognised.

1.3 Aged receivable analysis

 Definition

An aged receivable analysis shows when the elements of the total debt owed by each customer were incurred.

An aged receivable analysis should be produced on a regular basis and studied with care. If a customer has old outstanding debts or if the customer has stopped paying the debts owed regularly then there may be a problem with this receivable.

1.4 Other information about receivables

It is not uncommon for businesses to go into liquidation or receivership in which case it is often likely that any outstanding credit supplier will not receive payment. This will often be reported in the local or national newspapers or the information could be discovered informally from conversation with other parties in the same line of business.

If information is gathered about a receivable with potential problems which may mean that your organisation will not receive full payment of the amounts due then this must be investigated.

However care should be taken as customers are very important to a business and any discussion or correspondence with the customer must be carried out with tact and courtesy.

2 Irrecoverable debts

2.1 Information

If information is reliably gathered that a receivable is having problems paying the amounts due then a decision has to be made about how to account for the amount due from that receivable. This will normally take the form of deciding whether the debt is an irrecoverable debt or a doubtful debt.

2.2 What is an irrecoverable debt?

 Definition

An irrecoverable debt is a debt that is not going to be received from the receivable.

Therefore an irrecoverable debt is one that the organisation is reasonably certain will not be received at all from the receivable. This may be decided after discussions with the receivable, after legal advice if the customer has gone into liquidation or simply because the receivable has disappeared.

2.3 Accounting treatment of an irrecoverable debt

An irrecoverable debt is one where it has been determined that it will never be recovered and therefore it is to be written out of the books totally.

The double entry reflects the fact that:

(a) the business no longer has the debt, so this asset must be removed from the books

(b) the business must put an expense equal to the debt as a charge to its statement of profit or loss because it has 'lost' this money. It does this by putting the expense initially through an 'irrecoverable debt expense' account.

The double entry for the irrecoverable debt is therefore:

Dr Irrecoverable debts expense account

Cr Sales ledger control account (SLCA)

There is also a credit entry in the individual receivable's account in the subsidiary sales ledger to match the entry in the SLCA.

Example

Lewis reviews his receivables (which total £10,000) and notices an amount due from John of £500. He knows that this will never be recovered so he wants to write it off.

Solution

Sales ledger control account

	£		£
Balance b/d	10,000	Irrecoverable debts expense	500
		Balance c/d	9,500
	———		———
	10,000		10,000
	———		———
Balance b/d	9,500		

Irrecoverable debts expense

	£		£
SLCA	500	I/S	500
	———		———

In the subsidiary sales ledger there will also be an entry in John's account:

John's account

	£		£
Balance b/d	500	Irrecoverable debts written off	500
	———		———

Activity 1

A business has total receivables of £117,489. One of these debts from J Casy totalling £2,448 is now considered to be bad and must be accounted for.

Record the accounting entries in the main ledger for the irrecoverable debt.

Sales ledger control account

	£		£
Balance b/d			
		Balance c/d	
	———		———
	———		———
Balance b/d			

Irrecoverable debts expense

	£		£
	——		——
	——		——

The accounting treatment of irrecoverable debts means that the debt is completely removed from the accounting records and the statement of profit or loss is charged with an expense.

3 Doubtful debts

3.1 Introduction

In the previous section we considered debts that we were reasonably certain would not be recovered. However the position with some receivables is not so clear cut. The organisation may have doubts about whether the debt may be received but may not be certain that it will not.

3.2 Doubtful debts

 Definition

Doubtful debts are receivables about which there is some question as to whether or not the debt will be received.

The situation here is not as clear cut as when a debt is determined to be irrecoverable and the accounting treatment is therefore different. If there is doubt about the recoverability of this debt then according to the prudence concept this must be recognised in the accounting records but not to the extreme of writing the debt out of the accounts totally.

3.3 Accounting treatment of doubtful debts

As the debt is only doubtful rather than irrecoverable we do not need to write it out of the accounting records totally but the doubt has to be reflected. This is done by setting up an allowance for doubtful debts.

 Definition

An allowance for doubtful debts is an amount that is netted off against the receivables balance in the statement of financial position to show that there is some doubt about the recoverability of these amounts.

An allowance for doubtful debts account is credited in order to net this off against the receivables balance and the debit entry is made to an allowance for doubtful debts adjustment account recognised in the statement of profit or loss.

The double entry therefore is:

Dr Allowance for doubtful debts adjustment account (SPL)

Cr Allowance for doubtful debts account (SFP)

Example

At the end of his first year of trading Roger has receivables of £120,000 and has decided that of these there is some doubt as to the recoverability of £5,000 of debts.

Set up the allowance for doubtful debts in the ledger accounts and show how the receivables would appear in the statement of financial position at the end of the year.

Solution

Allowance for doubtful debts account

	£		£
		Allowance for doubtful debts adjustments	5,000

Allowance for doubtful debt adjustment account

	£		£
Allowance for doubtful debts	5,000		

Statement of financial position extract

	£
Receivables	120,000
Less: Allowance for doubtful debts	(5,000)
	———
	115,000
	———

The accounting treatment of doubtful debts ensures that the statement of financial position clearly shows that there is some doubt about the collectability of some of the debts and the statement of profit or loss is charged with the possible loss from not collecting these debts.

3.4 Changes in the allowance

As the allowance for doubtful debts account is a statement of financial position balance, the balance on that account will remain in the ledger accounts until it is changed. When the allowance is altered, **only the increase or the decrease** is charged or credited to the allowance for doubtful debt adjustment.

Increase in allowance:

Dr Allowance for doubtful debt **adjustment** account with increase in allowance

Cr Allowance for doubtful debts account with increase in provision

Decrease in allowance:

Dr Allowance for doubtful debts account with decrease in provision

Cr Allowance for doubtful debt **adjustment** account with decrease in provision.

 Example

At the end of the second year of trading Roger feels that the allowance should be increased to £7,000. At the end of the third year of trading Roger wishes to decrease the allowance to £4,000.

Show the entries in the ledger accounts required at the end of year 2 and year 3 of trading.

Solution

Allowance for doubtful debts account

	£		£
		Balance b/d	5,000
End of year 2 balance c/d	7,000	Year 2 – Allowance for doubtful debts adjustment account	2,000
	7,000		7,000
Year 3 – Allowance for doubtful debts adjustment account	3,000	Balance b/d	7,000
End of year 3 balance c/d	4,000		
	7,000		7,000
		Balance b/d	4,000

Allowance for doubtful debts adjustment account			
	£		£
Year 2 Allowance for doubtful debt account	2,000	Statement of profit or loss year 2	2,000
	2,000		2,000
Statement of profit or loss year 3	3,000	Year 3 Allowance for doubtful debt account	3,000
	3,000		3,000

Take care that the statement of profit or loss is only charged or credited with the increase or decrease in the allowance each year.

---

4 Types of allowances for doubtful debts

4.1 Introduction

There are two main types of allowances for doubtful debts:

- specific allowances
- general allowances.

This does not affect the accounting for allowance for doubtful debts but it does affect the calculation of the allowance.

4.2 Specific allowances

 Definition

A specific allowance is an allowance against identified specific debts.

This will normally be determined by close scrutiny of the aged receivable analysis in order to determine whether there are specific debts that the organisation feels may not be paid.

4.3 General allowance

 Definition

A general allowance is an allowance against receivables as a whole normally expressed as a percentage of the receivable balance.

Most businesses will find that not all of their receivables pay their debts. Experience may indicate that generally a percentage of debts, say 3%, will not be paid.

The organisation may not know which debts these are going to be but they will maintain an allowance for 3% of the receivable balance at the year end.

Care should be taken with the calculation of this allowance as the percentage should be of the receivable balance after deducting any specific allowances as well as any irrecoverable debts written off.

Order of dealing with a general allowance:

1 Write off irrecoverable debts

2 Create specific allowances

3 Calculate the net receivables figures after both irrecoverable debts and specific allowances

4 Calculate the general provision using the net receivables figure from point 3.

 Example

A business has receivables of £356,000 of which £16,000 are to be written off as irrecoverable debts.

Of the remainder a specific allowance is to be made against a debt of £2,000 and a general allowance of 4% is required against the remaining receivables.

The opening balance on the allowance for doubtful debts account is £12,000.

Show the entries in the allowance for doubtful debts account, the allowance for doubtful debts adjustment account and the irrecoverable debts expense account.

Solution

Calculation of allowance required:

		£
	Receivables	356,000
1	Less: irrecoverable debt to be written off	(16,000)
2	Less: specific allowances	(2,000)
3	Remaining receivables	338,000
4	General allowance 4% × £338,000	13,520
	Specific allowance	2,000
	Allowance at year end	15,520

Allowance for doubtful debts (note 1)

	£		£
		Balance b/d	12,000
Balance c/d	15,520	Allowance for doubtful debts adjustment – increase in allowance	3,520
	15,520		15,520
		Balance b/d	15,520

Sales ledger control account (note 2)

	£		£
Balance b/d	356,000	Irrecoverable debt expense – written off	16,000
		Balance c/d	340,000
	356,000		356,000
Balance b/d	340,000		

Irrecoverable debt expense account

	£		£
Receivables (Note 2)	16,000	Statement of profit or loss	16,000
	16,000		16,000

Allowance for doubtful debts adjustment account

	£		£
Allowance for doubtful debts account (Note 1)	3,520	Statement of profit or loss	3,520
	_____		_____
	3,520		3,520
	_____		_____

Note 1

The balance on the allowance account is simply 'topped-up' (or down) at each year end. In this case the required allowance has been calculated to be £15,520. The existing allowance is £12,000 so the increase is calculated as:

	£
Allowance at start of year b/f	12,000
Allowance required at year end	15,520
	_____
Increase in allowance	3,520
	_____

This is credited to the allowance account and debited to the allowance for doubtful debt adjustment account.

Note 2

The £16,000 irrecoverable debt is written out of the books. The double entry for this is to credit the SLCA and debit the irrecoverable debt expense.

Note that the allowance does not affect the SLCA.

Any specific allowance must be deducted from the receivables balance before the general allowance percentage is applied.

 Activity 2

DD makes an allowance for doubtful debts of 5% of receivables.

On 1 January 20X5 the balance on the allowance for doubtful debts account was £1,680.

During the year the business incurred irrecoverable debts amounting to £1,950. On 31 December 20X5 receivables amounted to £32,000 after writing off the irrecoverable debts of £1,950.

Required:

Write up the relevant accounts for the year ended 31 December 20X5.

Activity 3

Peter had the following balances in his trial balance at 31 March 20X4:

	£
Total receivables	61,000
Allowance for doubtful debts at 1 April 20X3	1,490

After the trial balance had been prepared it was decided to carry forward at 31 March 20X4 a specific allowance of £800 and a general allowance equal to 1% of remaining receivables. It was also decided to write off debts amounting to £1,000.

What is the total charge for irrecoverable and doubtful debts which should appear in the company's statement of profit or loss for the year ended 31 March 20X4?

5 Writing off a debt already provided for

5.1 Introduction

It may happen that a doubtful debt allowance is made at a year end, and then it is decided in a later year to write the debt off completely as an irrecoverable debt as it will not be received.

 Example

At 31 December 20X2, John has a balance on the SLCA of £20,000 and an allowance for doubtful debts of £1,000 which was created in 20X1.

This £1,000 relates to A whose debt was thought to be doubtful. There is no general allowance.

At 31 December 20X2, A has still not paid and John has decided to write the debt off as irrecoverable.

Make the related entries in the books.

Solution

Step 1

Open the SLCA and the allowance account.

SLCA

	£		£
Balance b/d	20,000		

Allowance for doubtful debts

	£		£
		Balance b/d	1,000

Step 2

Remove A's debt from the accounts.

A's £1,000 is included in the £20,000 balance on the SLCA, and this has to be removed. Similarly, the £1,000 in the allowance account related to A.

The double entry is simply to:

Debit   Allowance account with £1,000

Credit   SLCA with £1,000

SLCA

	£		£
Balance b/d	20,000	Allowance	1,000

Allowance for doubtful debts

	£		£
SLCA	1,000	Balance b/d	1,000

Note that there is no impact on the statement of profit or loss. The profits were charged with £1,000 when an allowance was made for A's debt, and there is no need to charge profits with another £1,000.

6   Money received from irrecoverable and doubtful debts

6.1   Receipt of a debt previously written off as irrecoverable

Occasionally money may be received from a receivable whose balance has already been written off as an irrecoverable debt.

The full double entry for this receipt has two elements:

Dr   Sales ledger control account

Cr   Irrecoverable debt expense account

In order to reinstate the receivable that has been previously written off.

Dr   Bank account

Cr   Sales ledger control account

To account for the cash received from this receivable.

However this double entry can be simplified to:

Dr   Bank account

Cr   Irrecoverable debts expense account (or a separate irrecoverable debts recovered account)

Note that the receivable is not reinstated as there is both a debit and credit to the sales ledger control account which cancel each other out.

6.2   Receipt of a debt previously provided against

On occasion money may be received from a receivable for whose balance a specific allowance was previously made.

The double entry for this receipt is:

Dr   Bank account

Cr   Sales ledger control account

This is accounted for as a normal receipt from a receivable (that has not been written out of the books) and at the year end, the requirement for an allowance against this debt will no longer be necessary.

☼ Example

At the end of 20X6 Bjorn had made an allowance of £500 against doubtful receivables. This was made up as follows:

		£
Specific allowance	A	300
Specific allowance	50% × B	200
		500

At the end of 20X7 Bjorn's receivables total £18,450. After reviewing each debt he discovers the following, none of which have been entered in the books:

(1)   A has paid £50 of the debt outstanding at the beginning of the year.
(2)   B has paid his debt in full.

Show the ledger entries required to record the above.

Step 1

Calculate the new allowance required at the year end.

	£
A	250
B	Nil
	250

Step 2

Enter the cash on the SLCA.

Sales ledger control account

	£		£
Balance b/d	18,450	Cash – A	50
		Cash – B	400
		Balance c/d	18,000
	18,450		18,450
Balance b/d	18,000		

Step 3

Bring down the new allowance required in the allowance account.

Allowance for doubtful debts adjustment account

	£		£
		Allowance for doubtful debts	250

Allowance for doubtful debts account

	£		£
Allowance for doubtful debt adjustment	250	Balance b/d	500
Balance c/d	250		
	500		500
		Balance b/d	250

Note: Because the allowance has been reduced from £500 to £250, there is a credit entry in the allowance for doubtful debt adjustment account which will be taken to the statement of profit or loss.

6.3 Journal entries

As with the depreciation charge for the year and any accrual or prepayment adjustments at the year end, any irrecoverable debts or doubtful debt allowances are transactions that will not appear in any of the books of prime entry.

Therefore, the source document for any irrecoverable debt write offs or increases or decreases in doubtful debt allowances must be the transfer journal. The necessary journals must be written up and then posted to the relevant ledger accounts at the year end.

Activity 4

Record the following journal entries needed in the general ledger to deal with the items below.

(a)   Entries need to be made for an irrecoverable debt of £240.

Journal	Dr £	Cr £

(b)   Entries need to be made for a doubtful debt allowance. The receivable's balance at the year end is £18,000 and an allowance is to be made against 2% of these.

Journal	Dr £	Cr £

(c)   A sole trader has an opening balance on his allowance for doubtful debts account of £2,500. At his year end he wishes to make an allowance for 2% of his year end receivables of £100,000.

Journal	Dr £	Cr £

(d)   Entries need to be made for an amount of £200 that has been recovered, it was previously written off in the last accounting period.

Journal	Dr £	Cr £

---

7 Summary

When sales are made on credit they are recognised as income when the invoice is sent out on the assumption that the money due will eventually be received from the receivable.

However according to the prudence concept if there is any doubt about the recoverability of any of the debts this must be recognised in the accounting records.

The accounting treatment will depend upon whether the debt is considered to be an irrecoverable debt or a doubtful debt.

Irrecoverable debts are written out of the sales ledger control account.

However, for doubtful debts an allowance is set up which is netted off against the receivables figure in the statement of financial position. The charge or credit to the statement of profit or loss each year for doubtful debts is either the increase or decrease in the allowance for doubtful debts required at the end of the each year.

Answers to chapter activities

Activity 1

Sales ledger control account

	£		£
Balance b/d	117,489	Irrecoverable debts expense	2,448
		Balance c/d	115,041
	117,489		117,489
Balance b/d	115,041		

Irrecoverable debts expense account

	£		£
Sales ledger control account	2,448	SPL	2,448

Activity 2

Allowance for doubtful debts account

	£		£
Irrecoverable debts exps	80	Balance b/d	1,680
Balance c/d	1,600		
	1,680		1,680

Note: The allowance required at 31 December 20X5 is calculated by taking 5% of the total receivables at 31 December 20X5 (i.e. 5% × £32,000 = £1,600). As there is already an allowance of £1,680, there will be a release of the allowance (decrease) of £80.

Irrecoverable debt expense account

	£		£
Receivables	1,950	Allowance for doubtful debts	80
		Profit and loss a/c	1,870
	1,950		1,950

Note

Only one account is being used to record the reduction in the allowance and also the irrecoverable debt.

Activity 3

Allowance for doubtful debts accounts

	£		£
Irrecoverable debt expense account (bal fig)	98	Balance b/d	1,490
Balance c/d			
Specific	800		
Allowance 1% × (61,000 – 1,000 – 800)	592		
	1,490		1,490
		Balance b/d (800 + 592)	1,392

Irrecoverable debts expense

	£		£
Irrecoverable debts written off	1,000		
		Statement of profit or loss	1,000
	1,000		1,000

Allowance for doubtful debts adjustment

	£		£
		Allowance for doubtful debts	98
Statement of profit or loss	98		
	98		98

Activity 4

(a) Entries need to be made for an irrecoverable debt of £240; main ledger accounts therefore will be as below.

Journal	Dr £	Cr £
Irrecoverable debts expense account	240	
Sales ledger control account		240

(b) Allowance is calculated as £18,000 × 2%.

Journal	Dr £	Cr £
Allowance for doubtful debt adjustment account	360	
Allowance for doubtful debts account		360

(c) Allowance for doubtful debts are ((100,000 × 2%) – 2,500)

Journal	Dr £	Cr £
Allowance for doubtful debts	500	
Allowance for doubtful debt adjustment account		500

(d) Entries need to be made for an amount of £200 in the bank and irrecoverable debt expense account.

Journal	Dr £	Cr £
Bank account	200	
Irrecoverable debt expense account		200

8   Test your knowledge

 Workbook Activity 5

John Stamp has opening balances at 1 January 20X6 on his receivables account and allowance for doubtful debts account of £68,000 and £3,400 respectively.

During the year to 31 December 20X6 John Stamp makes credit sales of £354,000 and receives cash from his receivables of £340,000.

At 31 December 20X6 John Stamp reviews his receivables listing and acknowledges that he is unlikely ever to receive debts totalling £2,000. These are to be written off as irrecoverable.

John also wishes to provide an allowance against 5% of his remaining receivables after writing off the irrecoverable debts.

You are required to write up the:

- Receivables account

- Allowance for doubtful debts account and the irrecoverable debts expense account for the year to 31 December 20X6

- Show the receivables and allowance for doubtful debts extract from the statement of financial position at that date.

Workbook Activity 6

Angola

Angola started a business on 1 January 20X7 and during the first year of business it was necessary to write off the following debts as irrecoverable:

			£
10 April	Cuba		46
4 October	Kenya		29
6 November	Peru		106

On 31 December 20X7, after examination of the sales ledger, it was decided to provide an allowance against two specific debts of £110 and £240 from Chad and Chile respectively and to make a general allowance of 4% against the remaining debts.

On 31 December 20X7, the total of the receivables balances stood at £5,031; Angola had not yet adjusted this total for the irrecoverable debts written off.

Required:

Show the accounts for irrecoverable debts expense and allowance for doubtful debts.

Workbook Activity 7

Zambia

On 1 January 20X8 Angola sold his business, including the receivables, to Zambia. During the year ended 31 December 20X8 Zambia found it necessary to write off the following debts as irrecoverable:

		£
26 February	Fiji	125
8 August	Mexico	362

He also received on 7 July an amount of £54 as a final dividend against the debt of Peru which had been written off during 20X7.

No specific allowance were required at 31 December 20X8 but it was decided to make a general allowance of 5% against outstanding receivables.

On 31 December 20X8 the total of the receivables balances stood at £12,500 (before making any adjustments for irrecoverable debts written off during the year) and the balance b/d on the allowance for doubtful debts account stood at £530.

Required:

Show the accounts for irrecoverable debt expense and allowance for doubtful debts, bringing forward any adjustments for Angola.

 Workbook Activity 8

Julie Owens is a credit customer of Explosives and currently owes approximately £5,000.

She has recently become very slow in paying for purchases and has been sent numerous reminders for most of the larger invoices issued to her.

A cheque for £2,500 sent to Explosives has now been returned by Julie Owens' bankers marked 'refer to drawer'.

Which accounting concept would suggest that an allowance for doubtful debts should be created to cover the debt of Julie Owens?

Control account reconciliations

Introduction

Before the preparation of a trial balance or extended trial balance, we should consider reconciling the sales ledger control account and the purchases ledger control account.

The purpose of these is to detect any errors made in accounting for sales, purchases or cash book and to ensure that the correct figure is used for receivables and payables in the statement of financial position.

KNOWLEDGE	CONTENTS
Explain the purpose and use of books of prime entry and ledger accounts (2.3)	1 Subsidiary ledgers
	2 Contra entries
	3 Sales and purchases ledger control accounts
Explain the purpose of reconciling the sales and purchases ledgers, and the cash book (2.4)	4 Control account reconciliations
SKILLS	
Prepare ledger account balances, reconciling them, identifying any discrepancies and taking appropriate action (8.1)	

1 Subsidiary ledgers

1.1   Introduction

As you have seen in your earlier studies double entry bookkeeping is performed in the ledger accounts in the general ledger. This means that when double entry is performed with regard to credit sales and purchases this takes place in the sales ledger control account and purchases ledger control account.

The details of each transaction with each customer and supplier are also recorded in the subsidiary ledgers. There will be a subsidiary ledger for receivables (called the sales ledger) and a subsidiary ledger for payables (called the purchases ledger).

Note: The sales ledger control account can also be called the receivables ledger control account, while the purchases ledger control account can also be called the payables ledger control account.

1.2   Sales ledger

Definition

The sales ledger is a collection of records for each individual receivable of the organisation. It may alternatively be called the receivables ledger.

The record for each receivable is normally in the form of a ledger account and each individual sales invoice, credit note and receipt from the receivable is recorded in the account. These accounts are known as subsidiary (memorandum) accounts as they are not part of the double entry system.

This means that at any time it is possible to access the details of all the transactions with a particular receivable and the balance on that receivable's account.

1.3   Purchases ledger

Definition

The purchases ledger is a collection of records for each individual payable of the organisation. It may alternatively be called the payables ledger.

The record for each payable is normally in the form of a ledger account and each individual purchase invoice, credit note and payment to the payable is recorded in the account. These accounts are again known as subsidiary (memorandum) accounts as they are not part of the double entry system.

This means that at any time it is possible to access the details of all of the transactions with a particular payable and the balance on that payable's account.

1.4 Credit sales

In the general ledger the double entry for credit sales is:

Dr   Sales ledger control account

Cr   Sales account

The figure that is used for the posting is the total of the sales day book for the period.

Each individual invoice from the sales day book is then debited to the individual receivable accounts in the sales ledger.

Example

Celia started business on 1 January 20X5 and made all of her sales on credit terms. No discount was offered for prompt payment. During January 20X5, Celia made the following credit sales:

	£
To Shelagh	50
To John	30
To Shelagh	25
To Godfrey	40
To Shelagh	15
To Godfrey	10

Solution

By the end of January 20X5 the **sales day book (SDB)** will appear as follows:

Customer	Invoice No.	£
Shelagh	1	50
John	2	30
Shelagh	3	25
Godfrey	4	40
Shelagh	5	15
Godfrey	6	10
		────
		170
		────

At the end of the month, the following **double-entry in the general ledger** will be made:

		£	£
Debit	Sales ledger control account	170	
Credit	Sales account		170

Also the following postings will be made to the **memorandum accounts in the sales ledger:**

		£
Debit	Shelagh	50
Debit	John	30
Debit	Shelagh	25
Debit	Godfrey	40
Debit	Shelagh	15
Debit	Godfrey	10

The **sales ledger** will now show:

John

	£		£
SDB	30		

Shelagh

	£		£
SDB	50		
SDB	25		
SDB	15		

Godfrey

	£		£
SDB	40		
SDB	10		

The **general ledger** will include:

Sales ledger control account

	£		£
SDB	170		

Sales

	£		£
		SDB	170

1.5 Cash receipts from receivables

The cash receipts from receivables are initially recorded in the cash receipts book. The double entry in the general ledger is:

Dr   Bank account

Cr   Sales ledger control account

The figure used for the posting is the total from the cash receipts book.

Each individual receipt is then credited to the individual receivable accounts in the sales ledger.

Example

Continuing with Celia's business. During January 20X5, the following amounts of cash were received:

	£
From John	30
From Godfrey	10
From Shelagh	50

Solution

By the end of the month the analysed cash book will show:

Debit side

Date	Narrative	Total £	Sales ledger £	Cash sales £	Other £
1/X5	John	30	30		
1/X5	Godfrey	10	10		
1/X5	Shelagh	50	50		
		90	90		

Now for the double-entry. At the end of the month, the bank account in the general ledger will be debited and the sales ledger control account in the general ledger will be credited with £90.

Memorandum entries will be made to the individual accounts in the sales ledger as follows:

		£
Credit	John	30
Credit	Godfrey	10
Credit	Shelagh	50

The sales ledger will now show:

John

	£			£
SDB	30	Analysed cash book		30

Shelagh

	£		£
SDB	50	Analysed cash book	50
SDB	25	Balance c/d	40
SDB	15		
	90		90
Balance b/d	40		

Godfrey

	£		£
SDB	40	Analysed cash book	10
SDB	10	Balance c/d	40
	50		50
Balance b/d	40		

The general ledger will include:

Sales ledger control account

	£		£
SDB	170	Analysed cash book	90
		Balance c/d	80
	170		170
Balance b/d	80		

Sales account

	£		£
		SDB	170

Cash account

	£		£
Analysed cash book	90		

The trial balance will show:

	Dr £	Cr £
Sales ledger control account	80	
Sales		170
Cash	90	
	170	170

Notes

- As the individual accounts in the sales ledger are not part of the double-entry, they will not appear in the trial balance.

- The total of the individual balances in the sales ledger should agree to the balance on the sales ledger control account. Normally before the trial balance is prepared a reconciliation will be performed between the individual accounts and the sales ledger control account:

	£
John	–
Shelagh	40
Godfrey	40
Total per individual accounts	80
Balance per sales ledger control account	80

This reconciliation will help to ensure the accuracy of our postings. We shall look at this in more detail later in this chapter.

If all of the entries in the control account and the sales ledger have been made correctly then the total of the individual balances in the sales ledger should equal the balance on the sales ledger control account in the general ledger.

1.6 Sales returns

The double entry for sales returns is:

Dr Sales returns account

Cr Sales ledger control account

Each return is also credited to the individual receivable's account in the sales ledger.

 KAPLAN PUBLISHING

1.7 Discounts allowed

Discounts allowed to receivables are recorded in the cash receipts book if a receivable pays after taking advantage of a cash or settlement discount. The double entry for these discounts is:

Dr   Discounts allowed account

Cr   Sales ledger control account

The discount is also credited to the individual receivable's account in the sales ledger.

1.8 Accounting for purchases on credit

The accounting system for purchases on credit works in the same manner as for sales on credit and is summarised as follows.

The total of the purchases day book is used for the double entry in the general ledger:

Dr   Purchases account

Cr   Purchases ledger control account

Each individual invoice is also credited to the individual payable accounts in the purchases ledger.

The total of the cash payments book is used for the double entry in the general ledger:

Dr   Purchases ledger control account

Cr   Bank account

Each individual payment is then debited to the payable's individual account in the purchases ledger.

1.9 Purchases returns

The double entry for purchases returns is:

Dr   Purchases ledger control account

Cr   Purchases returns account

Each purchase return is also debited to the individual payable's account in the purchases ledger.

1.10   Discounts received

Discounts received from suppliers are recorded in the cash payments book when they are deducted from payments made to the supplier. They are then posted in the general ledger as:

Dr   Purchases ledger control account

Cr   Discounts received account

Each discount is also debited to the individual payable's account in the purchases ledger.

2   Contra entries

2.1   Introduction

In the previous paragraphs the double entry learned in your earlier studies has been revisited. In this paragraph a new piece of double entry will be introduced.

2.2   Contras

A business sometimes sells goods to, and purchases goods from, the same person, i.e. one of the receivables is also a payable. As it would seem pointless to pay the payable and then receive payment for the debt, a business will often offset as much as is possible of the receivable and the payable balances. The entry that results is called a contra entry and the double entry for this is:

Dr   Purchases ledger control account

Cr   Sales ledger control account

Example

Celia sells goods to Godfrey but also purchases some supplies from him. At the end of the period, Godfrey owes Celia £40 but Celia also owes Godfrey £50. The balances on the accounts in the subsidiary sales and purchases ledgers in Celia's books will be:

Sales ledger

Godfrey

	£		£
Balance b/d	40		

Purchases ledger

Godfrey

	£		£
		Balance b/d	50

The maximum amount which can be offset is £40 and after recording the contra entries the accounts will show:

Sales ledger

Godfrey

	£		£
Balance b/d	40	Contra with purchase ledger	40
	——		——

Purchases ledger

Godfrey

	£		£
Contra with sales ledger	40	Balance b/d	50
Balance c/d	10		
	——		——
	50		50
	——		——
		Balance b/d	10

I.e. Celia still owes Godfrey £10.

We have so far considered only the individual receivables' and payables' accounts but we know that every entry which is put through an individual account must also be recorded in the control accounts in the general ledger. Assuming that the balances before the contras on the sales ledger control account (SLCA) and the purchases ledger control account (PLCA) were £15,460 and £12,575 respectively, they will now show:

SLCA

	£		£
Balance b/d	15,460	Contra with PLCA	40
		Balance c/d	15,420
	———		———
	15,460		15,460
	———		———
Balance b/d	15,420		

PLCA

	£		£
Contra with SLCA	40	Balance b/d	12,575
Balance c/d	12,535		
	———		———
	12,575		12,575
	———		———
		Balance b/d	12,535

i.e. receivables and payables have both been reduced by £40.

3 Sales and purchases ledger control accounts

3.1 Introduction

Now that we have reminded you of the entries to the sales ledger and purchases ledger control accounts we will summarise the typical entries in these accounts.

3.2 Proforma sales ledger control account

Sales ledger control account

	£		£
Balance b/d	X	Returns per returns day book	X
Sales per sales day book	X	Cash from receivables *	X
		Discounts allowed *	X
		Irrecoverable debts written off	X
		Contra with purchases ledger control a/c	X
		Balance c/d	X
	X		X
Balance b/d	X		

3.3 Proforma purchases ledger control account

Purchases ledger control account

	£		£
		Balance b/d	X
Cash to suppliers *	X	Purchases per purchase day book	X
Discounts received *	X		
Returns per returns day book	X		
Contra with sales ledger control a/c	X		
Balance c/d	X		
	X		X
		Balance b/d	X

* Per cash book

Activity 1

The following information is available concerning Meads' sales ledger:

	£
Receivables 1.1.X7	3,752
Returns inwards	449
Cheques received from customers, subsequently dishonoured	25
Credit sales in year to 31.12.X7	24,918
Cheques from receivables	21,037
Cash from receivables	561
Purchases ledger contra	126
Cash sales	3,009

Required:

Write up the sales ledger control account for the year ended 31 December 20X7.

Sales ledger control account

	£		£
	____		____
	____		____

4 Control account reconciliations

4.1 Introduction

As we have seen earlier in the chapter the totals of the balances on the sales or purchases ledgers should agree with the balance on the sales ledger control account and purchases ledger control account respectively.

If the balances do not agree then there has been an error in the accounting which must be investigated and corrected.

Therefore this reconciliation of the total of the subsidiary ledger balances to the control account total should take place on a regular basis, usually monthly, and certainly should take place before the preparation of a trial balance.

KAPLAN PUBLISHING

4.2   Procedure

The steps involved in performing a control account reconciliation are as follows:

Step 1

Determine the balance on the control account.

Step 2

Total the individual balances in the subsidiary ledger.

Step 3

Compare the two totals as they should agree.

Step 4

If the totals do not agree then the difference must be investigated and corrected.

4.3   Possible reasons for differences

Errors could have taken place in the accounting in the control account or in the individual customer or supplier accounts in the subsidiary ledgers. Possible errors include:

- Errors in casting (i.e. adding up) of the day books – this means that the totals posted to the control accounts are incorrect but the individual entries to the subsidiary ledgers are correct.

- A transposition error made in posting to either the control account or the individual accounts in the subsidiary ledger.

- A contra entry has not been recorded in all of the relevant accounts i.e. the control accounts and the subsidiary ledger accounts.

- A balance has been omitted from the list of subsidiary ledger balances.

- A balance in the subsidiary ledger has been included in the list of balances as a debit when it was a credit, or vice versa.

4.4 Treatment of the differences in the control account reconciliation

When the reasons for the difference have been discovered the following procedure takes place:

- the control account balance is adjusted for any errors affecting the control account

- the list of subsidiary ledger balances is adjusted for any errors that affect the list of individual balances

- after these adjustments the balance on the control account should agree to the total of the list of individual balances.

The key to these reconciliations is to be able to determine which types of error affect the control account and which affect the list of balances.

 Example

The balance on Diana's sales ledger control account at 31 December 20X6 was £15,450. The balances on the individual accounts in the sales ledger have been extracted and total £15,705. On investigation the following errors are discovered:

(1) a debit balance of £65 has been omitted from the list of balances

(2) a contra between the subsidiary purchases and sales ledgers of £40 has not been recorded in the control accounts

(3) discounts allowed totalling £70 have been recorded in the individual accounts but not in the control account

(4) the sales day book was 'overcast' by £200 (this means the total was added up as £200 too high), and

(5) an invoice for £180 was recorded correctly in the sales day book but was posted to the receivables' individual account as £810.

Solution

Step 1

We must first look for those errors which will mean that the control account is incorrectly stated: they will be points 2, 3 and 4 above.

The control account is then adjusted as follows.

Sales ledger control account

	£		£
Balance b/d	15,450	Contra	40
		Discounts allowed	70
		Overcast of SDB	200
		Adjusted balance c/d	15,140
	15,450		15,450
Balance b/d	15,140		

Step 2

There will be errors in the total of the individual balances per the sales ledger as a result of points 1 and 5. The extracted list of balances must be adjusted as follows:

	£
Original total of list of balances	15,705
Debit balance omitted	65
Transposition error (810 – 180)	(630)
	15,140

Step 3

As can be seen, the adjusted total of the list of balances now agrees with the adjusted balance per the sales ledger control account.

Activity 2

The balance on Mead's sales ledger control account is £6,522.

Mead extracts his list of receivables' balances at 31 December 20X7 and they total £6,617.

He discovers the following:

(1)   The sales day book has been under cast by £100

(2)   A contra with the purchase ledger of £20 with the account of Going has not been entered in the control account

(3)   The account of Murdoch in the sales ledger which shows a credit balance of £65 has been shown as a debit balance in the list of balances

(4)   McCormack's account with a debit balance of £80 has been omitted from the list of balances

(5)   Discounts allowed of £35 recorded in the sales ledger were not shown in the sales ledger control account.

Required:

Show the necessary adjustment to the sales ledger control account and prepare a statement reconciling the list of balances with the balance on the sales ledger control account.

Sales ledger control account			
	£		£
	___		___
	___		___

List of balances per sales ledger

	£
Total per draft list	
Less:	
	___
Add:	
	___
Total per receivables' control account	
	___

4.5　Purchases ledger control account reconciliation

The procedure for a purchases ledger control account reconciliation is just the same as for the sales ledger control account reconciliation however you must remember that the entries are all the other way around.

 Example

The balance on John's purchases ledger control account at 31 May 20X5 was £14,667. However the total of the list of balances from the purchases ledger totalled £14,512.

Upon investigation the following errors were noted:

(1)　an invoice from J Kilpin was credited to his account in the purchases ledger as £210 whereas it was correctly entered into the purchases day book as £120

(2)　the cash payments book was under cast by £100

(3)　a transfer of £50 from a receivables' account in the sales ledger to their account in the purchases ledger has been correctly made in the subsidiary ledgers but not in the control accounts (a contra entry)

(4)　a debit balance of £40 on a payable's account in the subsidiary ledger was included in the list of balances as a credit balance

(5)　the discounts received total of £175 was not posted to the control account in the general ledger.

Required:

Reconcile the corrected balance on the purchases ledger control account with the correct total of the list of payables' balances from the subsidiary ledger.

Solution

Purchases ledger control account

	£		£
Under cast of CPB (2)	100	Balance b/d	14,667
Contra (3)	50		
Discounts received (5)	175		
Adjusted balance c/d	14,342		
	14,667		14,667
		Balance b/d	14,342

List of balances per purchase ledger

	£
Total per draft list	14,512
Transposition error (210 – 210) (1)	(90)
Debit balance included as a credit balance (2 × 40) (4)	(80)
	14,342

 Activity 3

The total of the list of balances extracted from Morphy's purchases ledger on 30 September 20X1 amounted to £5,676 which did not agree with the balance on the purchases ledger control account of £6,124.

(1)   An item of £20 being purchases from R Fischer had been posted from the purchases day book to the credit of Lasker's account

(2)   On 30 June 20X1 Spasskey had been debited for goods returned to him, £85, and no other entry had been made

(3)   Credit balances in the purchases ledger amounting to £562 and debit balances amounting to £12 (Golombek, £7, Alexander £5) had been omitted from the list of balances

(4)   Morphy had correctly recorded returns outwards of £60. However, these returns were later disallowed. No record was made when the returns were disallowed

(5) A contra of £90 with the sales ledger had been recorded twice in the control account

(6) The purchases day book has been undercast by £100

(7) A payment to Steinitz of £3 for a cash purchase of goods had been recorded in the petty cash book and posted to his account in the purchases ledger, no other entry having been made.

Required:

(a) Prepare the purchases ledger control account showing the necessary adjustments.

(b) Prepare a statement reconciling the original balances extracted from the purchases ledger with the corrected balance on the purchases ledger control account.

Purchases ledger control account

£	£

List of balances per purchases ledger

£

Total per draft list

Activity 4

1   What is the double entry in the general ledger for sales returns?

2   What is the double entry in the general ledger for discounts received?

3   When preparing the sales ledger control account reconciliation it was discovered that discounts allowed had been under cast in the cash receipts book by £100. What is the double entry required to correct this?

4   A credit note sent to a credit customer for £340 had been entered in the customer's account in the sales ledger at £430. How would this be adjusted for in the sales ledger control account reconciliation?

5   When preparing the purchases ledger control account reconciliation it was discovered that the total of the purchases returns day book had been posted as £1,300 rather than £300. What is the double entry required to correct this?

6   A payment to a credit supplier was correctly recorded in the cash payments book at £185 but was posted to the payable's individual account in the purchase ledger as £158. How would this be adjusted for in the purchases ledger control account reconciliation?

7   A contra entry for £100 had only been entered in the general ledger accounts and not in the subsidiary ledger accounts. How would this be adjusted for in the purchases ledger control account reconciliation?

5 Summary

The chapter began with a revision of the entries from the books of prime entry to the sales ledger and purchases ledger control accounts and to the sales ledger and purchases ledger.

If the entries are all correctly made the balance on the control account should agree to the total of the list of balances in the appropriate subsidiary ledger. This must however be checked on a regular basis by carrying out a reconciliation of the control account and the total of the list of balances.

The process of carrying out a control account reconciliation is to consider each error and determine whether it affects the control account, the individual receivable/payable accounts in the subsidiary ledger or both. The control account will then be adjusted to find a corrected balance and this should agree to the corrected total of the individual accounts from the subsidiary ledger.

Answers to chapter activities

Activity 1

Sales ledger control account

	£		£
Balance b/d	3,752	Returns inwards	449
Cheques dishonoured	25	Cheques	21,037
Credit sales	24,918	Cash	561
		Contra with purchases ledger	126
		Balance c/d	6,522
	28,695		28,695
Balance b/d	6,522		

NB: cash sales do not affect the SLCA

Activity 2

Sales ledger control account

	£		£
Balance b/d	6,522	Contra with purchases ledger (2)	20
Sales day book (1)	100	Discounts (5)	35
		Balance c/d	6,567
	6,622		6,622
Balance b/d	6,567		

List of balances per sales ledger

	£
Total per draft list	6,617
Less: Murdoch's balance included as a credit (3) (£65 × 2)	(130)
	6,487
Add: McCormack's balance (4)	80
Total per receivables' control account	6,567

Activity 3

Purchases ledger control account

	£		£
Returns allowed (2)	85	Balance b/d	6,124
Balance c/d	6,289	Returns disallowed (4)	60
		Correction of contra recorded twice (5)	90
		Under cast of purchases day book (6)	100
	6,374		6,374
		Balance b/d	6,289

List of balances per purchases ledger

	£
Total per draft list	5,676
Credit balances omitted (3)	562
Debit balances omitted (3)	(12)
Returns disallowed (4)	60
Petty cash purchase (7) (used incorrectly to reduce amount owing for credit purchases)	3
	6,289

(**Note** point (1) in the question does not affect the overall balance of the accounts. It has been treated correctly but posted to the wrong suppliers account)

Activity 4

1	Debit	Sales returns account	
	Credit	Sales ledger control account	
2	Debit	Purchases ledger control account	
	Credit	Discounts received account	
3	Debit	Discounts allowed account	£100
	Credit	Sales ledger control account	£100

4 The total of the list of receivable balances would be increased by £90 (£430 – £340).

5	Debit	Purchases returns account	£1,000
	Credit	Purchases ledger control account	£1,000

6 The total of the list of payable balances would be reduced by £27 (£185 – £158).

7 The total of the list of payable balances would be reduced by £100.

6 Test your knowledge

 Workbook Activity 5

Mortimer Wheeler

Mortimer Wheeler is a general dealer. The following is an extract from the opening trial balance of his business at 1 January 20X6:

	Dr £	Cr £
Cash	1,066	
Trade receivables	5,783	
Trade payables		5,531
Allowance for doubtful debts		950

Receivables and payables are listed below:		£
Receivables	Pitt-Rivers	1,900
	Evans	1,941
	Petrie	1,942
		5,783
Payables	Cunliffe	1,827
	Atkinson	1,851
	Piggott	1,853
		5,531

In January the following purchases, sales and cash transactions were made:

		£			£
Purchases	Cunliffe	950	Payments	Cuncliffe	900
	Atkinson	685		Atkinson	50
	Piggott	1,120		Piggott	823
		2,755			1,773

		£			£
Sales	Pitt-Rivers	50	Receipts	Pitt-Rivers	–
	Evans	1,760		Evans	1,900
	Petrie	1,665		Petrie	1,942
		3,475			3,842

The £950 allowance was against 50% of Pitt-Rivers' debt. Pitt-Rivers was declared bankrupt half way through the year.

Evans denied knowledge of £41 of the balance outstanding at 1 January 20X6 and Mortimer felt that this amount should be provided for as a doubtful debt.

Mortimer received £15 discount from Cunliffe for prompt payment.

Required:

Write up:

(a) Sales and purchases accounts, sales and purchases ledger control accounts, the allowance for doubtful debts account and the irrecoverable debts expense account, the sales and purchases ledgers;

(b) Lists of receivables and payables balances at the end of January.

Workbook Activity 6

Robin & Co

The balance on the sales ledger control account of Robin & Co on 30 September 20X0 amounted to £3,800 which did not agree with the net total of the list of sales ledger balances at that date which totalled £3,362.

Errors were found and the appropriate adjustments when made balanced the books.

The items were as follows:

1. Debit balances in the sales ledger, amounting to £103, had been omitted from the list of balances.

2. An irrecoverable debt amounting to £400 had been written off in the sales ledger but had not been posted to the irrecoverable debts expense account or entered in the control accounts.

3. An item of goods sold to Sparrow, £250, had been entered once in the sales day book but posted to his account twice.

4. £25 discount allowed to Wren had been correctly recorded and posted in the books. This sum had been subsequently disallowed, debited to Wren's account, and entered in the discount received column of the cash book.

5. No entry had been made in the control account in respect of the transfer of a debit of £70 from Quail's account in the sales ledger to his account in the purchases ledger.

6. The discount allowed column in the cash account had been undercast by £140.

Required:

(a) Make the necessary adjustments in the sales ledger control account and bring down the balance.

(b) Show the adjustments to the net total of the original list of balances to reconcile with the amended balance on the sales ledger control account

Workbook Activity 7

Data

The individual balances of the accounts in the sales ledger of a business were listed, totalled and compared with the £73,450 balance of the sales ledger control account.

The total of the list came to £76,780 and after investigation the following errors were found:

(a)   A customer account with a balance of £400 was omitted from the list.

(b)   A £50 discount allowed had been debited to a customer's account.

(c)   A customer's account with a balance of £2,410 was included twice in the list.

(d)   A customer's balance of £320 was entered in the list as £230.

(e)   A customer with a balance of £540 had been written off as an irrecoverable debt during the year but the balance was still included in the list.

(f)   Sales returns totalling £770 (including VAT) had been omitted from the relevant customer accounts.

Task

Make appropriate adjustments to the total of the list using the table below. For each adjustment show clearly the amount involved and whether the amount is to be added or subtracted.

	£
Total from listing of balances	76,780
Adjustment for (a) add/(subtract)	....
Adjustment for (b) add/(subtract)	....
Adjustment for (c) add/(subtract)	....
Adjustment for (d) add/(subtract)	....
Adjustment for (e) add/(subtract)	....
Adjustment for (f) add/(subtract)	....
Revised total to agree with sales ledger control account	....

Workbook Activity 8

On 30 November 20X3 the balances of the accounts in the purchases ledger of a business were listed, totalled and then compared with the updated balance of the purchases ledger control account. The total of the list of balances amounted to £76,670. After investigation the following errors were found:

(a) A credit purchase of £235 (inclusive of VAT) had been omitted from a supplier's account in the purchases ledger.

(b) A payment of £1,600 to a supplier had been credited to the supplier's account in the purchases ledger.

(c) A supplier's balance of £1,194 had been listed as £1,914.

Enter the appropriate adjustments in the table shown below. For each adjustment show clearly the amount involved and whether the amount is to be added or subtracted.

	£
Total from listing of balances	76,670
Adjustment for (a) add/subtract*	....
Adjustment for (b) add/subtract*	....
Adjustment for (c) add/subtract*	....
Revised total to agree with purchases ledger control account	....

 Workbook Activity 9

A credit sale, made by The Pine Warehouse, was correctly entered into the general ledger but was then credited to the customer's memorandum account in the sales ledger.

(a) Would the error be detected by drawing up a trial balance?

Yes / No

(b) Briefly explain the reason for your answer to (a).

Bank reconciliations

Introduction

In addition to reconciling the sales and purchases ledger control accounts, before the preparation of a trial balance or extended trial balance, we must also perform a bank reconciliation. A bank reconciliation compares the bank statement (external document) and the cash book (internal document).

KNOWLEDGE	CONTENTS
Explain the purpose and use of books of prime entry and ledger accounts (2.3)	1 Bank reconciliations
Explain the purpose of reconciling the sales and purchases ledgers, and the cash book (2.4)	
SKILLS	
Prepare ledger account balances, reconciling them, identifying any discrepancies and taking appropriate action (8.1)	

1 Bank reconciliations

1.1 Introduction

At regular intervals the cashier must check that the cash book is correct by comparing the cash book with the bank statement.

Why might they not agree?

- Uncleared Lodgements

  Cheques we have paid into the bank have not yet cleared.

  The cash book is up to date.

- Unpresented cheques

  Cheques we have written have not yet been taken to the bank or have not yet cleared. The cash book is up to date.

- Unrecorded transactions

  Bank charges or direct credits that appear in the bank statement have not been updated in the cash book.

1.2 Bank reconciliation process

(1) Tick off outstanding items from previous reconciliation and agree the opening balance between the cash book and bank statement

(2) Tick off items in the debit side of the cash book (cash received) to the bank statement

(3) Tick off items in the credit side of the cash book (cash payments) to the bank statement

(4) Update the cash book with any items not ticked in the bank statement – i.e. unrecorded transactions

(5) Any items that are now remaining unticked in the cash book should be included in the reconciliation – i.e. uncleared lodgements or unpresented cheques.

1.3   Bank reconciliation proforma

	£	£
Balance per bank statement		X
Add: uncleared lodgements		
Details		X
Less: unpresented cheques		
Details	X	
Details	X	(X)
Balance per cash book		X

 Example

The balance showing on Pinkie's bank statement is a credit of £19,774 and the balance on the cash book is a debit balance of £7,396.

The bank statement is compared to the cash book and the following differences were identified:

(1)   Bank charges paid of £52 were not entered in the cash book

(2)   A cheque payment for £650 has been incorrectly recorded in the cash book as £560

(3)   Cheque payments to suppliers totalling an amount of £7,400 have been written but are not yet showing in the bank statement

(4)   A BACS receipt of £5,120 from a customer has not been entered in the cash book.

Required:

Identify the THREE adjustments you need to make to the cash book and record these adjustments in the cash book ledger. Reconcile the bank statement to the cash book.

Solution

Cash book

	£		£
Balance b/d	7,396	Bank charges (1)	52
BACS receipt (4)	5,120	Cheque (650 – 560) (2)	90
		Balance c/d	12,374
	12,516		12,516
Balance b/d	12,374		

Bank reconciliation

	£
Balance per bank statement	19,774
Less unpresented cheques (3)	(7,400)
Balance per cash book	12,374

2 Summary

The bank reconciliation also needs to be prepared. It is a comparison between the bank statement (external document) and the cash book (internal document). It is necessary to complete the reconciliation on a regular basis to ensure that the cash book is updated and any errors are identified.

Accruals and prepayments

Introduction

In this chapter we review the need to account for accruals and prepayments of income and expenses.

KNOWLEDGE

Explain the accounting principles of going concern, accruals, prudence and consistency (1.1)

Explain the accounting treatment of accruals and prepayments to expenses and revenue (7.1)

SKILLS

Record the journal entries for accrued and prepaid expenses and income (7.4)

Accounts for these adjustments, including:

Accruals and prepayments to expenses and income (8.3)

CONTENTS

1　Recording income and expenditure
2　Accruals
3　Prepayments
4　Income accounts
5　Journal entries

1 Recording income and expenditure

1.1 Introduction

We saw in an earlier chapter that one of the fundamental accounting concepts is the accruals concept. This states that the income and expenses recognised in the accounting period should be that which has been earned or incurred during the period rather than the amounts received or paid in cash in the period.

1.2 Recording sales and purchases on credit

Sales on credit are recorded in the ledger accounts from the sales day book. The double entry is to credit sales and debit the sales ledger control account (receivables account).

Therefore all sales made in the period are accounted for in the period whether the money has yet been received by the seller or not.

Purchases on credit are recorded in ledger accounts from the purchases day book and debited to purchases and credited to the purchases ledger control account (payables account).

Again this means that the purchases are already recorded whether or not the payable has yet been paid.

1.3 Recording expenses of the business

Most of the expenses of the business such as rent, rates, telephone, power costs etc will tend to be entered into the ledger accounts from the cash payments book. This means that the amount recorded in the ledger accounts is only the cash payment.

In order to accord with the accruals concept the amount of the expense to be recognised in the statement of profit or loss may be different to this cash payment made in the period.

Expenses should be charged to the statement of profit or loss as the amount that has been incurred in the accounting period rather than the amount of cash that has been paid during the period.

2 Accruals

2.1 Introduction

If an expense is to be adjusted then the adjustment may be an accrual or a prepayment. Note, that even if the business does not know the exact amount, they must make a prudent estimate of accrued costs.

 Definition

An accrual is an expense that has been incurred during the period but has not been paid by the period end, i.e. a liability.

Example

A business has a year end of 31 December. During the year 20X1 the following electricity bills were paid:

		£
15 May	4 months to 30 April	400
18 July	2 months to 30 June	180
14 Sept	2 months to 30 August	150
15 Nov	2 months to 31 October	210

It is estimated that the average monthly electricity bill is £100.

What is the total charge for the year 20X1 for electricity?

Solution

	£
Jan to April	400
May to June	180
July to August	150
Sept to Oct	210
Accrual for Nov/Dec (2 × 100)	200
	———
Total charge	1,140
	———

Activity 1

Olwen commenced business on 1 May 20X0 and is charged rent at the rate of £6,000 per annum. During the period to 31 December 20X0, he actually paid £3,400.

What should his charge in the statement of profit or loss for the period to 31 December 20X0 be in respect of rent?

2.2 Accounting for accruals

The method of accounting for an accrual is to:

(a) **debit the expense account**

to increase the expense to reflect the fact that an expense has been incurred; and

(b) **credit an accruals account** (or the same expense account)

to reflect the fact that there is a liability for the expense.

Note that the credit entry can be made in one of two ways:

Method 1:   credit a separate accruals account; or

Method 2:   carry down a credit balance on the expense account.

 Example

Using the electricity example from above, the accounting entries will now be made in the ledger accounts.

Solution

Method 1 – separate accruals account

Electricity account

	£		£
15 May CPB	400		
18 July CPB	180		
14 Sept CPB	150		
15 Nov CPB	210		
31 Dec Accrual a/c	200	SPL	1,140
	1,140		1,140

Accruals account

	£		£
		Electricity account	200

Using this method the statement of profit or loss is charged with the full amount of electricity used in the period and there is an accrual or payable to be shown in the statement of financial position of £200 in the accruals account. Any other accruals such as telephone, rent, etc would also appear in the accruals account as a credit balance. The total of the accruals would appear in the statement of financial position as a payable.

Method 2 – using the expense account

Electricity account

		£		£
15 May	CPB	400		
18 July	CPB	180		
14 Sept	CPB	150		
15 Nov	CPB	210		
31 Dec	Accrual c/d	200	SPL	1,140
		———		———
		1,140		1,140
		———		———
			Balance b/d	200

Again with this method the statement of profit or loss charge is the amount of electricity used in the period and the credit balance on the expense account is shown as an accrual or payable in the statement of financial position.

 Activity 2

Olwen commenced business on 1 May 20X0 and is charged rent at the rate of £6,000 per annum. During the period to 31 December 20X0, he actually paid £3,400.

Write up the ledger account for rent for the period to 31 December 20X0 using method 2 (as explained above).Clearly state whether the year-end adjustment is an accrual or prepayment.

Rent account

	£		£

2.3 Opening and closing balances

When the accrual is accounted for in the expense account then care has to be taken to ensure that the accrual brought down is included as the opening balance on the expense account at the start of the following year.

Example

Continuing with our earlier electricity expense example the closing accrual at the end of 20X0 was £200. During 20X1 £950 of electricity bills were paid and a further accrual of £220 was estimated at the end of 20X1.

Write up the ledger account for electricity for 20X1 clearly showing the charge to the statement of profit or loss and any accrual balance.

Solution

Electricity account

	£		£
Cash paid during the year	950	Balance b/d – opening accrual	200
Balance c/d – closing accrual	220	SPL	970
	─────		─────
	1,170		1,170
	─────		─────
		Balance b/d	220

The opening balance b/d of £200 relates to expenses incurred in the prior year. Therefore of the £950 cash paid, £200 relates to the prior year and £750 to the current year. In addition the company owes a further £220 for the current year that it has not yet paid.

Activity 3

The insurance account of a business has an opening accrual of £340 at 1 July X0. During the year insurance payments of £3,700 were made and it has been calculated that there is a closing accrual of £400.

Prepare the insurance expense account for the year ended 30th June X1 and close it off by showing the transfer to the statement of profit or loss

Insurance expenses

£		£
‾‾‾		‾‾‾
‾‾‾		‾‾‾

3 Prepayments

3.1 Introduction

The other type of adjustment that might need to be made to an expense account is to adjust for a prepayment.

 Definition

A prepayment is a payment made during the period (and therefore debited to the expense account) for an expense that relates to a period after the year end.

Example

The rent of a business is £3,000 per quarter payable in advance. During 20X0 the rent ledger account shows that £15,000 of rent has been paid during the year.

What is the correct charge to the statement of profit or loss for the year and what is the amount of any prepayment at 31st December 20X0?

Solution

The statement of profit or loss charge should be £12,000 for the year, four quarterly charges of £3,000 each. The prepayment is £3,000 (£15,000 – £12,000), rent paid in advance for next year.

 Activity 4

Julie paid £1,300 insurance during the year to 31 March 20X6. The charge in the statement of profit or loss for the year to 31 March 20X6 is £1,200.

What is the amount of the prepayment at 31 March 20X6?

3.2 Accounting for prepayments

The accounting for prepayments is the mirror image of accounting for accruals.

(a) **credit the expense account**

to reduce the expense by the amount of the prepayment; and

(b) **debit a prepayment account**

to show that the business has an asset (the prepayment) at the period end.

The debit entry can appear in one of two places:

Method 1: a debit to a separate prepayments account; or

Method 2: a debit balance carried down on the expense account.

Example

The rent of a business is £3,000 per quarter payable in advance. During 20X0 the rent ledger account shows that £15,000 of rent has been paid during the year.

Show how these entries would be made in the ledger accounts.

Solution

Method one – separate prepayments account and rent account

Rent account

	£		£
Cash payments	15,000	Prepayments account	3,000
		SPL	12,000
	———		———
	15,000		15,000
	———		———

Prepayments account

	£		£
Rent account	3,000		

The charge to the statement of profit or loss is now the correct figure of £12,000 and there is a debit balance on the prepayments account.

This balance on the prepayments account will appear as a receivable or prepayment in the statement of financial position.

Method two – balance shown on the expense account.

Rent account

	£		£
Cash payments	15,000	SPL	12,000
		Balance c/d – prepayment	3,000
	———		———
	15,000		15,000
	———		———
Balance b/d – prepayment	3,000		

The expense to the statement of profit or loss is again £12,000 and the debit balance on the account would appear as the prepayment on the statement of financial position.

3.3 Opening and closing balances

Again as with accounting for accruals, care must be taken with opening prepayment balances on the expense account. If there is a closing prepayment balance on an expense account then this must be included as an opening balance at the start of the following year.

 Example

Continuing with the previous rent example the prepayment at the end of 20X0 was £3,000. The payments for rent during the following year were £15,000 and the charge for the year was £14,000.

Write up the ledger account for rent clearly showing the charge to the statement of profit or loss and the closing prepayment at 31 December 20X1.

Solution

Rent account

	£		£
Balance b/d – opening prepayment	3,000	SPL charge	14,000
Cash payments	15,000	Balance c/d – prepayment (bal fig)	4,000
	———		———
	18,000		18,000
	———		———
Balance b/d – prepayment	4,000		

Note that you were given the charge for the year in the question and therefore the prepayment figure is the balancing amount.

The opening balance b/d relates to £3,000 of cash paid in the prior year. This relates to this year's rent and is therefore added to this year's rental expense (i.e. the year the cost was incurred).

Activity 5

The following information relates to a company's rent and rates account:

Balances as at:	1 April 20X0 £	31 March 20X1 £
Prepayment for rates expenses	20	30
Accrual for rent expense	100	120

The bank summary for the year shows payments for rent and rates of £840.

Prepare the rent and rates account for the year ended 31st March 20X1 and close it off by showing the transfer to the statement of profit or loss.

Rent and rates expense account

£	£
___	___
___	___

3.4 Approach to accruals and prepayments

There are two approaches to writing up expenses accounts with accruals or prepayments. This will depend upon whether the charge to the statement of profit or loss is the balancing figure or whether the accrual or prepayment is the balancing figure.

Approach 1 – enter any opening accrual /prepayment

– enter the cash paid during the period

– enter the closing accrual/prepayment that has been given or calculated

– enter the charge to the statement of profit or loss as a balancing figure

Approach 2 – enter any opening accrual/prepayment

      – enter the cash paid during the period

      – enter the statement of profit or loss charge for the period

      – enter the closing accrual/prepayment as the balancing figure

4 Income accounts

4.1 Introduction

As well as having expenses some businesses will also have sundry forms of income. The cash received from this income may not always be the same as the income earned in the period and therefore similar adjustments to those for accruals and prepayments in the expense accounts will be required.

4.2 Accruals of income

If the amount of income received in cash is less than the income earned for the period then this additional income must be accrued for. This is done by:

- a credit entry in the income account (i.e. an increase in income)

- a debit entry/receivable in the statement of financial position (for the amount of cash due).

4.3 Income prepaid

If the amount of cash received is greater than the income earned in the period then this income has been prepaid by the payer. The accounting entries required here are:

- a debit entry to the income account (to reduce income)

- a credit entry/payable shown in the statement of financial position for the amount of income that has been prepaid.

Example

Minnie's business has two properties, A and B, that are rented out to other parties. The rental on property A for the year is £12,000 but only £10,000 has been received. The rental on property B is £15,000 and the client has paid £16,000 this year.

Write up separate rent accounts for properties A and B showing the income credited to the statement of profit or loss and any closing balances on the income accounts.

Explain what each balance means.

Solution

Rent account – A

	£		£
SPL	12,000	Cash received	10,000
		Balance c/d – income accrued	2,000
	———		———
	12,000		12,000
	———		———
Balance b/d income accrued	2,000		

This would be a receivable balance in the statement of financial position showing that Minnie is owed £2,000 for rent on this property.

Rent account – B

	£		£
SPL	15,000	Cash received	16,000
Balance c/d – income prepaid	1,000		
	———		———
	16,000		16,000
	———		———
		Balance b/d – income prepaid	1,000

This would be a payable balance in the statement of financial position indicating that too much cash has been received for this rental.

Activity 6

Hyde, an acquaintance wishes to use your shop to display and sell framed photographs. He will pay £40 per month for this service in cash.

(a)   How would you account for this transaction each month?

(b)   If, at the end of the year, the acquaintance owed one month's rental, how would this be treated in the accounts?

(c)   Which accounting concept is being applied?

5 Journal entries

5.1 Introduction

As with the depreciation expense, the accruals and prepayments are adjustments to the accounts which do not appear in the accounting records from the primary records. Therefore the adjustments for accruals and prepayments must be entered into the accounting records by means of a journal entry.

 Example

An accrual for electricity is to be made at the year-end of £200. Show the journal entry required for this adjustment.

Solution

Journal entry			No:
Date			
Prepared by			
Authorised by			
Account	Code	Debit £	Credit £
Electricity account	0442	200	
Accruals	1155		200
Totals		200	200

Activity 7

A prepayment adjustment is to be made at the year end of £1,250 for insurance expense.

Record the journal entry required for this adjustment.

The following account codes and account names should be used.

0445 Insurance

1000 Prepayment

Journal entry			No:
Date			
Prepared by			
Authorised by			
Account	**Code**	**Debit £**	**Credit £**
Totals			

6 Summary

In order for the final accounts of an organisation to accord with the accruals concept, the cash receipts and payments for income and expenses must be adjusted to ensure that they include all of the income earned during the year and expenses incurred during the year.

The sales and purchases are automatically dealt with through the sales ledger and purchases ledger control account.

However the expenses and sundry income of the business are recorded in the ledger accounts on a cash paid and received basis and therefore adjustments for accruals and prepayments must be made by journal entries.

Answers to chapter activities

Activity 1

$(\frac{8}{12} \times £6,000) = £4,000$ The expense should reflect the proportion of the year's £6,000 charge consumed, not what has been paid.

Activity 2

Rent account

	£		£
Cash payments	3,400	Statement of profit or loss (6,000 × $\frac{8}{12}$)	4,000
Balance c/d – accrual	600		
	4,000		4,000
		Balance b/d – accrual	600

Activity 3

Insurance expenses

	£		£
Cash payments	3,700	Balance b/d – opening accrual	340
Balance c/d – closing accrual	400	SPL charge (bal fig)	3,760
	4,100		4,100
		Balance b/d – accrual	400

Activity 4

The prepayment is £1,300 – 1,200 = £100

 Activity 5

Rent and rates expenses

	£		£
Balance b/d	20	Balance b/d	100
Cash	840	Statement of profit or loss	850
Balance c/d	120	(bal fig)	
		Balance c/d	30
	___		___
	980		980
	___		___
Balance b/d	30	Balance b/d	120

Activity 6

(a)　Dr　Cash account

　　　Cr　Sundry Income a/c (or any other sensible account name)

(b)　A sundry receivable

　　　Dr　sundry receivable (SoFP)

　　　Cr　sundry income (SPL)

(c)　Accruals concept

Activity 7

Journal entry			No:
Date			
Prepared by			
Authorised by			
Account	**Code**	**Debit** £	**Credit** £
Prepayment	1000	1,250	
Insurance	0445		1,250
Totals		1,250	1,250

7 Test your knowledge

Workbook Activity 8

Siobhan

Siobhan, the proprietor of a sweet shop, provides you with the following information in respect of sundry expenditure and income of her business for the year ended 31 December 20X4:

1 **Rent payable**

£15,000 was paid during 20X4 to cover the 15 months ending 31 March 20X5.

2 **Gas**

£840 was paid during 20X4 to cover gas charges from 1 January 20X4 to 31 July 20X4. Gas charges can be assumed to accrue evenly over the year. There was no outstanding balance at 1 January 20X4.

3 **Advertising**

Included in the payments totalling £3,850 made during 20X4 is an amount of £500 payable in respect of a planned campaign for 20X5.

4 **Bank interest**

The bank statements of the business show that the following interest has been charged to the account.

For period up to 31 May 20X4   Nil (no overdraft)
For 1 June – 31 August 20X4   £28
1 September – 30 November 20X4 £45

The bank statements for 20X5 show that £69 was charged to the account on 28 February 20X5.

5 **Rates**

Towards the end of 20X3 £4,800 was paid to cover the six months ended 31 March 20X4.

In May 20X4 £5,600 was paid to cover the six months ended 30 September 20X4.

In early 20X5 £6,600 was paid for the six months ending 31 March 20X5.

6   **Rent receivable**

During 20X4, Siobhan received £250 rent from Joe Soap for the use of a lock-up garage attached to the shop, in respect of the six months ended 31 March 20X4.

She increased the rent to £600 pa from 1 April 20X4, and during 20X4 Joe Soap paid her rent for the full year ending 31 March 20X5.

Required:

Write up ledger accounts for each of the above items, showing:

(a)   the opening balance at 1 January 20X4, if any

(b)   any cash paid or received

(c)   the closing balance at 31 December 20X4

(d)   the charge or credit for the year to the statement of profit or loss.

 Workbook Activity 9

A Crew

The following is an extract from the trial balance of A Crew at 31 December 20X1:

	Dr £
Stationery	560
Rent	900
Rates	380
Lighting and heating	590
Insurance	260
Wages and salaries	2,970

Stationery which had cost £15 was still in hand at 31 December 20X1.

Rent of £300 for the last three months of 20X1 had not been paid and no entry has been made in the books for it.

£280 of the rates was for the 12 months ended 31 March 20X2. The remaining £100 was for the three months ended 31 March 20X1.

Fuel had been delivered on 18 December 20X1 at a cost of £15 and had been consumed before the end of 20X1. No invoice had been received for the £15 fuel in 20X1 and no entry has been made in the records of the business.

£70 of the insurance paid was in respect of insurance cover for the year 20X2. Nothing was owing to employees for wages and salaries at the close of 20X1.

Required:

Record the above information in the relevant accounts, showing the transfers to the statement of profit or loss for the year ended 31 December 20X1.

 ## Workbook Activity 10

A Metro

A Metro owns a number of antique shops and, in connection with this business, he runs a small fleet of motor vans. He prepares his accounts to 31 December in each year.

On 1 January 20X0 the amount prepaid for motor tax and insurance was £570.

On 1 April 20X0 he paid £420 which represented motor tax on six of the vans for the year ended 31 March 20X1.

On 1 May 20X0 he paid £1,770 insurance for all ten vans for the year ended 30 April 20X1.

On 1 July 20X0 he paid £280 which represented motor tax for the other four vans for the year ended 30 June 20X1.

Required:

Write up the account for 'motor tax and insurance' for the year ended 31 December 20X0.

Suspense accounts and errors

Introduction

When preparing a trial balance or an extended trial balance it is likely that a suspense account will have to be opened and then any errors and omissions adjusted for and the suspense account cleared.

There are a variety of different types of errors that candidates need to be aware of. Some of the errors are detected by a trial balance and some are not.

Before the final accounts are prepared the suspense account must be cleared by correcting each of the errors that have caused the trial balance not to balance.

SKILLS
Prepare ledger account balances, reconciling them, identifying any discrepancies and taking appropriate action (8.1) Check for errors and/or inaccuracies in the trial balance, taking appropriate action (8.5)

CONTENTS

1 The trial balance

1.1 Introduction

We saw in an earlier chapter that one of the purposes of the trial balance is to provide a check on the accuracy of the double entry bookkeeping and it is important that this is done regularly. Once all ledger balances have been extracted and the trial balance has been prepared, it might be that the trial balance does not balance – i.e. total debits do not equal total credits. If the trial balance does not balance then an error or a number of errors have occurred and this must be investigated and the errors corrected.

However if the trial balance does balance this does not necessarily mean that all of the double entry is correct as there are some types of errors that are not detected by the trial balance.

1.2 Errors where the trial balance does not balance

The following types of error will cause a difference in the trial balance and therefore will be detected by the trial balance and can be investigated and corrected:

A single entry – if only one side of a double entry has been made then this means that the trial balance will not balance e.g. if only the debit entry for receipts from receivables has been made then the debit total on the trial balance will exceed the credit balance.

A casting error – if a ledger account has not been balanced correctly due to a casting error then this will mean that the trial balance will not balance.

A transposition error – if an amount in a ledger account or a balance on a ledger account has been transposed and incorrectly recorded then the trial balance will not balance e.g. a debit entry was recorded correctly as £5,276, but the related credit entry was entered as £5,726.

An extraction error – if a ledger account balance is incorrectly recorded on the trial balance, either by recording the wrong figure or putting the balance on the wrong side of the trial balance, then the trial balance will not balance.

An omission error – if a ledger account balance is inadvertently omitted from the trial balance then the trial balance will not balance.

Two entries on one side – if a transaction is entered as a debit in two accounts, or as a credit in two accounts, instead of the normal debit and credit entry, then the trial balance will not balance.

1.3 Errors where the trial balance still balances

Certain other errors cannot be detected by preparing a trial balance, as these errors will not cause a difference between the total debits and total credits in that trial balance.

An error of original entry – this is where the wrong figure is entered as both the debit and credit entry e.g. a payment of the electricity expense was correctly recorded as a debit in the electricity account and a credit to the bank account but it was recorded as £300 instead of £330.

A compensating error – this is where two separate errors are made, one on the debit side of a particular ledger account and the other on the credit side of a different ledger account. By coincidence the two errors are of the same amount and therefore cancel each other out when the trial balance is prepared.

An error of omission – this is where an entire double entry is omitted from the ledger accounts. As both the debit and credit have been omitted the trial balance will still balance.

An error of commission – with this type of error a debit entry and an equal credit entry have been made. However one of the entries has been to the wrong account e.g. if the electricity expense was debited to the rent account but the credit entry was correctly made in the bank account – here both the electricity account and rent account will be incorrect but the trial balance will still balance.

An error of principle – this is similar to an error of commission in that part of an entry has been posted to the wrong account. However, the error is one of principle. For example, instead of capitalising the cost of a non-current asset on the statement of financial position (by debiting non-current assets) the cost has been debited to a statement of profit or loss expense account. This is fundamentally incorrect but the trial balance will still balance.

1.4 Correction of errors

Whatever type of error is discovered, either by producing the trial balance or by other checks on the ledger accounts, it will need to be corrected. Errors will normally be corrected by putting through a double entry journal for the correction.

The procedure for identifying what journal is required to correct those errors is as follows:

Step 1: What did they do?

Determine the precise nature of the incorrect double entry that has been made.

Step 2: What should they have done?

Determine the correct entries that should have been made.

Step 3: What is the correction?

Produce a journal entry that cancels the incorrect part and puts through the correct entries.

 Example

The electricity expense of £450 has been correctly credited to the bank account but has been debited to the rent account.

Step 1 – What did they do?

Dr	Rent account	£450
Cr	Bank account	£450

Step 2 – What should they have done?

Dr	Electricity account	£450
Cr	Bank account	£450

Step 3 – What is the correction?

The journal entry required is:

Dr	Electricity account	£450
Cr	Rent account	£450

Note that this removes the incorrect debit from the rent account and puts the correct debit into the electricity account.

 Activity 1

Colin returned some goods to a supplier because they were faulty. The original purchase price of these goods was £8,260.

The ledger clerk has correctly accounted for the transaction but has used the figure £8,620 in error.

Required:

What is the correcting entry which needs to be made?

---

2 Opening a suspense account

2.1 Introduction

A suspense account is a temporary account that can be created to deal with any errors or omissions arising in our general ledger accounting. It means that it is possible to continue with the production of financial accounts whilst the reasons for any errors are investigated and then corrected.

2.2 Reasons for opening a suspense account

A suspense account will be opened in two main circumstances:

(a) an unknown entry – i.e. the bookkeeper does not know how to deal with one side of a transaction

(b) the trial balance does not balance.

2.3 Unknown entry

In some circumstances the bookkeeper may come across a transaction for which he is not certain of the correct double entry and therefore, rather than making an error, one side of the entry will be posted to a suspense account until the correct entry can be determined.

Example

A new bookkeeper is dealing with a cheque received from a garage for £800 for the sale of an old car. He correctly debits the bank account with the amount of the cheque but does not know what to do with the credit entry.

Solution

He will enter it in the suspense account:

Suspense account

	£		£
		Bank account – receipt from sale of car	800

2.4 Trial balance does not balance

If the total of the debits on the trial balance does not equal the total of the credits, then an error or a number of errors have been made. These must be investigated, identified and eventually corrected.

In the meantime, the difference between the debit total and the credit total is inserted as a suspense account balance in order to make the two totals agree.

Example

The totals of the trial balance are as follows:

	Debits £	*Credits* £
Totals as initially extracted	108,367	109,444
Suspense account, to make the TB balance	1,077	
	109,444	109,444

Suspense account

	£		£
Opening balance	1,077		

Activity 2

The debit balances on a trial balance exceed the credit balances by £2,600.

Required:

Open up a suspense account to record this difference.

3 Clearing the suspense account

3.1 Introduction

Whatever the reason for the suspense account being opened, it is only ever a temporary account. The reasons for the difference must be identified and then correcting entries should be put through the ledger accounts, via the journal, in order to correct the accounts and clear the suspense account balance to zero.

3.2 Procedure for clearing the suspense account

Step 1

Determine the incorrect entry that has been made or the omission from the ledger accounts – i.e. the reason for the creation of the suspense account balance.

Step 2

Determine the double entry journal required to correct the error or omission – this will not always require an entry to the suspense account e.g. when the electricity expense was debited to the rent account the journal entry did not require any entry to be made in the suspense account.

Step 3

Post the correcting journals through the ledger accounts and calculate any revised balances carried down. When all the corrections have been made the suspense account should normally have no remaining balance on it.

 Example

Some purchases for cash of £100 have been correctly entered into the cash account but no entry has been made in the purchases account. An entry of £100 was debited to the suspense account.

Draft a journal entry to correct this error.

Solution

Step 1 – Reason for suspense account

The cash account has been credited with £100 but no other entry was made. In this case the Dr would have been posted to the suspense account.

Did do:

Dr	Suspense	£100
Cr	Cash account	£100

Should have done:

Dr	Purchases	£100
Cr	Cash account	£100

Step 2 – Correction journal

A debit entry is required in the purchases account and the credit is to the suspense account to cancel the original debit and to clear the balance to nil.

		£	£
Dr	Purchases account	100	
Cr	Suspense account		100

Being correction of double entry for cash purchases.

Remember that normally a journal entry needs a narrative to explain what it is for – however in most examinations you are told not to provide the narratives so always read the requirements carefully.

Example

On 31 December 20X0 the trial balance of John Jones, a small manufacturer, failed to agree and the difference of £967 was entered as a debit balance on a suspense account. After the final accounts had been prepared, the following errors were discovered and the balance on the suspense account was eliminated.

(1)   A purchase of goods from A Smith for £170 had been credited in error to the account of H Smith.

(2)   The purchase day book was under cast by £200.

(3)   Machinery purchased for £150 had been debited to the purchases account.

(4)   Discounts received of £130 had been debited to the discounts received account.

(5)   Rates paid by a cheque for £46 had been debited to the rates account as £64.

(6)   Cash drawings by the owner of £45 had been posted to the cash account correctly but not posted to the drawings account.

(7)   A non-current asset balance of £1,200 had been omitted from the trial balance.

Note: The control accounts are part of the double-entry.

Required:

(a)   Show the journal entries necessary to correct the above errors.

(b)   Show the entries in the suspense account to eliminate the differences entered in the suspense account.

Solution

Tuition note: Not all the errors relate to the suspense account. Part of the way of dealing with these questions is to identify which entries do not relate to the suspense account. Do not assume that they all do just because this is a question about suspense accounts.

(a)   **Journal – John Jones**

		Dr £	Cr £
31 December 20X0			
1	H Smith	170	
	A Smith		170

Being adjustment of incorrect entry for purchases from A Smith – this correction takes place in the purchases ledger (no effect on suspense account).

2	Purchases	200	
	Purchases ledger control account		200

Being the correction of undercast purchases day book (no effect on suspense account as control account is the double entry, however the error should have been found during the reconciliation of the control account).

3	Machinery	150	
	Purchases		150

Being adjustment for wrong entry for machinery purchased (no effect on suspense account).

4	Suspense account	260	
	Discount received		260

Being correction of discounts received entered on wrong side of account.

5	Suspense account	18	
	Rates		18

Being correction of transposition error to rates account.

6	Drawings	45	
	Suspense account		45

Being completion of double entry for drawings.

7	Non-current asset	1,200	
	Suspense account		1,200

Being inclusion of non-current asset balance. There is no double entry for this error in the ledger as the mistake was to omit the item from the trial balance.

(b)   **Suspense account**

	£		£
Difference in trial balance	967	Drawings	45
Discounts received	260	Non-current asset per trial balance	1,200
Rates	18		
	1,245		1,245

Activity 3

GA extracted the following trial balance from his ledgers at 31 May 20X4.

	£	£
Petty cash	20	
Capital		1,596
Drawings	1,400	
Sales		20,607
Purchases	15,486	
Purchases returns		210
Inventory (1 January 20X4)	2,107	
Fixtures and fittings	710	
Sales ledger control	1,819	
Purchases ledger control		2,078
Carriage on purchases	109	
Carriage on sales	184	
Rent and rates	460	
Light and heat	75	
Postage and telephone	91	
Sundry expenses	190	
Cash at bank	1,804	
	24,455	24,491

The trial balance did not agree. On investigation, GA discovered the following errors which had occurred during the month of May.

(a) **Record the journal entries to correct the errors below.**

(1) In extracting the receivables balance the credit side of the sales ledger control account had been overcast by £10.

Journal	Dr £	Cr £

(2) An amount of £4 for carriage on sales had been posted in error to the carriage on purchases account.

Journal	Dr £	Cr £

(3) A credit note for £17 received from a payable had been entered in the purchase returns account but no entry had been made in the purchase ledger control account.

Journal	Dr £	Cr £

(4) £35 charged by Builders Ltd for repairs to GA's private residence had been charged, in error, to the sundry expenses account.

Journal	Dr £	Cr £

(5) A payment of a telephone bill of £21 had been entered correctly in the cash book but had been posted, in error, to the postage and telephone account as £12.

Journal	Dr £	Cr £

(b) **Show how the suspense account is cleared**

Suspense account		

(c) **Re-write the trial balance as it would appear after all the above corrections have been made.**

Trial balance for GA at 31 May 20X4

	£	£
Petty cash		
Capital		
Drawings		
Sales		
Purchases		
Purchases returns		
Inventory (1 January 20X4)		
Fixtures and fittings		
Sales ledger control		
Purchases ledger control		
Carriage on purchases		
Carriage on sales		
Rent and rates		
Light and heat		
Postage and telephone		
Sundry expenses		
Cash at bank		

Activity 4

The following questions are about errors and suspense accounts.

1   A telephone expense is debited to the rent expense account. This is an example of (tick the correct answer):

A casting error ☐

An error of commission ☐

A compensating error ☐

A single entry ☐

2   A repair expense is debited to a non-current asset account. This is an example of (tick the correct answer):

A casting error ☐

An error of commission ☐

A compensating error ☐

An error of principle ☐

3   Discounts received of £400 have been entered as a credit into the discount allowed account. What is the journal entry required to correct this?

Debit	Credit	
Discounts received	Discounts allowed	☐
Discounts allowed	Discounts received	☐

4   The total of the debit balances on a trial balance are £312,563 whilst the credit balances total to £313,682. Will the suspense account balance be a debit or a credit balance?

Debit of £1,119 ☐

Credit of £1,119 ☐

5   Purchases returns of £210 had been correctly posted to the purchases ledger control account but had been debited to the purchases returns account. What is the journal entry required to correct this?

Debit	Credit	
Purchase returns account	Purchase ledger control account	☐
Suspense account	Purchase returns account	☐

6   An invoice from a supplier for £485 had been entered in the purchases day book as £458. What journal entry is required to correct this?

Debit	Credit	
Purchase account	Purchase ledger control account	☐
Purchases account	Suspense account	☐

7   When producing the trial balance the telephone account expense of £300 was omitted from the trial balance. What journal entry is required to correct this?

Debit	Credit	
Suspense account	Telephone account	☐
Telephone account	Suspense account	☐

8   Motor expenses of £500 were correctly dealt with in the bank account but were debited to the motor vehicles non-current asset account. What journal entry is required to correct this?

Debit	Credit	
Bank account	Motor vehicles at cost account	☐
Motor expenses account	Motor vehicles at cost account	☐

4 Summary

Preparation of the trial balance is an important element of control over the double entry system but it will not detect all errors.

The trial balance will still balance if a number of types of error are made. If the trial balance does not balance then a suspense account will be opened temporarily to make the debits equal the credits in the trial balance.

The errors or omissions that have caused the difference on the trial balance must be discovered and then corrected using journal entries.

Not all errors will require an entry to the suspense account. However, any that do should be put through the suspense account in order to try to eliminate the balance on the account.

Answers to chapter activities

 Activity 1

Step 1 – What did they do?

The purchases ledger control account has been debited and the purchases returns account credited but with £8,620 rather than £8,260.

Dr	Purchases ledger control account	£8,620
Cr	Purchases returns account	£8,620

Step 2 – What should they have done?

Dr	Purchases ledger control account	£8,260
Cr	Purchases returns account	£8,260

Step 3 – What is the correction?

Both of the entries need to be reduced by the difference between the amount used and the correct amount (8,620 – 8,260) = £360

Journal entry:		£	£
Dr	Purchases returns account	360	
Cr	Purchases ledger control account		360

Being correction of misposting of purchase returns

 Activity 2

As the debit balances exceed the credit balances the balance needed is a credit balance to make the two totals equal.

Suspense account

£		£
	Opening balance	2,600

Activity 3

			Dr	Cr
			£	£
1	Debit	Sales ledger control account	10	
	Credit	Suspense account		10

being correction of overcast in receivables' control account

2	Debit	Carriage on sales	4	
	Credit	Carriage on purchases		4

being correction of posting to the wrong account

3	Debit	Purchases ledger control account	17	
	Credit	Suspense account		17

being correction of omitted credit note entry

4	Debit	Drawings	35	
	Credit	Sundry expenses		35

being correction to posting of payment for private expenses

5	Debit	Postage and telephone	9	
	Credit	Suspense account		9

being correction of transposition error

Suspense account

	£		£
Difference per trial balance (24,455 – 24,491)	36	Receivables	10
		Payables	17
		Postage	9
	───		───
	36		36
	───		───

Trial balance after adjustments

	Dr £	Cr £
Petty cash	20	
Capital		1,596
Drawings	1,435	
Sales		20,607
Purchases	15,486	
Purchases returns		210
Inventory (1 January 20X4)	2,107	
Fixtures and fittings	710	
Sales ledger control	1,829	
Purchases ledger control		2,061
Carriage on purchases	105	
Carriage on sales	188	
Rent and rates	460	
Light and heat	75	
Postage and telephone	100	
Sundry expenses	155	
Cash at bank	1,804	
	24,474	24,474

Activity 4

1	An error of commission.		
2	An error of principle.		
3	Debit	Discount allowed account	£400
	Credit	Discount received account	£400
4	£1,119 debit balance		
5	Debit	Suspense account	£420
	Credit	Purchases returns account	£420
6	Debit	Purchases account	£27
	Credit	Purchases ledger control account	£27
7	Debit	Telephone account (TB)	£300
	Credit	Suspense account	£300
8	Debit	Motor expenses account	£500
	Credit	Motor vehicles at cost account	£500

5 Test your knowledge

 Workbook Activity 5

On extracting a trial balance the accountant of ETT discovered a suspense account with a debit balance of £1,075 included; he also found that the debits (including the suspense account) exceeded the credits by £957.

He posted this difference to the suspense account and then investigated the situation.

He discovered:

(a) A debit balance of £75 on the postages account had been incorrectly extracted on the trial balance as £750 debit.

(b) A payment of £500 to a payable, X, had been correctly entered in the bank account, but no entry had been made in the payables control account.

(c) When a motor vehicle had been purchased during the year the bookkeeper did not know what to do with the debit entry so he made the entry Dr Suspense, Cr bank £1,575.

(d) A credit balance of £81 in the sundry income account had been incorrectly extracted on the trial balance as a debit balance.

(e) A receipt of £5 from a receivable had been correctly posted to the receivables control account but had been entered in the cash account as £625.

(f) The bookkeeper was not able to deal with the receipt of £500 from the proprietor of ETT's own bank account, and he made the entry Dr Bank and Cr Suspense.

(g) No entry has been made for a cheque of £120 received from a receivable.

(h) A receipt of £50 from a receivable had been entered into the receivables control account as £5 and into the cash at bank account as £5.

Task

Show how the suspense account balance is cleared by means of a ledger account.

Workbook Activity 6

Julia

The difference on the trial balance of Julia's business whereby the credit column exceeded the debit by £144 has been transferred to a suspense account.

The following errors had been made:

1   Purchase of goods from A Myers for £120 had been credited to the account of H Myers.

2   A total from the sales day book of £27 had been credited to the control account.

3   Sale of plant for £190 had been credited to sales.

4   One total of £120 from the sales day book had been debited to the sales ledger control account as £12.

5   Sales day book undercast by £200.

6   Rent payable accrued as £30 in the previous period had not been entered as an opening balance in the current period.

7   Petty cash balance of £12 omitted from the trial balance.

Required:

Prepare the necessary journal entries, and the entries in the suspense account to clear it.

The extended trial balance – in action

Introduction

As discussed in chapter 6 'The extended trial balance – an introduction', the examination will contain an exercise involving preparation or completion of an extended trial balance. You need to be familiar with the technique for entering adjustments to the initial trial balance and extending the figures into the statement of financial position and statement of profit or loss columns.

The relevant adjustments (accruals, prepayments, depreciation charges, irrecoverable and doubtful debts, errors and closing inventory), have all been covered in previous chapters.

In this chapter we will bring all of this knowledge together in preparation of an extended trial balance.

SKILLS

Record the journal entries to close off revenue accounts in preparation for the transfer of balances to the final accounts (7.6)

Prepare ledger account balances, reconciling them, identifying any discrepancies and taking appropriate action (8.1)

Prepare a trial balance (8.2)

Account for these adjustments (8.3)

Closing inventory

Accruals and prepayments to expenses and income

Provisions for depreciation on non-current assets

Irrecoverable debts

Allowance for doubtful debts

CONTENTS

1 Procedure for preparing an extended trial balance

Use the appropriate columns in the extended trial balance or produce journal entries

Prepare the trial balance after adjustments (8.4)

Check for errors and/or inaccuracies in the trial balance, taking appropriate action (8.5)

1 Procedure for preparing an extended trial balance

1.1 Procedure for preparing an extended trial balance

Step 1

Each ledger account name and its balance is initially entered in the trial balance columns.

Total the debit and credit columns to ensure they equal; i.e. that all balances have been transferred across. Any difference should be put to a suspense account.

Step 2

The adjustments required are then entered into the adjustments column. The typical adjustments required are:

- correction of any errors
- depreciation charges for the period
- write off any irrecoverable debts
- increase or decrease in allowance for doubtful debts
- accruals or prepayments
- accrued income or deferred income
- closing inventory

Note: it is always important to ensure that all adjustments have an equal and opposite debit and credit. Never enter a one sided journal.

Step 3

Total the adjustments columns to ensure that the double entry has been correctly made in these columns.

Step 4

All the entries on the line of each account are then cross-cast and the total is entered into the correct column in either the statement of profit or loss columns or statement of financial position columns.

Step 5

The statement of profit or loss column totals are totalled in order to determine the profit (or loss) for the period. This profit (or loss) is entered in the statement of profit or loss columns as the balancing figure. See example below for further clarification on the adjustment required.

Step 6

The profit (or loss) for the period calculated in step 5 is entered in the statement of financial position columns and the statement of financial position columns are then totalled.

Example

Set out below is the trial balance of Lyttleton, a sole trader, extracted at 31 December 20X5.

	Dr £	Cr £
Capital account		7,830
Cash at bank	2,010	
Non-current assets at cost	9,420	
Accumulated depreciation at 31.12.X4		3,470
Sales ledger control account	1,830	
Inventory at 31.12.X4	1,680	
Purchases ledger control account		390
Revenue		14,420
Purchases	8,180	
Rent	1,100	
Electricity	940	
Rates	950	
	26,110	26,110

On examination of the accounts, the following points are noted:

(1) Depreciation for the year of £942 is to be charged.

(2) An allowance for doubtful debts of 3% of total debts is to be set up.

(3) Purchases include £1,500 of goods which were bought for the proprietor's personal use.

(4) The rent account shows the monthly payments of £100 made from 1 January to 1 November 20X5 inclusive. Due to an oversight, the payment due on 1 December 20X5 was not made.

(5) The rates account shows the prepayment of £150 brought forward at the beginning of 20X5 (and representing rates from 1 January 20X5 to 31 March 20X5) together with the £800 payment made on 1 April 20X5 and relating to the period from 1 April 20X5 to 31 March 20X6.

(6) The electricity charge for the last three months of 20X5 is outstanding and is estimated to be £400.

(7) Inventory at 31.12.X5 was valued at £1,140.

Solution

Step 1

The balances from the trial balance are entered into the trial balance columns.

Account name	Trial balance		Adjustments		Statement of profit or loss		Statement of fin. pos.	
	Dr £	Cr £	Dr £	Cr £	Dr £	Cr £	Dr £	Cr £
Capital		7,830						
Cash	2,010							
Non-current asset cost	9,420							
Accumulated depreciation		3,470						
SLCA	1,830							
Inventory	1,680							
PLCA		390						
Revenue		14,420						
Purchases	8,180							
Rent	1,100							
Electricity	940							
Rates	950							
Total	26,110	26,110						

There are a number of points to note here:

- the accumulated depreciation is the balance at the end of the previous year as this year's depreciation charge has not yet been accounted for;

- the figure for inventory is the inventory at the start of the year – the opening inventory; the inventory at the end of the year, the closing inventory, will be dealt with later.

Make sure you total each column at this stage to ensure that you have entered the figures correctly, and nothing has been missed.

Step 2

Deal with all of the adjustments required from the additional information given.

Adjustment 1 – Depreciation charge

The double entry for the annual depreciation charge is:

Dr Depreciation expense account   £942

Cr Accumulated depreciation account   £942

You will need to open up a new account line for the depreciation expense account at the bottom of the extended trial balance.

Account name	Trial balance		Adjustments		Statement of profit or loss		Statement of fin. pos.	
	Dr £	Cr £	Dr £	Cr £	Dr £	Cr £	Dr £	Cr £
Capital		7,830						
Cash	2,010							
Non-current asset cost	9,420							
Accumulated depreciation		3,470		942				
SLCA	1,830							
Inventory	1,680							
PLCA		390						
Revenue		14,420						
Purchases	8,180							
Rent	1,100							
Electricity	940							
Rates	950							
Depreciation expense			942					

Adjustment 2 – Allowance for doubtful debts

There is no allowance in the accounts yet so this will need to be set up. The amount of the allowance is 3% of receivables therefore £1,830 × 3% = £55

The double entry for this is:

　　Dr Allowance for doubtful debt adjustment　　　£55

　　Cr Allowance for doubtful debts　　　　　　　　£55

As neither of these accounts yet exists they will be added in at the bottom of the ETB.

Revision point: If an allowance for doubtful debts account already exists then only the increase or decrease is accounted for as the adjustment.

Account name	Trial balance		Adjustments		Statement of profit or loss		Statement of fin. pos.	
	Dr £	Cr £	Dr £	Cr £	Dr £	Cr £	Dr £	Cr £
Capital		7,830						
Cash	2,010							
Non-current asset cost	9,420							
Accumulated depreciation		3,470		942				
SLCA	1,830							
Inventory	1,680							
PLCA		390						
Revenue		14,420						
Purchases	8,180							
Rent	1,100							
Electricity	940							
Rates	950							
Depreciation expense			942					
Allowance for doubtful debts adjustment			55					
Allowance for doubtful debts				55				

Adjustment 3 – Owner taking goods for own use

If the owner of a business takes either cash or goods out of the business these are known as drawings. Where goods have been taken by the owner then they are not available for resale and must be taken out of the purchases figure and recorded as drawings.

The double entry is:

Dr Drawings account	£1,500
Cr Purchases account	£1,500

A drawings account must be added to the list of balances:

Account name	Trial balance		Adjustments		Statement of profit or loss		Statement of fin. pos.	
	Dr £	Cr £	Dr £	Cr £	Dr £	Cr £	Dr £	Cr £
Capital		7,830						
Cash	2,010							
Non-current asset cost	9,420							
Accumulated depreciation		3,470		942				
SLCA	1,830							
Inventory	1,680							
PLCA		390						
Revenue		14,420						
Purchases	8,180			1,500				
Rent	1,100							
Electricity	940							
Rates	950							
Depreciation expense			942					
Allowance for doubtful debts adjustment			55					
Allowance doubtful debts				55				
Drawings			1,500					

Adjustment 4 – Rent

The rent charges for the year should be £1,200 (£100 per month) therefore an accrual is required for the December rent of £100.

The double entry is:

Dr Rent account	£100
Cr Accruals account	£100

An accruals account must be added at the bottom of the extended trial balance.

Revision note: The treatment for an accrued expense is to increase the charge to the statement of profit or loss, so that the cost for all goods / services used in the period is captured; and to set up a payable account known as an accrual.

Account name	Trial balance		Adjustments		Statement of profit or loss		Statement of fin. pos.	
	Dr £	Cr £	Dr £	Cr £	Dr £	Cr £	Dr £	Cr £
Capital		7,830						
Cash	2,010							
Non-current asset cost	9,420							
Accumulated depreciation		3,470		942				
SLCA	1,830							
Inventory	1,680							
PLCA		390						
Revenue		14,420						
Purchases	8,180			1,500				
Rent	1,100		100					
Electricity	940							
Rates	950							
Depreciation expense			942					
Allowance for doubtful debt adjustments			55					
Allowance for doubtful debts				55				
Drawings			1,500					
Accruals				100				

Adjustment 5 – Rates

The charge for rates for the year should be:

	£
1 Jan to 31 March	150
1 April to 31 Dec (800 × 9/12)	600
	750

As the invoice of £800 covers 1 April 20X5 to 31 March 20X6, a prepayment should be recognised for the period 1 Jan X6–31 March X6 as this relates to costs incurred outside of the accounting period. (£800 × 3/12 = £200)

This is accounted for by the following double entry:

Dr Prepayments account £200

Cr Rates account £200

A prepayment account must be set up at the bottom of the extended trial balance.

Revision note: The accounting treatment for a prepayment is to reduce the charge to the statement of profit or loss, as the expense is too high because it includes a payment for another period's costs; and to set up a receivable account in the statement of financial position known as a prepayment.

Account name	Trial balance		Adjustments		Statement of profit or loss		Statement of fin. pos.	
	Dr £	Cr £	Dr £	Cr £	Dr £	Cr £	Dr £	Cr £
Capital		7,830						
Cash	2,010							
Non-current asset cost	9,420							
Accumulated depreciation		3,470		942				
SLCA	1,830							
Inventory	1,680							
PLCA		390						
Revenue		14,420						
Purchases	8,180			1,500				
Rent	1,100		100					
Electricity	940							
Rates	950			200				
Depreciation expense			942					
Allowance for doubtful debts adjustment				55				
Allowance for doubtful debts				55				
Drawings			1,500					
Accruals				100				
Prepayments			200					

Adjustment 6 – Electricity

There needs to be a further accrual of £400 for electricity.

The double entry for this is:

  Dr Electricity account   £400

  Cr Accruals account   £400

Therefore £400 needs to be added to the accruals account balance of £100 to bring it up to £500.

Account name	Trial balance		Adjustments		Statement of profit or loss		Statement of fin. pos.	
	Dr £	Cr £	Dr £	Cr £	Dr £	Cr £	Dr £	Cr £
Capital		7,830						
Cash	2,010							
Non-current asset cost	9,420							
Accumulated depreciation		3,470		942				
SLCA	1,830							
Inventory	1,680							
PLCA		390						
Revenue		14,420						
Purchases	8,180			1,500				
Rent	1,100		100					
Electricity	940		400					
Rates	950			200				
Depreciation expense			942					
Allowance for doubtful debt adjustments			55					
Allowance for doubtful debts				55				
Drawings			1,500					
Accruals				500				
Prepayments			200					

Adjustment 7 – Closing inventory

We saw in a previous chapter on inventory that the closing inventory appears in both the statement of financial position as a debit (as a current asset), and in the statement of profit or loss as a credit (a reduction to cost of sales). Therefore two entries will be made in the ETB:

Dr Inventory – statement of financial position £1,140

Cr Inventory – statement of profit or loss £1,140

Account name	Trial balance		Adjustments		Statement of profit or loss		Statement of fin. pos.	
	Dr £	Cr £	Dr £	Cr £	Dr £	Cr £	Dr £	Cr £
Capital		7,830						
Cash	2,010							
Non-current asset cost	9,420							
Accumulated depreciation		3,470		942				
SLCA	1,830							
Inventory	1,680							
PLCA		390						
Revenue		14,420						
Purchases	8,180			1,500				
Rent	1,100		100					
Electricity	940		400					
Rates	950			200				
Depreciation expense			942					
Allowance for doubtful debts adjustment			55					
Allowance for doubtful debts				55				
Drawings			1,500					
Accruals				500				
Prepayments			200					
Closing inventory SPL				1,140				
Closing inventory SoFP			1,140					

Step 3

The adjustments columns must now be totalled. Each adjustment was made in double entry form and therefore the total of the debit column should equal the total of the credit column. Leave a spare line before putting in the total as there will be a further balance to enter, the profit or loss for the period.

Account name	Trial balance		Adjustments		Statement of profit or loss		Statement of fin. pos.	
	Dr £	Cr £	Dr £	Cr £	Dr £	Cr £	Dr £	Cr £
Capital		7,830						
Cash	2,010							
Non-current asset cost	9,420							
Accumulated depreciation		3,470		942				
SLCA	1,830							
Opening inventory	1,680							
PLCA		390						
Revenue		14,420						
Purchases	8,180			1,500				
Rent	1,100		100					
Electricity	940		400					
Rates	950			200				
Depreciation expense			942					
Allowance for doubtful debts adjustments			55					
Allowance for doubtful debts				55				
Drawings			1,500					
Accruals				500				
Prepayments			200					
Closing inventory SoFP			1,140					
Closing inventory SPL				1,140				
	26,110	26,110	4,337	4,337				

Step 4

Each of the account balances must now be cross-cast (added across) and then entered as a debit or credit in either the statement of profit or loss columns or the statement of financial position columns.

Income and expenses are entered in the statement of profit or loss columns and assets and liabilities are entered in the statement of financial position columns.

This is how it works taking each account balance in turn:

- capital account: there are no adjustments to this therefore the balance is entered in the credit column of the statement of financial position – the liability of the business owed back to the owner

- cash account: again no adjustments here therefore this is entered into the debit column of the statement of financial position – an asset

- non-current asset cost account: no adjustments therefore entered in the debit column of the statement of financial position – an asset

- accumulated depreciation: (£3,470 + 942 = £4,412) this is the amount that has to be deducted from the non-current asset cost total in the statement of financial position, as it is the accumulated depreciation, and therefore the credit entry is to the statement of financial position – part of non-current asset net book value

- SLCA: no adjustments therefore entered in the debit column of the statement of financial position – an asset

- opening inventory account: entered as a debit in the statement of profit or loss as it increases expenses – part of cost of sales

- PLCA: no adjustment and so is entered as a credit in the statement of financial position – a liability

- sales account: no adjustments therefore a credit in the statement of profit or loss – income

- purchases account: (£8,180 – 1,500 = £6,680) note that the £1,500 is deducted from the initial balance, as the £8,180 is a debit and the £1,500 a credit. The total is then entered as a debit in the statement of profit or loss – part of cost of sales

- rent account: (£1,100 + 100 = £1,200) these two amounts are added together as they are both debits and the total is entered in the debit column of the statement of profit or loss – an expense

- electricity account: (£940 + 400 = £1,340) again two debits so added together and the total entered in the debit column of the statement of profit or loss – an expense

- rates account: (£950 – 200 = £750) the balance of £950 is a debit therefore the credit of £200 must be deducted and the final total is entered in the debit column of the statement of profit or loss – an expense

- depreciation expense account: adjustment is entered in the statement of profit or loss debit column – an expense

- allowance for doubtful debts adjustment – another expense account to the statement of profit or loss debit column

- allowance for doubtful debts account: this is the amount that is deducted from receivables in the statement of financial position and is therefore entered in the credit column of the statement of financial position

- drawings account – this is a reduction of the amount the business owes to the owner and is therefore a debit in the statement of financial position, it is a reduction of the amount of overall capital

- accruals account: this balance is an extra payable in the statement of financial position therefore is entered into the credit column in the statement of financial position – a liability

- prepayments account: this balance is an extra receivable in the statement of financial position and is therefore a debit in the statement of financial position columns – an asset

Account name	Trial balance		Adjustments		Statement of profit or loss		Statement of fin. pos.	
	Dr £	Cr £	Dr £	Cr £	Dr £	Cr £	Dr £	Cr £
Capital		7,830						7,830
Cash	2,010						2,010	
Non-current asset cost	9,420						9,420	
Accumulated depreciation		3,470		942				4,412
SLCA	1,830						1,830	
Opening inventory	1,680				1,680			
PLCA		390						390
Revenue		14,420				14,420		
Purchases	8,180			1,500	6,680			
Rent	1,100		100		1,200			
Electricity	940		400		1,340			
Rates	950			200	750			
Depreciation expense			942		942			
Allowance for doubtful debts adjustment			55		55			
Allowance doubtful debts				55				55
Drawings			1,500				1,500	
Accruals				500				500
Prepayments			200				200	
Closing inventory SoFP			1,140				1,140	
Closing inventory SPL				1,140		1,140		
	26,110	26,110	4,337	4,337	12,647	15,560	16,100	13,187

Steps 5 and 6

- Total the debit and credit columns of the statement of profit or loss – they will not be equal as the difference between them is any profit or loss.

- If the credit total exceeds the debits the difference is a profit which must be entered in the last line of the ETB and put into the debit column of the statement of profit or loss columns in order to make them equal.

- To complete the double entry the same figure is also entered as a credit in the statement of financial position columns – the profit owed back to the owner.

- If the debit total of the statement of profit or loss columns exceeds the credit total then a loss has been made – this is entered as a credit in the statement of profit or loss and a debit in the statement of financial position columns. Finally total the statement of financial position debit and credit columns, these should now be equal.

Account name	Trial balance		Adjustments		Statement of profit or loss		Statement of fin. pos.	
	Dr £	Cr £	Dr £	Cr £	Dr £	Cr £	Dr £	Cr £
Capital		7,830						7,830
Cash	2,010						2,010	
NCA cost	9,420						9,420	
Accumulated depreciation		3,470		942				4,412
SLCA	1,830						1,830	
Open. inventory	1,680				1,680			
PLCA		390						390
Revenue		14,420				14,420		
Purchases	8,180			1,500	6,680			
Rent	1,100		100		1,200			
Electricity	940		400		1,340			
Rates	950			200	750			
Depreciation expense			942		942			
Allowance for doubtful debts adjustment			55		55			
Allowance for doubtful debts				55				55
Drawings			1,500				1,500	
Accruals				500				500
Prepayments			200				200	
Closing inventory SoFP			1,140				1,140	
Closing inventory SPL				1,140		1,140		
Profit (15,560 – 12,647)					2,913			2,913
	26,110	26,110	4,337	4,337	15,560	15,560	16,100	16,100

Activity 1

The following is the trial balance of Hick at 31 December 20X6

	Dr £	Cr £
Shop fittings at cost	7,300	
Accumulated shop fitting depreciation at 1 January 20X6		2,500
Leasehold premises at cost	30,000	
Accumulated leasehold depreciation at 1 January 20X6		6,000
Inventory at 1 January 20X6	15,000	
Sales ledger control account at 31 December 20X6	10,000	
Allowance for doubtful debts at 1 January 20X6		800
Cash in hand	50	
Cash in bank	1,250	
Purchases ledger control account at 31 Dec 20X6		18,000
Proprietor's capital at 1 January 20X6		19,050
Drawings to 31 December 20X6	4,750	
Purchases	80,000	
Revenue		120,000
Wages	12,000	
Advertising	4,000	
Rates for 15 months	1,800	
Bank charges	200	
	166,350	166,350

Complete the journal entries for the adjustments below.

Depreciation of shop fittings: £400; depreciation of leasehold: £1,000.

Journal	Dr £	Cr £

Journal	Dr £	Cr £

A debt of £500 is irrecoverable and is to be written off; the doubtful debts allowance is to be 3% of the receivables.

Journal	Dr £	Cr £

Journal	Dr £	Cr £

Advertising fees of £200 have been treated incorrectly as wages.

Journal	Dr £	Cr £

The proprietor has withdrawn goods costing £1,200 for his personal use; these have not been recorded as drawings.

Journal	Dr £	Cr £

The inventory at 31 December 20X6 is valued at £21,000.

Journal	Dr £	Cr £

Prepayment adjustment for rates, as 15 months has been included in the trial balance.

Journal	Dr £	Cr £

Prepare an extended trial balance at 31 December 20X6.

Extended trial balance at 31 December 20X6

Account name	Trial balance		Adjustments		Statement of profit or loss		Statement of fin. pos.	
	Dr	Cr	Dr	Cr	Dr	Cr	Dr	Cr
	£	£	£	£	£	£	£	£
Shop fittings cost								
Accumulated shop fitting dep'n								
Leasehold								
Accumulated leasehold dep'n								
Open. inventory								
SLCA								
Allowance for doubtful debt 1.1.X6								
Cash in hand								
Cash at bank								
PLCA								
Capital								
Drawings								
Purchases								
Revenue								
Wages								
Advertising								
Rates								
Bank charges								
Dep'n expenses								
– Fittings								
– Lease								
Irrecoverable debts expense								
Allowance for doubtful debt adjustment								
Prepayments								
Closing Inventory SoFP								
Closing Inventory SPL								
Net profit								

Activity 2

Michael carries on business as a clothing manufacturer. The trial balance of the business as on 31 December 20X6 was as follows:

	Dr £	Cr £
Capital account – Michael		30,000
Freehold factory at cost (including land £4,000)	20,000	
Factory plant and machinery at cost	4,800	
Sales reps' cars at cost	2,600	
Accumulated depreciation, 1 January 20X6		
Freehold factory		1,920
Factory plant and machinery		1,600
Sales reps' cars		1,200
Inventories, 1 January 20X6	8,900	
Trade receivables and payables	3,600	4,200
Allowance for doubtful debts		280
Purchases	36,600	
Wages and salaries	19,800	
Rates and insurance	1,510	
Sundry expenses	1,500	
Motor expenses	400	
Revenue		72,000
Balance at bank	11,490	
	111,200	111,200

Complete the journal entries for the adjustments below.

Inventories on hand at 31 December were £10,800.

Journal	Dr £	Cr £

Wages and salaries include the following:

Michael – drawings £2,400

Motor expenses £600

Journal	Dr £	Cr £

Journal	Dr £	Cr £

Provision is to be made for depreciation on the freehold factory, plant and machinery and sales reps' cars at 2%, 10% and 25% respectively, calculated on a straight line basis.

Journal	Dr £	Cr £

Journal	Dr £	Cr £

Journal	Dr £	Cr £

On 31 December 20X6 £120 was owed for sundry expenses and rates paid in advance amounted to £260. Neither of these had been adjusted for in the trial balance.

Journal	Dr £	Cr £

Journal	Dr £	Cr £

Of the trade receivables £60, for which an allowance had previously been made, is to be written off. The closing allowance for doubtful debts is to be reduced to reflect this write off.

Journal	Dr £	Cr £

Prepare an extended trial balance at 31 December 20X6 dealing with the above information.

Extended trial balance at 31 December 20X6

Account name	Trial balance		Adjustments		Statement of profit or loss		Statement of financial position	
	Dr £	Cr £	Dr £	Cr £	Dr £	Cr £	Dr £	Cr £
Capital account								
Freehold factory cost								
Plant cost								
Sales Reps' Cars Cost								
Accum dep'n								
– factory								
– Plant								
– Sales Reps' cars								
Open. inventory								
Sales ledger control account								
Purchase ledger control account								
Allowance doubtful debts								
Purchases								
Wages & salaries								
Rates & insurance								
Sundry expenses								
Motor expenses								
Revenue								
Cash at bank								
Drawings								
Closing Inventory – SoFP								
Closing Inventory – SPL								
Depreciation								
– factory								
– Plant								
– Sales Reps' cars								
Accruals								
Prepayments								
Net profit								

1.2   Treatment of goods taken by the owner

In the earlier example we saw how goods taken for use by the owner must be taken out of purchases and transferred to drawings. The double entry was:

Dr   Drawings account

Cr   Purchases account

With the cost of the goods taken.

There is however an alternative method which may be required by some examinations:

Dr   Drawings account with the selling price plus VAT (Gross)

Cr   Sales account with the net of VAT selling price (Net)

Cr   VAT account with the VAT

As a general guide use the first method when the goods are stated at cost price and the second method when the goods are stated at selling price. If both methods are possible from the information given use the first method as it is simpler.

Activity 3

You have been asked to prepare the 20X0 accounts of Rugg, a retail merchant. Rugg has balanced the books at 31 December 20X0 and gives you the following list of balances:

	£
Capital account at 1 January 20X0	2,377
Rent	500
Inventory as at 1 January 20X0	510
Rates	240
Insurance	120
Wages	1,634
Receivables	672
Revenue	15,542
Repairs	635
Purchases	9,876
Discounts received	129
Drawings	1,200
Petty cash in hand 31 December 20X0	5
Bank balance 31 December 20X0	763
Motor vehicles, at cost	1,740
Fixtures and fittings at cost	829
Accumulated depreciation at 1 January 20X0	
– Motor vehicles	435
– Fixtures and fittings	166
Travel and entertaining	192
Payables	700
Sundry expenses	433

Complete the journal entries for the adjustments below.

Closing inventory, valued at cost, amounts to £647.

Journal	Dr £	Cr £

Rugg has drawn £10 a month and these drawings have been charged to wages.

Journal	Dr £	Cr £

Depreciation is to be provided at 25% straight line on motor vehicles and 20% straight line on fixtures and fittings.

Journal	Dr £	Cr £

Journal	Dr £	Cr £

Irrecoverable debts totalling £37 are to be written off.

Journal	Dr £	Cr £

Sundry expenses include £27 spent on electrical repairs and cash purchases of goods for resale of £72.

Journal	Dr £	Cr £

Journal	Dr £	Cr £

KAPLAN PUBLISHING

Rugg has taken goods from inventory for his own use. When purchased by his business, these goods cost £63 and would have been sold for £91.

Journal	Dr £	Cr £

The annual rental of the business premises is £600; in addition £180 of rates charges paid in August 20X0 covers the year ending 30 June 20X1.

Journal	Dr £	Cr £

Journal	Dr £	Cr £

Prepare an extended trial balance reflecting the above information

Extended trial balance at 31 December 20X0

Account name	Trial balance		Adjustments		Statement of profit or loss		Statement of fin. pos.	
	Dr	Cr	Dr	Cr	Dr	Cr	Dr	Cr
	£	£	£	£	£	£	£	£
Capital 1.1.X0								
Rent								
Open. inventory								
Rates								
Insurance								
Wages								
SLCA								
Revenue								
Repairs								
Purchases								
Discounts								
Drawings								
Petty cash								
Cash at bank								
Vehicles cost								
Fixtures cost								
Accum'd dep'n								
– Vehicles								
– Fixtures								
Travel								
PLCA								
Sundry expenses								
Closing Inventory SoFP								
Closing Inventory SPL								
Dep'n expense								
– Vehicles								
– Fixtures								
Irrecoverable debts								
Accruals								
Prepayments								
Net profit								

Activity 4

1   What is the double entry for a depreciation charge for the year of £640? (record the account name and amount)

Account name	£	£
Debit		
Credit		

2   The owner of a business takes goods costing £1,000 out of the business for his own use. What is the double entry for this? (record the account name and amount)

Account name	£	£
Debit		
Credit		

3   What is the double entry required to put closing inventory into the adjustment columns of the extended trial balance? (record the account names)

Account name	£	£
Debit		
Credit		

4   Does the accumulated depreciation appear in the statement of profit or loss or statement of financial position columns of the ETB?

Statement of profit or loss   ☐

Statement of financial position   ☐

5   Does opening inventory appear in the statement of profit or loss or statement of financial position columns of the ETB?

Statement of profit or loss   ☐

Statement of financial position   ☐

2 Summary

Once the initial trial balance has been taken out then it is necessary to correct any errors in the ledger accounts and to put through the various year end adjustments that we have considered. These adjustments will be closing inventory, depreciation, irrecoverable and doubtful debts, accruals and prepayments. These can all be conveniently put through on the extended trial balance.

The ETB is then extended and the totals shown in the appropriate statement of profit or loss and statement of financial position columns. Finally the profit or loss is calculated and the statement of financial position columns totalled.

Answers to chapter activities

 Activity 1

Extended trial balance at 31 December 20X6

Account name	Trial balance		Adjustments		Statement of profit or loss		Statement of fin. pos.	
	Dr	Cr	Dr	Cr	Dr	Cr	Dr	Cr
	£	£	£	£	£	£	£	£
Shop fittings cost	7,300						7,300	
Accumulated shop fitting dep'n		2,500		400				2,900
Leasehold	30,000						30,000	
Accumulated leasehold dep'n		6,000		1,000				7,000
Opening Inventory	15,000				15,000			
SLCA	10,000			500			9,500	
Allowance for doubtful debt 1.1.X6		800	515					285
Cash in hand	50						50	
Cash at bank	1,250						1,250	
PLCA		18,000						18,000
Capital		19,050						19,050
Drawings	4,750		1,200				5,950	
Purchases	80,000			1,200	78,800			
Revenue		120,000				120,000		
Wages	12,000			200	11,800			
Advertising	4,000		200		4,200			
Rates	1,800			360	1,440			
Bank charges	200				200			
Dep'n expenses								
– Fittings			400		400			
– Lease			1,000		1,000			
Irrecoverable debts			500		500			
Allowance for doubtful debt adjustment				515		515		
Prepayments			360				360	
Closing Inventory SoFP			21,000				21,000	
Closing Inventory SPL				21,000		21,000		
Sub Total					113,340	141,515		
Net profit					28,175			28,175
TOTAL	**166,350**	**166,350**	**25,175**	**25,175**	**141,515**	**141,515**	**75,410**	**75,410**

Revision point: Take care with the doubtful debt allowance.

Allowance required is 3% of receivables after writing off the irrecoverable debt.

	£
Allowance 3% × (10,000 – 500)	285
Allowance in trial balance	800
Decrease in allowance	515

 Activity 2

Extended trial balance at 31 December 20X6

Account name	Trial balance Dr £	Trial balance Cr £	Adjustments Dr £	Adjustments Cr £	Statement of profit or loss Dr £	Statement of profit or loss Cr £	Statement of fin. pos. Dr £	Statement of fin. pos. Cr £
Capital account		30,000						30,000
Freehold factory cost	20,000						20,000	
Plant cost	4,800						4,800	
Sales Reps' Cars cost	2,600						2,600	
Accum dep'n – factory *1		1,920		320				2,240
– Plant		1,600		480				2,080
– Sales Reps' cars cost		1,200		650				1,850
Open. inventory	8,900				8,900			
SLCA	3,600			60			3,540	
PLCA		4,200						4,200
Allowance doubtful debts		280	60					220
Purchases	36,600				36,600			
Wages & salaries	19,800			3,000	16,800			
Rates & insurance	1,510			260	1,250			
Sundry expenses	1,500		120		1,620			
Motor expenses	400		600		1,000			
Sales		72,000				72,000		
Cash at bank	11,490						11,490	
Closing Inventory SoFP			10,800				10,800	
Closing Inventory SPL				10,800		10,800		

	Dr	Cr	Dr	Cr	Dr	Cr	Dr	Cr
Drawings			2,400				2,400	
Depreciation								
– factory			320		320			
– plant			480		480			
– Sales Reps' cars			650		650			
Accruals				120				120
Prepayments			260				260	
Sub total					67,620	82,800	55,890	40,710
Net profit					15,180			15,180
TOTAL	111,200	111,200	15,690	15,690	82,800	82,800	55,890	55,890

NOTE:

*1 – as the factory also includes land, the depreciation charge is (20,000 – 4,000) × 2% = 320

*2 – including an irrecoverable debt expense line and having a Dr and Cr of £60 is an alternative answer

Activity 3

Extended trial balance at 31 December 20X0

Account name	Trial balance		Adjustments		Statement of profit or loss		Statement of fin. pos.	
	Dr	Cr	Dr	Cr	Dr	Cr	Dr	Cr
	£	£	£	£	£	£	£	£
Capital 1.1.X0		2,377						2,377
Rent	500		100		600			
Open. inventory	510				510			
Rates	240			90	150			
Insurance	120				120			
Wages	1,634			120	1,514			
SLCA	672			37			635	
Revenue		15,542				15,542		
Repairs	635		27		662			
Purchases	9,876		72	63	9,885			
Discounts Received		129				129		
Drawings	1,200		63 120				1,383	
Petty cash	5						5	
Cash at bank	763						763	
Vehicles cost	1,740						1,740	
Fixtures cost	829						829	

					27			
Accumulated dep'n								
– Vehicles		435		435				870
– Fixtures		166		166				332
Travel	192				192			
PLCA		700						700
Sundry expenses	433			27 / 72	334			
Closing Inventory SoFP			647				647	
Closing Inventory SPL				647		647		
Dep'n expense								
– Vehicles			435		435			
– Fixtures			166		166			
Irrecoverable debts			37		37			
Accruals				100				100
Prepayments			90				90	
Sub Total					14,605			
Net Profit					1,713			1,713
TOTAL	**19,349**	**19,349**	**1,757**	**1,757**	**16,318**	**16,318**	**6,092**	**6,092**

Activity 4

1 Debit   Depreciation expense account   £640
   Credit   Accumulated depreciation account   £640

2 Debit   Drawings account   £1,000
   Credit   Purchases account   £1,000

3 Debit   Closing inventory – statement of financial position
   Credit   Closing inventory – statement of profit or loss

4 Statement of financial position

5 Statement of profit or loss

KAPLAN PUBLISHING

3 Test your knowledge

Workbook Activity 5

Randall

Trial balance at 31 December 20X6

	Dr £	Cr £
Shop fittings at cost	2,000	
Depreciation accumulated at 1 January 20X6		100
Leasehold premises at cost	12,500	
Depreciation accumulated at 1 January 20X6		625
Inventory in trade at 1 January 20X6	26,000	
Receivables at 31 December 20X6	53,000	
Allowance for doubtful debts at 1 January 20X6		960
Cash in hand	50	
Cash at bank	4,050	
Payables for supplies		65,000
Proprietor's capital at 1 January 20X6		28,115
Drawings to 31 December 20X6	2,000	
Purchases	102,000	
Revenue		129,000
Wages	18,200	
Advertising	2,300	
Rates for 15 months to 31 March 20X7	1,500	
Bank charges	200	
	223,800	223,800

The following adjustments are to be made:

1 Depreciation of shop fittings £100

Depreciation of leasehold £625

2 A debt of £500 is irrecoverable and is to be written off; the doubtful debts allowance is to be increased to 2% of the receivables.

3 Advertising fees of £200 have been treated incorrectly as wages.

4 The proprietor has withdrawn goods costing £1,000 for his personal use; these have not been recorded as drawings.

5 The inventory in trade at 31 December 20X6 is valued at £30,000.

Required:

Prepare an extended trial balance at 31 December 20X6.

Workbook Activity 6

Willis

Willis extracts the following trial balance at 31 December 20X6.

	Dr £	Cr £
Capital		3,112
Cash at bank		2,240
Petty cash	25	
Plant and machinery at cost	2,750	
Accumulated depreciation at 1 January 20X6		1,360
Motor vehicles at cost	2,400	
Accumulated depreciation at 1 January 20X6		600
Fixtures and fittings at cost	840	
Accumulated depreciation at 1 January 20X6		510
Inventory at 1 January 20X6	1,090	
Receivables	1,750	
Allowance for doubtful debts		50
Payables		1,184
Purchases	18,586	
Revenue		25,795
Selling and distribution expenses	330	
Establishment and administration expenses	520	
Financial expenses	60	
	28,351	34,851

You discover the following:

1   Closing inventory is valued at £1,480.

2   The difference on the trial balance is a result of Willis' omission of the balance on his deposit account of £6,500. Willis transferred this amount on 30 September 20X6 by 31 December 20X6 the account had earned £50 interest, which has not yet been reflected in the ledgers.

3   All non-current assets are to be depreciated at 25% per annum on net book value.

4   The allowance for doubtful debts has been carried forward from last year. It is felt that receivables of £30 should be written off and the allowance increased to 5% of receivables.

5   Included in the selling and distribution expenses are £20 of payments which are better described as 'purchases'.

6   In establishment expenses are prepaid rent and rates of £30.

7   Also in establishment expenses are amounts paid for electricity. At 31 December 20X6 £28 was due for electricity.

8   An accrual of £50 should be made to cover accountancy fees.

9   The cash book does not reconcile with the bank statement since bank charges and interest have been omitted from the former, totalling £18.

10   On enquiring into Willis' drawings, you discover that £4,000 of the amount transferred to a deposit account on 30 September 20X6 was then immediately switched to Willis' private bank account.

Required:

Prepare an extended trial balance at 31 December 20X6.

 Workbook Activity 7

Data

Phil Townsend is the proprietor of Infortec Computers, a wholesale business which buys and sells computer hardware and software.

- You are employed by Phil Townsend to assist with the bookkeeping.

- The business currently operates a manual system consisting of a general ledger, a sales ledger and a purchase ledger.

- Double entry takes place in the general ledger and the individual accounts of receivables and payables are therefore regarded as memoranda accounts.

- Day books consisting of a purchases day book, a sales day book, a purchases returns day book and a sales returns day book are used. Totals from the various columns of the day books are transferred into the general ledger.

At the end of the financial year, on 30 November 20X3, the following balances were extracted from the main ledger:

	£
Capital	134,230
Purchases	695,640
Revenue	836,320
Inventory at 1 December 20X2	84,300
Rent paid	36,000
Salaries	37,860
Motor vehicles (MV) at cost	32,400
Accumulated depreciation (MV)	8,730
Fixtures and fittings (F&F) at cost	50,610
Accumulated depreciation (F&F)	12,340
Purchases returns	10,780
Sales returns	5,270
Drawings	55,910
Insurance	4,760
Sales ledger control account	73,450
Purchases ledger control account	56,590
Irrecoverable debts	3,670
Allowance for doubtful debts	3,060
Bank overdraft	10,800
Cash	1,980
VAT (credit balance)	5,410
Discounts allowed	6,770
Discounts received	4,380

Task 1

Enter the balances into the columns of the trial balance provided below. Total the two columns and enter an appropriate suspense account balance to ensure that the two totals agree.

Trial balance as at 30 November 20X3

Description	Dr £	Cr £
Capital		
Purchases		
Revenue		
Inventory at 1 December 20X2		
Rent paid		
Salaries		
Motor vehicles (MV) at cost		
Accumulated depreciation (MV)		
Fixtures and fittings (F&F) at cost		
Accumulated depreciation (F&F)		
Purchases returns		
Sales returns		
Drawings		
Insurance		
Sales ledger control account		
Purchases ledger control account		
Irrecoverable debts		
Allowance for doubtful debts		
Bank overdraft		
Cash		
VAT (credit balance)		
Discounts allowed		
Discounts received		
Suspense account		

Data

Subsequent to the preparation of the trial balance, a number of errors were discovered which are detailed below.

(a) Drawings of £400 had been debited to the salaries account.

(b) The net column of the sales day book had been undercast by £100.

(c) The VAT column of the sales returns day book had been overcast by £60.

(d) A cheque for £120 paid to a credit supplier had been entered in the cash book but not in the relevant control account.

(e) A £3,000 cheque paid for rent had been debited to both the bank account and the rent paid account.

(f) The total column of the purchases day book had been overcast by £10.

(g) The discounts received ledger account had been overstated by £40.

(h) A £65 cheque paid for insurance, although correctly entered in the cash book, had been entered in the insurance account as £55.

Task 2

Prepare journal entries to record the correction of these errors. Dates and narratives are not required. Use the blank journal below.

JOURNAL		
	Dr £	Cr £

Workbook Activity 8

Data

Amanda Carver is the proprietor of Automania, a business which supplies car parts to garages to use in servicing and repair work.

- You are employed by Amanda Carver to assist with the bookkeeping.
- The business currently operates a manual system consisting of a main ledger, a sales ledger and a purchases ledger.
- Double entry takes place in the main ledger and the individual accounts of receivables and payables are therefore regarded as memoranda accounts.
- Day books consisting of a purchases day book, a sales day book, a purchases returns day book and a sales returns day book are used. Totals from the various columns of the day books are transferred into the general ledger.

At the end of the financial year, on 30 April 20X3, the balances were extracted from the general ledger and entered into an extended trial balance as shown below.

Task

Make appropriate entries in the adjustments columns of the extended trial balance to take account of the following:

(a)   Rent payable by the business is as follows:
      For period to 31 July 20X2   – £1,500 per month
      From 1 August 20X2   – £1,600 per month

(b)   The insurance balance includes £100 paid for the period of 1 May 20X3 to 31 May 20X3.

(c)   Depreciation is to be calculated as follows:
      Motor vehicles   – 20% per annum straight line method

      Fixtures and fittings   – 10% per annum reducing balance method

(d)   The allowance for doubtful debts is to be adjusted to a figure representing 2% of receivables.

(e)   Inventory has been valued at cost on 30 April 20X3 at £119,360. However, this figure includes old inventory, the details of which are as follows:
      Cost price of old inventory   – £3,660
      Net realisable value of old inventory – £2,060

Also included is a badly damaged car door which was to have been sold for £80 but will now have to be scrapped. The cost price of the door was £60.

(f) A credit note received from a supplier on 5 April 20X3 for goods returned was filed away with no entries having been made. The credit note has now been discovered and is for £200 net plus £35 VAT.

Extended trial balance at 30 April 20X3

Description	Ledger balances		Adjustments	
	Dr £	Cr £	Dr £	Cr £
Capital		135,000		
Drawings	42,150			
Rent	17,300			
Purchases	606,600			
Revenue		857,300		
Sales returns	2,400			
Purchases returns		1,260		
Salaries and wages	136,970			
Motor vehicles (MV) at cost	60,800			
Accumulated depreciation (MV)		16,740		
Office equipment (F&F) at cost	40,380			
Accumulated depreciation (F&F)		21,600		
Bank		3,170		
Cash	2,100			
Lighting and heating	4,700			
VAT		9,200		
Inventory at 1 May 20X2	116,100			
Irrecoverable debts	1,410			
Allowance for doubtful debts		1,050		
Sales ledger control account	56,850			
Purchases ledger control account		50,550		
Sundry expenses	6,810			
Insurance	1,300			
Accruals				
Prepayments				
Depreciation				
Allowance for doubtful debts adjustments				
Closing inventory – SPL				
Closing inventory – SoFP				
Totals	**1,095,870**	**1,095,870**		

Note: Only the above columns of the extended trial balance are required for this question.

WORKBOOK ACTIVITIES
ANSWERS

Workbook Activities Answers

1 Double entry bookkeeping

Workbook Activity 5

Assets	Non-current assets (5,000 + 6,000)	11,000
	Cash (15,000 – 6,000)	9,000
	Inventory (4,000 – 1,500)	2,500
	Receivables	2,000
		24,500

Assets – Liabilities = Ownership interest

£24,500 – £4,000 = £20,500

Ownership interest has increased by the profit made on the sale of inventory.

Workbook Activity 6

The balance on the capital account represents the investment made in the business by the owner. It is a special liability of the business, showing the amount payable to the owner at the statement of financial position date.

Workbook Activity 7

Tony

Cash

	£		£
Capital (a)	20,000	Purchases (b)	1,000
Revenue (g)	1,500	Purchases (c)	3,000
Revenue (i)	4,000	Insurance (d)	200
		Storage units (e)	700
		Advertising (f)	150
		Telephone (h)	120
		Stationery (j)	80
		Drawings (k)	500
		Balance c/d	19,750
	25,500		25,500
Balance b/d	19,750		

Capital

	£		£
Balance c/d	20,000	Cash (a)	20,000
	20,000		20,000
		Balance b/d	20,000

Purchases

	£		£
Cash (b)	1,000	Balance c/d	4,000
Cash (c)	3,000		
	4,000		4,000
Balance b/d	4,000		

Insurance

	£		£
Cash (d)	200	Balance c/d	200
	200		200
Balance b/d	200		

Storage units – cost

	£		£
Cash (e)	700	Balance c/d	700
	700		700
Balance b/d	700		

Advertising

	£		£
Cash (f)	150	Balance c/d	150
	150		150
Balance b/d	150		

Telephone

	£		£
Cash (h)	120	Balance c/d	120
	120		120
Balance b/d	120		

Revenue

	£		£
Balance c/d	5,500	Cash (g)	1,500
		Cash (i)	4,000
	5,500		5,500
		Balance b/d	5,500

Stationery

	£		£
Cash (j)	80	Balance c/d	80
	80		80
Balance b/d	80		

Drawings

	£		£
Cash (k)	500	Balance c/d	500
	500		500
Balance b/d	500		

Workbook Activity 8

Dave

Cash

	£		£
Capital	500	Rent	20
Revenue	210	Electricity	50
		Drawings	30
		Car	100
		Balance c/d	510
	710		710
Balance b/d	510		

Capital

	£		£
Balance c/d	500	Cash	500
	500		500
		Balance b/d	500

Purchases

	£		£
Payables (A Ltd)	200	Balance c/d	200
	___		___
	200		200
	___		___
Balance b/d	200		

Payables

	£		£
Balance c/d	200	Purchases	200
	___		___
	200		200
	___		___
		Balance b/d	200

Revenue

	£		£
Balance c/d	385	Receivables (X Ltd)	175
		Cash	210
	___		___
	385		385
	___		___
		Balance b/d	385

Receivables

	£		£
Revenue	175	Balance c/d	175
	___		___
	175		175
	___		___
Balance b/d	175		

Electricity

	£		£
Cash	50	Balance c/d	50
	___		___
	50		50
	___		___
Balance b/d	50		

Rent

	£		£
Cash	20	Balance c/d	20
	20		20
Balance b/d	20		

Motor car

	£		£
Cash	100	Balance c/d	100
	100		100
Balance b/d	100		

Drawings

	£		£
Cash	30	Balance c/d	30
	30		30
Balance b/d	30		

Workbook Activity 9

Audrey Line

Cash

	£		£
Capital	6,000	Rent	500
Revenue	3,700	Shop fittings	600
		Payables	1,200
		Wages	600
		Electricity	250
		Telephone	110
		Drawings	1,600
		Balance c/d	4,840
	9,700		9,700
Balance b/d	4,840		

Capital

	£		£
		Cash	6,000

Revenue

	£		£
		Cash	3,700

Shop fittings

	£		£
Cash	600		

Rent

	£		£
Cash	500		

Telephone

	£		£
Cash	110		

Drawings

	£		£
Cash	1,600		

Purchases

	£		£
Payables	2,000		

Payables

	£		£
Cash	1,200	Purchases	2,000
Balance c/d	800		
	2,000		2,000
		Balance b/d	800

Wages

	£		£
Cash	600		

Electricity

	£		£
Cash	250		

2 Accounting for VAT (sales tax)

Workbook Activity 3

VAT control account

	£		£
Bank	8,455	Opening balance	8,455
Input VAT 143,600 × 20%	28,720	Output VAT	39,362
Balance carried down	10,642	236,175 × 20/120	
	———		———
	47,817		47,817
	———		———
		Balance brought down	10,642

The closing balance on the account represents the amount of VAT (sales tax) owing to HM Revenue and Customs.

3 Capital and revenue expenditure

Workbook Activity 7

Stapling machine

(a) No.

(b) Although, by definition, since the stapler will last a few years, it might seem to be a non-current asset, its treatment would come within the remit of the concept of materiality and would probably be treated as office expenses.

Workbook Activity 8

Office equipment

The item will have value in future years and could therefore be regarded as a non-current asset. However, the stronger argument is that this is not justified by the relatively small amount involved and the concept of materiality would suggest treatment as an expense of the year.

 ## Workbook Activity 9

Engine

This would typically represent capital expenditure. As the engine is being depreciated separately from the rest of the plane it is effectively an asset in its own right. Therefore the replacement of the separate component is like the purchase of a new asset.

If, on the other hand, the engine was depreciated as part of the plane as a whole it is likely that the replacement cost would simply be treated as a repair/refurbishment cost and would be accounted for as an expense.

4 Depreciation

Workbook Activity 9

Motor car cost

	£		£
20X3		**20X3**	
1 Jan Purchase ledger control	12,000	31 Dec Balance c/d	12,000
20X4		**20X4**	
1 Jan Balance b/d	12,000	31 Dec Balance c/d	12,000
20X5		**20X5**	
1 Jan Balance b/d	12,000	31 Dec Balance c/d	12,000
20X6			
1 Jan Balance b/d	12,000		

$$\text{Annual depreciation charge} = \frac{12,000 - 2,400}{4}$$

$$= £2,400$$

Motor car – accumulated depreciation account

	£		£
20X3		**20X3**	
31 Dec Balance c/d	2,400	31 Dec Depreciation expense	2,400
20X4		**20X4**	
31 Dec Balance c/d	4,800	1 Jan Balance b/d	2,400
		31 Jan Depreciation expense	2,400
	4,800		4,800
20X5		**20X5**	
31 Dec Balance c/d	7,200	1 Jan Balance b/d	4,800
		31 Dec Depreciation expense	2,400
	7,200		7,200
		20X6	
		1 Jan Balance b/d	7,200

Depreciation expense account

	£		£
20X3		**20X3**	
31 Dec Motor car accumulated depreciation	2,400	31 Dec SPL	2,400
20X4		**20X4**	
31 Dec Motor car accumulated depreciation	2,400	31 Dec SPL	2,400
20X5		**20X5**	
31 Dec Motor car accumulated depreciation	2,400	31 Dec SPL	2,400

Workbook Activity 10

(1)   Straight line method

$$\text{Annual depreciation} = \frac{\text{Cost} - \text{Scrap value}}{\text{Estimated life}}$$

$$= \frac{£6,000 - £1,000}{8 \text{ years}}$$

$$= £625 \text{ p.a.}$$

Machine account

	£		£
Year 1:			
Cost	6,000		

Accumulated depreciation

	£		£
Year 1:		**Year 1:**	
Balance c/d	625	Depreciation expense	625
Year 2:		**Year 2:**	
Balance c/d	1,250	Balance b/d	625
		Depreciation expense	625
	1,250		1,250
Year 3:		**Year 3:**	
Balance c/d	1,875	Balance b/d	1,250
		Depreciation expense	625
	1,875		1,875
		Year 4:	
		Balance b/d	1,875

Statement of financial position extract:

		Cost £	Accumulated depreciation £	Carrying value £
Non-current asset:				
Year 1	Machine	6,000	625	5,375
Year 2	Machine	6,000	1,250	4,750
Year 3	Machine	6,000	1,875	4,125

(2) Reducing balance method

		£
Cost		6,000
Year 1	Depreciation 20% × £6,000	1,200
		4,800
Year 2	Depreciation 20% × £4,800	960
		3,840
Year 3	Depreciation 20% × £3,840	768
Carrying value		3,072

Workbook Activity 11

Hilton

(a)

Workings

		Chopper £	Mincer £	Stuffer £	Total £
Cost		4,000	6,000	8,000	18,000
Depreciation	20X6 – 25%	(1,000)			(1,000)
Depreciation	20X7 – 25%	(1,000)	(1,500)		(2,500)
Depreciation	20X8 – 25%	(1,000)	(1,500)	(2,000)	(4,500)
Carrying value at 31 Dec 20X8		1,000	3,000	6,000	10,000

Machinery

	£		£
20X6		**20X6**	
Cash – chopper	4,000	Balance c/d	4,000
20X7		**20X7**	
Balance b/d	4,000		
Cash – mincer	6,000	Balance c/d	10,000
	10,000		10,000
20X8		**20X8**	
Balance b/d	10,000		
Cash – stuffer	8,000	Balance c/d	18,000
	18,000		18,000
20X9			
Balance b/d	18,000		

Accumulated depreciation (machinery)

	£		£
20X6		20X6	
Balance c/d	1,000	Depreciation expense (25% × £4,000)	1,000
20X7		20X7	
Balance c/d	3,500	Balance b/d	1,000
		Depreciation expense (25% × £10,000)	2,500
	3,500		3,500
20X8		20X8	
Balance c/d	8,000	Balance b/d	3,500
		Depreciation expense (25% × £18,000)	4,500
	8,000		8,000
		20X9	
		Balance b/d	8,000

Depreciation expense (machinery)

	£		£
20X6		20X6	
Accumulated depreciation	1,000	Statement of profit or loss	1,000
20X7		20X7	
Accumulated depreciation	2,500	Statement of profit or loss	2,500
20X8		20X8	
Accumulated depreciation	4,500	Statement of profit or loss	4,500

(b)

Workings

	Metro £	Transit £	Astra £	Total £
Cost	3,200	6,000	4,200	13,400
Depreciation 20X6 – 40%	(1,280)			(1,280)
CV 31.12.X6	1,920			
Depreciation 20X7 – 40%	(768)	(2,400)		(3,168)
CV 31.12.X7	1,152	3,600		
Depreciation 20X8 – 40%	(461)	(1,440)	(1,680)	(3,581)
Carrying value at 31 Dec 20X8	691	2,160	2,520	5,371

Motor vehicles

	£		£
20X6		**20X6**	
Cash – Metro	3,200	Balance c/d	3,200
20X7		**20X7**	
Balance b/d	3,200		
Cash – Transit	6,000	Balance c/d	9,200
	9,200		9,200
20X8		**20X8**	
Balance b/d	9,200		
Cash – Astra	4,200	Balance c/d	13,400
	13,400		13,400
20X9			
Balance b/d	13,400		

Accumulated depreciation (machinery)

	£		£
20X6		**20X6**	
Balance c/d	1,280	Depreciation charge	1,280
	1,280		1,280
20X7		**20X7**	
		Balance b/d	1,280
Balance c/d	4,448	Depreciation charge	3,168
	4,448		4,448
20X8		**20X8**	
		Balance b/d	4,448
Balance c/d	8,029	Depreciation charge	3,581
	8,029		8,029
		Balance b/d	8,029

Depreciation expense (motor vehicles)

	£		£
20X6		**20X6**	
Accumulated depreciation	1,280	Statement of profit or loss	1,280
20X7		**20X7**	
Accumulated depreciation	3,168	Statement of profit or loss	3,168
20X8		**20X8**	
Accumulated depreciation	3,581	Statement of profit or loss	3,581

Workbook Activity 12

Depreciation for vehicle sold 1 March 20X3 (18,000 × 20% × 3/12)	900
Depreciation for vehicle purchased 1 June 20X3 (10,000 × 20% × 6/12)	1,000
Depreciation for vehicle purchased 1 September 20X3 (12,000 × 20% × 3/12)	600
Depreciation for other vehicles owned during the year ((28,400 – 18,000) × 20%)	2,080
	——
Total depreciation for the year ended 30 November 20X3	4,580
	——

---

5 Disposal of capital assets

Workbook Activity 4

(a) **Profit or loss on disposal**

	£
Cost	12,000
Depreciation	(5,000)
	——
CV	7,000
	——

Comparing the carrying value of £7,000 with the sale proceeds of £4,000, there is a loss of (7,000 – 4,000) = £3,000.

(b) **Ledger account entries**

Disposal of non-current assets account

	£		£
Car cost	12,000	Accumulated depreciation	5,000
		Cash at bank a/c (sales proceeds)	4,000
		Loss on disposal	3,000
	——		——
	12,000		12,000
	——		——

Car account

	£		£
Balance b/d	12,000	Disposal a/c	12,000

Car accumulated depreciation account

	£		£
Disposal a/c	5,000	Balance b/d	5,000

Cash at bank account

	£		£
Disposal a/c	4,000		

Workbook Activity 5

Machinery

	£		£
20X7		20X7	
Cash	2,700	Balance c/d	2,700
20X8		20X8	
Balance b/d	2,700	Balance c/d	2,700
20X9		20X9	
Balance b/d	2,700	Disposals account	2,700

Accumulated depreciation (machinery)

	£		£
20X7		20X7	
Balance c/d	675	Depreciation expense (25% × £2,700)	675
20X8		20X8	
		Balance b/d	675
Balance c/d	1,181	Depreciation expense (25% × (£2,700 – £675))	506
20X9		20X9	
Disposals account	1,181	Balance b/d	1,181

Depreciation expense (machinery)

	£		£
20X7		**20X7**	
Accumulated depreciation	675	Statement of profit or loss	675
20X8		**20X8**	
Accumulated depreciation	506	Statement of profit or loss	506

Disposals

	£		£
20X9		**20X9**	
Machinery – cost	2,700	Accumulated depreciation	1,181
		Cash	1,300
		SPL – loss on disposal	219
	2,700		2,700

Workbook Activity 6

Keith

1   Calculate the Balance b/d position at 1 January 20X7:

		Cost	Accumulated depreciation		Accumulated depreciation at 1 Jan 20X7
		£		£	£
Piece machine	(1 June 20X5)	10,000	$\dfrac{£10,000}{5}$	2,000	4,000
Acrylic machine	(1 Jan 20X6)	5,000	$\dfrac{£5,000 - £1,000}{5}$	800	800
Heat seal machine	(1 June 20X6)	6,000	$\dfrac{£6,000}{5}$	1,200	1,200
		21,000		4,000	6,000

2   Calculate the annual depreciation on the new assets:

	Cost	Annual depreciation	
	£		£
20X7			
Lathe machine (1 Jan 20X7)	10,000	$\dfrac{£10,000}{4}$	2,500
Cutting machine (1 Apr 20X7)	12,000	$\dfrac{£12,000 - £1,000}{5}$	2,200
Assets b/d at 1 January 20X7	(calc from part 1)		4,000
Charge for the year (20X7)			8,700
20X8			
Lathe machine			2,500
Cutting machine			2,200
Laser machine (1 Jun 20X8)	28,000	$\dfrac{£28,000 - £2,800}{7}$	3,600
Assets b/d at 1 January 20X7			4,000
Charge for the year (20X8)			12,300
20X9			
Lathe machine			2,500
Cutting machine – disposed of			–
Laser machine			3,600
Micro-cutter (1 Apr 20X9)	20,000		
Add: Installation	1,500		
	21,500	$\dfrac{£21,500 - 3,000}{5}$	3,700
Assets b/d at 1 January 20X7			4,000
Charge for the year (20X9)			13,800

3   Show the ledger accounts

Plant and machinery account

	£		£
20X7			
Assets Balance b/d	21,000		
Lathe machine	10,000		
Cutting machine	12,000	Balance c/d 31.12.X7	43,000
	43,000		43,000
20X8			
Assets Balance b/d	43,000		
Laser machine	28,000	Balance c/d 31.12.X8	71,000
	71,000		71,000
20X9			
Assets Balance b/d	71,000	Disposal account	12,000
Micro-cutter			
Disposal	3,000		
Bank account	17,000		
Installation costs	1,500 21,500	Balance c/d 31.12.X9	80,500
	92,500		92,500

Accumulated depreciation

	£		£
20X7		**20X7**	
		Balance b/d (1)	6,000
Balance c/d	14,700	Depreciation account (2)	8,700
	14,700		14,700
		20X8	
		Balance b/d	14,700
Balance c/d	27,000	Depreciation account	12,300
	27,000		27,000
		20X9	
Disposal account (4)	4,400	Balance b/d	27,000
Balance c/d	36,400	Depreciation account	13,800
	40,800		40,800

4   Calculate the accumulated depreciation on the cutting machine disposed of:

Cutting machine	purchased	1 April 20X7
	disposed	1 March 20X9

Therefore depreciation should have been charged for 20X7 and 20X8 and none in 20X9, the year of sale.

Accumulated depreciation is £2,200 × 2 = £4,400.

Debit   Accumulated depreciation account   £4,400

Credit   Disposal account   £4,400

Depreciation expense

	£		£
20X7		**20X7**	
Accumulated depreciation	8,700	Statement of profit or loss	8,700
20X8		**20X8**	
Accumulated depreciation	12,300	Statement of profit or loss	12,300
20X9		**20X9**	
Accumulated depreciation	13,800	Statement of profit or loss	13,800

Disposals

	£		£
20X9			
Plant and machinery cost	12,000	Accumulated depreciation	4,400
		Part exchange – plant and machinery account	3,000
		Loss on disposal (bal fig)	4,600
	12,000		12,000

5   Disposal journal entries for part exchange:

Debit	Plant and machinery account	£3,000	
Credit	Disposal account		£3,000

Part exchange allowance.

Debit	Statement of profit or loss	£4,600	
Credit	Disposal account		£4,600

Loss on sale

Debit Cost	Plant and machinery (£20,000 – £3,000)	£17,000	
	Installation	£1,500	
		£18,500	
Credit	Bank account		£18,500

Balance on cost of new machine – micro-cutter

6   Show extracts from financial statements:

Statement of profit or loss extracts

	20X7 £	20X8 £	2009 £
Depreciation	8,700	12,300	13,800
Loss on disposal	–	–	4,600

Statement of financial position extracts

		Cost £	Accumulated depreciation £	Carrying value £
Non-current assets				
20X7	Plant and machinery	43,000	14,700	28,300
20X8	Plant and machinery	71,000	27,000	44,000
20X9	Plant and machinery	80,500	36,400	44,100

Workbook Activity 7

Disposals account

	£		£
Motor vehicles	12,000	Accumulated depreciation	3,800
Profit on disposal	1,800	Motor vehicles (part ex)	10,000
	13,800		13,800

Accumulated depreciation = £12,000 × 20% × 19/12 = 3,800

Workbook Activity 8

Motor van account

	£		£
Old van	16,400	Disposal account	16,400
Payables (21,000 – 5,500)	15,500		
Disposal account – trade in value	5,500	Balance c/d	21,000
	37,400		37,400
Balance b/d	21,000		

Accumulated depreciation

	£		£
Disposal account	9,840	Balance b/d (16,400 × 15% × 4)	9,840

Disposal account

	£		£
Cost	16,400	Accumulated depreciation	9,840
		Trade in value	5,500
		Loss on disposal	1,060
	16,400		16,400

7 Financial statements and accounting concepts

Workbook Activity 5

Lara

(a)

Cash

	£		£
Capital	200	Motor van	250
Marlar – loan account	1,000	Motor expenses	15
Revenue	105	Wages	18
Commission	15	Insurance	22
		Electricity	17
		Balance c/d	998
	1,320		1,320
Balance b/d	998		

Purchases

	£		£
Payables	296	Balance c/d	381
Payables	85		
	381		381
Balance b/d	381		

Capital

	£		£
Balance c/d	200	Cash book	200
	200		200
		Balance b/d	200

Marlar – loan

	£		£
Balance c/d	1,000	Cash book	1,000
	1,000		1,000
		Balance b/d	1,000

Motor van

	£		£
Cash book	250	Balance c/d	250
	250		250
Balance b/d	250		

Revenue

	£		£
Balance c/d	105	Cash book	105
	105		105
		Balance b/d	105

Motor expenses

	£		£
Cash book	15	Balance c/d	15
	15		15
Balance b/d	15		

Wages

	£		£
Cash book	18	Balance c/d	18
	18		18
Balance b/d	18		

Insurance

	£		£
Cash book	22	Balance c/d	22
	22		22
Balance b/d	22		

Commission

	£		£
Balance c/d	15	Cash book	15
	15		15
		Balance b/d	15

Electricity

	£		£
Cash book	17	Balance c/d	17
	17		17
Balance b/d	17		

Payables

	£		£
Balance c/d	381	Purchases	296
		Purchases	85
	381		381
		Balance b/d	381

(b)

Lara

Trial balance at 31 July 20X6

	£	£
Cash	998	
Purchases	381	
Capital		200
Loan		1,000
Motor van	250	
Revenue		105
Motor expenses	15	
Wages	18	
Insurance	22	
Commission		15
Electricity	17	
Payables		381
	1,701	1,701

Workbook Activity 6

Peter

Trial balance at 31 December 20X8

	£	£
Fixtures and fittings	6,430	
Delivery vans	5,790	
Cash at bank	3,720	
General expenses	1,450	
Receivables	2,760	
Payables		3,250
Purchases	10,670	
Revenue		25,340
Wages	4,550	
Drawings	5,000	
Lighting and heating	1,250	
Rent, rates and insurance	2,070	
Capital		15,100
	43,690	43,690

Workbook Activity 7

Peter Wall

(a)

Cash

	£		£
Capital	10,000	Equipment	7,000
Loan	10,000	Ink	10
Revenue	200	Rent and rates	25
Receivables	60	Insurance	40
		Loan	400
		Loan interest	50
		Payables	200
		Payables	50
		Payables	100
		Balance c/d	12,385
	20,260		20,260
Balance b/d	12,385		

Payables

	£		£
Cash	200	Van	400
Cash	50	Purchases of paper	100
Cash	100		
Balance c/d	150		
	500		500
		Balance b/d	150

Capital

	£		£
		Cash	10,000

Loan account

	£		£
Cash	400	Cash	10,000
Balance c/d	9,600		
	10,000		10,000
		Balance b/d	9,600

Equipment

	£		£
Cash	7,000		

Van

	£		£
Payables (Arnold)	400		

Purchases of paper

	£		£
Payables (Butcher)	100		

Ink

	£		£
Cash	10		

Rent and rates

	£		£
Cash	25		

Loan interest

	£		£
Cash	50		

Insurance

	£		£
Cash	40		

Revenue

	£		£
Balance c/d	300	Cash	200
		Receivables (Constantine)	100
	___		___
	300		300
	___		___
		Balance b/d	300

Receivables

	£		£
Revenue	100	Cash	60
		Balance c/d	40
	___		___
	100		100
	___		___
Balance b/d	40		

(b)

Trial balance at 31 March 20X8

	Debit £	Credit £
Cash	12,385	
Payables		150
Capital		10,000
Loan		9,600
Equipment	7,000	
Van	400	
Purchases of paper	100	
Purchases of ink	10	
Rent and rates	25	
Loan interest	50	
Insurance	40	
Revenue		300
Receivables	40	
	_____	_____
	20,050	20,050
	_____	_____

8 Accounting for inventory

Workbook Activity 4

M E M O

To: Phil Townsend   **Ref:** Valuation of inventory

From: Accounting Technician   **Date:** 29 November 20XX

I note your observations concerning the inventory valuation and the issue of the Mica 40z PCs.

IAS 2 Inventory, states that inventory should be valued at the lower of cost and net realisable value. The NRV of a Mica 40z is £480.

If we were confident that we could sell them at that price then that would be the value for inventory purposes as this is lower than their cost of £500.

However, as you feel we are likely to scrap these computers, then I recommend we write them off to a zero inventory valuation immediately as the net realisable value is, in effect, zero.

Workbook Activity 5

MEMO

To: Melanie Langton   **Ref:** Closing inventory valuation
From: Accounting Technician   **Date:** X-X-20XX

I refer to your recent note concerning the valuation of the closing inventory. As far as the accounting concepts are concerned, the cost of inventory would normally be matched against income in compliance with the accruals concept (i.e. purchase costs of inventory are recognised in the same period as the revenue from selling those items). Most of your inventory will be valued at cost rather than net realisable value, as the latter is usually higher than cost due to the need to achieve profit margins, and IAS 2 requires inventory to be valued at the lower of cost and net realisable value. If, however, the estimated selling price were to fall below cost (for example if market conditions changed or if the goods became damaged) then the IAS 2 principle just identified would require you to impair the value of inventory down to the estimated NRV.

I hope this fully explains the points raised in your note.

9   Irrecoverable and doubtful debts

Workbook Activity 5

Step 1

Write up the receivables account showing the opening balance, the credit sales for the year and the cash received.

Receivables

20X6		£	20X6		£
1 Jan	Bal b/d	68,000	31 Dec	Cash	340,000
31 Dec	Revenue	354,000			

Step 2

Write off the irrecoverable debts for the period:

Dr   Irrecoverable debts expense account

Cr   Receivables account

Irrecoverable debts expense

20X6		£	20X6	£
31 Dec	Receivables	2,000		

Receivables

20X6		£	20X6		£
1 Jan	Balance b/d	68,000	31 Dec	Cash	340,000
			31 Dec	Irrecoverable	
31 Dec	Revenue	354,000		debts expense	2,000

Step 3

Balance off the receivables account to find the closing balance against which the allowance is required.

Receivables

20X6		£	20X6		£
1 Jan	Balance b/d	68,000	31 Dec	Cash	340,000
31 Dec	Revenue	354,000	31 Dec	Irrecoverable	
				debts expense	2,000
			31 Dec	Balance c/d	80,000
		422,000			422,000
20X7					
1 Jan	Balance b/d	80,000			

Step 4

Set up the allowance required of 5% of £80,000 = £4,000. Remember that there is already an opening balance on the allowance for doubtful debts account of £3,400 therefore only the increase in allowance required of £600 is credited to the allowance account and debited to the allowance for doubtful debt adjustment account.

Allowance for doubtful debt adjustment

20X6	£	20X6	£
Allowance for doubtful debts	600	31 Dec SPL	600
	600		600

Allowance for doubtful debts

20X6	£	20X6	£
		1 Jan Balance b/d	3,400
31 Dec Balance c/d		31 Dec Allowance for	
	4,000	doubtful debt adjustment	600
	4,000		4,000
		20X7	
		1 Jan Balance b/d	4,000

Step 5

The relevant extract from the statement of financial position at 31 December 20X6 would be as follows:

	£	£
Current assets		
Receivables	80,000	
Less: Allowance for doubtful debts	(4,000)	
		76,000

Workbook Activity 6

Angola

Allowance doubtful debts

	£		£
		Irrecoverable debts	
Balance c/d	530	expense account	530
	530		530
		Balance b/d	530

Irrecoverable debts expense

	£		£
Receivables written off		Statement of profit or loss	711
Cuba	46		
Kenya	29		
Peru	106		
Allowance account	530		
	711		711

Working – *Allowance carried down*

Specific:	£110 + £240	£350
General:	4% × (£5,031 – £46 – £29 – £106 – £350)	£180
		530

Note:

Only one account is being used for allowance for doubtful debt adjustment and irrecoverable debt expense. This is because the entries in the allowance for doubtful debt adjustment account and the irrecoverable debt expense account affect the statement of profit or loss.

Workbook Activity 7

Zambia

Allowance for doubtful debts

	£		£
		Balance b/d	530
Balance c/d (W1)	601	Irrecoverable debts expense account	
		extra charge required (W2)	71
	601		601
		Balance b/d	601

Working

1   **Allowance carried down**

		£
Specific:		
General:	5% × (£12,500 – £125 – £362)	601
		601

2   **Extra charge required**

	£
Allowance required at end of year	601
Allowance brought down and available	530
Increase required in allowance	71

Irrecoverable debts expense

	£		£
Receivables written off Fiji	125	Cash	54
Mexico	362	Statement of profit or loss	504
Allowance account	71		
	558		558

Workbook Activity 8

The accounting concept here is that of prudence.

---

10   Control account reconciliations

Workbook Activity 5

Mortimer Wheeler

(a)

Revenue

	£		£
SPL	3,475	Sales ledger control a/c	3,475

Purchases

	£		£
Purchases ledger control a/c	2,755	SPL	2,755

Sales ledger control account

	£		£
Balance b/d	5,783	Cash	3,842
Revenue	3,475	Irrecoverable debts – expense	1,950
		Balance c/d	3,466
	9,258		9,258
Balance b/d	3,466		

Purchases ledger control account

	£		£
Cash	1,773	Balance b/d	5,531
Discount	15	Purchases	2,755
Balance c/d	6,498		
	8,286		8,286
		Balance b/d	6,498

Allowance for doubtful debts

	£		£
Irrecoverable debt expense (bal figure)	909	Balance b/d	950
Balance c/d	41		
	950		950
		Balance b/d	41

Irrecoverable debt expense

	£		£
Sales ledger control account (Pitt-Rivers)	1,950	Allowance for doubtful debts	909
		SPL	1,041
	1,950		1,950

Sales ledger

Pitt-Rivers

	£		£
Balance b/d	1,900	Irrecoverable debt	1,950
Revenue	50		
	1,950		1,950

Evans

	£		£
Balance b/d	1,941	Cash	1,900
Revenue	1,760	Balance c/d	1,801
	3,701		3,701
Balance b/d	1,801		

Petrie

	£		£
Balance b/d	1,942	Cash	1,942
Revenue	1,665	Balance c/d	1,665
	3,607		3,607
Balance b/d	1,665		

Purchase ledger

Cunliffe

	£		£
Cash	900	Balance b/d	1,827
Discount	15	Purchases	950
Balance c/d	1,862		
	2,777		2,777
		Balance b/d	1,862

Atkinson

	£		£
Cash	50	Balance b/d	1,851
Balance c/d	2,486	Purchases	685
	2,536		2,536
		Balance b/d	2,486

Piggott

	£		£
Cash	823	Balance b/d	1,853
Balance c/d	2,150	Purchases	1,120
	2,973		2,973
		Balance b/d	2,150

(b) **List of receivables**

	£
Evans	1,801
Petrie	1,665
	3,466

List of payables

	£
Cunliffe	1,862
Atkinson	2,486
Piggott	2,150
	6,498

Workbook Activity 6

Robin & Co

(a)

Sales ledger control account

		£			£
30 Sep	Balance b/d	3,800	30 Sep irrecoverable debts account (2)		400
	Discounts allowed (4) (Wren)	25	Contra – Purchases ledger control account (5)		70
			Discount allow (6)		140
			Balance c/d		3,215
		3,825			3,825
1 Oct	Balance b/d	3,215			

(b) **List of sales ledger balances**

		£
Original total		3,362
Add	Debit balances previously omitted (1)	103
		3,465
Less	Item posted twice to Sparrow's account (3)	(250)
Amended total reconciling with balance on sales ledger control account		3,215

Workbook Activity 7

		£
Total from listing of balances		76,780
Adjustment for (a)	add/subtract*	400
Adjustment for (b)	add/subtract*	(100)
Adjustment for (c)	add/subtract*	(2,410)
Adjustment for (d)	add/subtract*	90
Adjustment for (e)	add/subtract*	(540)
Adjustment for (f)	add/subtract*	(770)
Revised total		73,450

Workbook Activity 8

	£
Total from listing of balances	76,670
Adjustment for (a) add/~~subtract~~	235
Adjustment for (b) ~~add~~/subtract	(3,200)
Adjustment for (c) ~~add~~/subtract	(720)
Revised total to agree with purchases ledger control account	72,985

Workbook Activity 9

(a) No

(b) The trial balance is constructed by extracting the various balances from the general ledger. If no errors have been made then the total of the debit balances should be equal to the total of the credit balances. In this case the error was made in the sales ledger and since the balances of the accounts in the sales ledger are not included in the trial balance, the error would not be detected.

12 Accruals and prepayments

Workbook Activity 8

Rent payable

	£		£
Cash paid	15,000	Statement of profit or loss	12,000
		Balance c/d (prepayment)	3,000
	15,000		15,000
Balance b/d (prepayment)	3,000		

Gas

	£		£
Gas paid	840	Statement of profit or loss	1,440
Balance c/d (840 × 5/7) (accrual)	600		
	1,440		1,440
		Balance b/d (accrual)	600

Advertising

	£		£
Cash	3,850	Statement of profit or loss	3,350
		Balance c/d (prepayment)	500
	3,850		3,850
Balance b/d (prepayment)	500		

Bank interest

	£		£
Cash	28	Statement of profit or loss	96
Cash	45		
Balance c/d ($^1/_3$ × 69) (accrual)	23		
	———		———
	96		96
	———		———
		Balance b/d (accrual)	23

Rates

	£		£
Balance b/d (prepayment $^3/_6$ × 4,800)	2,400	SPL	11,300
Cash	5,600		
Balance c/d ($^3/_6$ × 6,600) (accrual)	3,300		
	———		———
	11,300		11,300
	———		———
		Balance b/d (accrual)	3,300

Rent receivable

	£		£
Balance b/d (250 × 3/6) (receivable = accrued income)	125	Cash	250
Statement of profit or loss (W)	575	Cash	600
Balance c/d (3/12 × 600) (deferred income)	150		
	———		———
	850		850
	———		———
		Balance b/d (payable = deferred income)	150

Working – **Statement of profit or loss credit for rent receivable**

	£
1 January 20X4 – 31 March 20X4 ($^3/_6$ × 250)	125
1 April 20X4 – 31 December 20X4 ($^9/_{12}$ × 600)	450
	———
	575
	———

Workbook Activity 9

A Crew

Stationery

	£		£
31 Dec Balance per trial balance	560	31 Dec SPL	545
		31 Dec Balance c/d (prepayment)	15
	560		560
1 Jan Balance b/d (prepayment)	15		

Rent

	£		£
31 Dec Balance per trial balance	900	31 Dec SPL	1,200
31 Dec Balance c/d (accrual)	300		
	1,200		1,200
		1 Jan Balance b/d (accrual)	300

Rates

	£		£
31 Dec Balance per trial balance	380	31 Dec SPL	310
		31 Dec Balance c/d (prepayment (280 × 3/12)	70
	380		380
1 Jan Balance b/d (prepayment)	70		

Lighting and heating

	£		£
31 Dec Balance per trial balance	590	31 Dec SPL	605
31 Dec Balance c/d (accrual)	15		
	605		605
		1 Jan Balance b/d (accrual)	15

Insurance

	£		£
31 Dec Balance per trial balance	260	31 Dec SPL	190
		31 Dec Balance c/d (prepayment)	70
	260		260
1 Jan Balance b/d (prepayment)	70		

Wages and salaries

	£		£
31 Dec Balance per trial balance	2,970	31 Dec SPL	2,970

Workbook Activity 10

A Metro

Motor tax and insurance

	£		£
Balance b/d (prepayment)	570	SPL (W2)	2,205
Cash		Balance c/d (W1) (prepayment)	835
1 April	420		
1 May	1,770		
1 July	280		
	3,040		3,040
Balance b/d (prepayment)	835		

Workings

1 **Prepayment at the end of the year** £

Motor tax on six vans paid 1 April 20X0 ($\frac{3}{12} \times 420$)   105

Insurance on ten vans paid 1 May 20X0 ($\frac{4}{12} \times 1,770$)   590

Motor tax on four vans paid 1 July 20X0 ($\frac{6}{12} \times 280$)   140

Total prepayment   835

2 **SPL charge for the year**

There is no need to calculate this as it is the balancing figure, but it could be calculated as follows.

	£
Prepayment b/d	570
Motor tax ($\frac{9}{12} \times 420$)	315
Insurance ($\frac{8}{12} \times 1,770$)	1,180
Motor tax ($\frac{6}{12} \times 280$)	140
SPL charge	2,205

KAPLAN PUBLISHING

13 Suspense accounts and errors

Workbook Activity 5

Suspense account

	£		£
Balance b/d	1,075	Trial balance – difference	957
Postage (trial balance only) (a)	675	Payables control (b)	500
Sundry income (trial balance only) (d)	162	Non-current asset – cost (c)	1,575
Cash (e)	620		
Capital account – ETT (f)	500		
	3,032		3,032

Explanatory notes:

The £1,075 debit balance is already included in the books, whilst the £957 is entered on the credit side of the suspense account because the trial balance, as extracted, shows debits exceeding credits by £957. Although the two amounts arose in different ways they are both removed from suspense by the application of double entry

(a) The incorrect extraction is corrected by amending the balance on the trial balance and debiting the suspense account with £675. In this case the 'credit' entry is only on the trial balance, as the postages account itself shows the correct balance, the error coming in putting that balance on the trial balance.

(b) The non-entry of the £500 to the debit of X's account causes the account to be incorrectly stated and the trial balance to be unbalanced. To correct matters Dr Payables control Cr Suspense.

(c) The suspense entry here arose from adherence to double entry procedures, rather than a numerical error. In this case the bookkeeper should have Dr Non-current asset – cost, Cr Bank instead of Dr Suspense, Cr Bank, so to correct matters the entry Dr Non-current asset – cost, Cr Suspense is made.

(d) Is similar to (a), but note that the incorrect extraction of a credit balance as a debit balance means that twice the amount involved has to be amended on the trial balance and debited to suspense account.

(e) Is similar to (b) – on this occasion Dr Suspense, Cr Cash, and amend the cash account balance on the trial balance.

(f) Is similar to (c). The bookkeeper should have Dr Bank, Cr ETT – capital, but has instead Dr Bank, Cr Suspense, so to correct matters Dr Suspense, Cr Capital.

(g) Item (g) does not appear in the suspense account as the error does not affect the imbalance of the trial balance. As no entry has been made for the cheque, the correcting entry is

	£	£
Dr Cash at bank account	120	
Cr Receivables control account		120

(h) item (h) also does not appear in the suspense account. Although an entry has been made in the books which was wrong, the entry was incorrect for both the debit and credit entry. The correcting entry is

	£	£
Dr Cash at bank account	45	
Cr Receivables control account		45

Workbook Activity 6

Julia

Suspense account

	£		£
Difference on trial balance	144	SLCA (£27 × 2) (2)	54
Rent payable account (6)	30	SLCA (120 – 12) (4)	108
		Petty cash account (7)	12
	174		174

Journal entries

		£	£
Dr	H Myers' account	120	
	Cr A Myers' account		120

Correction of posting to incorrect personal account (1).

		£	£
Dr	Sales ledger control account	54	
	Cr Suspense account		54

Correction of posting to wrong side of SLCA (2).

		£	£
Dr	Revenue account	190	
	Cr Disposal account		190

Correction of error of principle – sales proceeds of plant previously posted to revenue account (3).

		£	£
Dr	SLCA	108	
	Cr Suspense account		108

Correction of posting £12 rather than £120 (4).

		£	£
Dr	Sales ledger control account	200	
	Cr Revenue account		200

Correction of undercasting of sales day book (5).

		£	£
Dr	Suspense account	30	
	Cr Rent payable account		30

Amount of accrual not Balance b/d on the account (6).

		£	£
Dr	Petty cash account (not posted)	12	
	Cr Suspense account		12

Balance omitted from trial balance (7).

14 The extended trial balance – in action

Workbook Activity 5

Extended trial balance of Randall at 31 Dec 20X6

Account	Trial balance Dr £	Trial balance Cr £	Adjustments Dr £	Adjustments Cr £	Statement of profit or loss Dr £	Statement of profit or loss Cr £	Statement of fin. pos. Dr £	Statement of fin. pos. Cr £
Fittings	2,000						2,000	
Accumulated depn 1 Jan 20X6		100		100				200
Leasehold	12,500						12,500	
Accumulated depn 1 Jan 20X6		625		625				1,250
Inventory 1 Jan 20X6	26,000				26,000			
Receivables	53,000			500			52,500	
Allowance doubtful debts 1 Jan 20X6		960		90				1,050
Cash in hand	50						50	
Cash at bank	4,050						4,050	
Payables		65,000						65,000
Capital		28,115						28,115
Drawings	2,000		1,000				3,000	
Purchases	102,000			1,000	101,000			
Revenue		129,000				129,000		
Wages	18,200			200	18,000			
Advertising	2,300		200		2,500			
Rates	1,500			300	1,200			
Bank charges	200				200			
Prepayments			300				300	
Depreciation Fittings			100		100			
Lease			625		625			
Irrecoverable debts			500		500			
Allowance for doubtful debts adjustment			90		90			
Closing inventory SoFP			30,000				30,000	
Closing inventory SPL				30,000		30,000		
Sub totals					150,215	159,000		
Net profit					8,785			8,785
Totals	223,800	223,800	32,815	32,815	159,000	159,000	104,400	104,400

Workbook Activity 6

Willis
Extended trial balance at 31 December 20X6

Account	Trial balance Dr £	Trial balance Cr £	Adjustments Dr £	Adjustments Cr £	Statement of profit or loss Dr £	Statement of profit or loss Cr £	Statement of fin. pos. Dr £	Statement of fin. pos. Cr £
Capital		3,112						3,112
Cash at bank		2,240		18				2,258
Petty cash	25						25	
Plant and machinery	2,750						2,750	
Accumulated depreciation		1,360		348				1,708
Motor vehicles	2,400						2,400	
Accumulated depreciation		600		450				1,050
Fixtures and fittings	840						840	
Accumulated depreciation		510		83				593
Inventory 1 Jan 20X6	1,090				1,090			
Receivables	1,750			30			1,720	
Allowance for doubtful debts		50		36				86
Payables		1,184						1,184
Purchases	18,586		20		18,606			
Revenue		25,795				25,795		
Selling and distribution	330			20	310			
Establishment and admin	520		28	30	518			
Financial expenses	60		18 50		128			
Deposit account	6,500		50	4,000			2,550	
Inventory at 31 Dec 20X6								
SoFP			1,480				1,480	
SPL				1,480		1,480		
Deposit interest				50		50		
Depreciation								
Plant and mach			348		348			
Motor vehicles			450		450			
F&F			83		83			
Irrecoverable debts expense			30					
Allowance for doubtful debts adjustment			36		66			
Drawings			4,000				4,000	
Accruals				28 50				78
Prepayments			30				30	
Profit					5,726			5,726
	34,851	34,851	6,623	6,623	27,325	27,325	15,795	15,795

Workbook Activity 7

Task 1

Trial balance as at 30 November 20X3

Description	Dr £	Cr £
Capital		134,230
Purchases	695,640	
Revenue		836,320
Inventory at 1 December 20X2	84,300	
Rent paid	36,000	
Salaries	37,860	
Motor vehicles (MV) at cost	32,400	
Accumulated depreciation (MV)		8,730
Fixtures and fittings (F&F) at cost	50,610	
Accumulated depreciation (F&F)		12,340
Purchases returns		10,780
Sales returns	5,270	
Drawings	55,910	
Insurance	4,760	
Sales ledger control account	73,450	
Purchases ledger control account		56,590
Irrecoverable debts	3,670	
Allowance for doubtful debts		3,060
Bank overdraft		10,800
Cash	1,980	
VAT (credit balance)		5,410
Discounts allowed	6,770	
Discounts received		4,380
Suspense account		5,980
	1,088,620	**1,088,620**

Task 2

Trial balance as at 30 November 20X3

JOURNAL		
	Dr £	Cr £
(a) Drawings account	400	
Salaries account		400
(b) Suspense account	100	
Revenue account		100
(c) Suspense account	60	
VAT account		60
(d) Purchases ledger control account	120	
Suspense account		120
(e) Suspense account	6,000	
Bank account		6,000
(f) Purchases ledger control account	10	
Suspense account		10
(g) Discounts received account	40	
Suspense account		40
(h) Insurance account	10	
Suspense account		10

Workbook Activity 8

Extended trial balance at 30 April 20X3

Description	Ledger balances		Adjustments	
	Dr	Cr	Dr	Cr
	£	£	£	£
Capital		135,000		
Drawings	42,150			
Rent	17,300		1,600	
Purchases	606,600			
Revenue		857,300		
Sales returns	2,400			
Purchases returns		1,260		200
Salaries and wages	136,970			
Motor vehicles (MV) at cost	60,800			
Accumulated depreciation (MV)		16,740		12,160
Office equipment (F&F) at cost	40,380			
Accumulated depreciation (F&F)		21,600		1,878
Bank		3,170		
Cash	2,100			
Lighting and heating	4,700			
VAT		9,200		35
Inventory at 1 May 20X2	116,100			
Irrecoverable debts	1,410			
Allowance for doubtful debts		1,050		87
Sales ledger control account	56,850			
Purchases ledger control account		50,550	235	
Sundry expenses	6,810			
Insurance	1,300			100
Accruals				1,600
Prepayments			100	
Depreciation			14,038	
Allowance for doubtful debts – adjustments			87	
Closing inventory – SPL				117,700
Closing inventory – SoFP			117,700	
TOTALS	**1,095,870**	**1,095,870**	**133,760**	**133,760**

MOCK ASSESSMENT

1 Mock Assessment Questions

Task 1.1

The following is a purchase invoice received by NFS Ltd:

Invoice 60754

To: NFS Ltd	Betty's	Date:
24 Roxburgh Place	42 Warwick Street	28 March 2009
Newcastle	Newcastle	
NE6 2HU	NE1 3TT	

		£
	Serial number 571GS90	
HP Printer		600.00
Delivery		10.00
Insurance		50.00
VAT @20%		132.00
Total		792.00

Settlement terms: strictly 30 days net

The following information relates to the sale of a vehicle:

Registration number	PQ09 NMH
Date of sale	20 March 09
Selling price excluding VAT	£4,600

- Bytes Technology Group has a policy of capitalising expenditure over £500.

- Vehicles are depreciated at 30% on a reducing balance basis.

- Computer Equipment is depreciated at 20% on a straight-line basis assuming no residual value.

- Non-current assets are depreciated in the year of acquisition but not in the year of disposal.

Record the following information in the non-current assets register below:

(a) Any acquisitions of non-current assets during the year ended 31 March 09

(b) Any disposals of non-current assets during the year ended 31 March 09

(c) Depreciation for the year ended 31 March 09

Non-current assets register

Description	Acquisition date	Cost £	Depreciation £	Carrying value £	Funding method	Disposal proceeds	Disposal date
Computer Equipment							
Mainframe Server	17/07/06	14,000.00			Cash		
Year end 31/03/07			2,800.00	11,200.00			
Year end 31/03/08			2,800.00	8,400.00			
Year end 31/03/09			2800	5600			
Printer	28/3/09	610			Cash		
Year end 31/03/09			122	488			
Motor Vehicles							
PQ09 NMH	14/09/07	9,000.00			Cash		
Year end 31/03/07			2,700.00	6,300.00			
Year end 31/03/08			1,890.00	4,410.00			
Year end 31/03/09						4600	20 3 9
EA55 SAR	12/02/08	10,000.00			Part-exchange		
Year end 31/03/08			3,000.00	7,000.00			
Year end 31/03/09			2100	4900			

Task 1.2

At the start of the financial year, the business had fixtures and fittings in the cost account of £35,000. The accumulated depreciation was £4,700 (see opening balances below).

During the year, the business disposed of fixtures and fittings. The original cost of the disposed asset was £1,700 and the carrying value was £1,200. They received a part-exchange value for this of £900 when they acquired new fixtures and fittings with total value of £3,000. The balance of the new purchase was paid for with a cheque.

Enter the Disposal and Acquisition into the Cost, Accumulated Depreciation, Disposals and Bank accounts below.

Balance the accounts and clearly show either the profit or loss on disposal.

Fixtures and fittings cost					
		£			£
Bal b/d		35,000			

Fixtures and fittings accumulated depreciation					
		£			£
			Bal b/d		4,700

Disposals					
		£			£

Bank					
		£			£

Task 1.3

Extending the trial balance

You are working on the final accounts of a business for year ended 31/12/09.

You have the following information. The figures below are net of VAT.

Balance at	01/01/09
Accrual telephone expenses	£90
Prepayment rent expenses	£400

(a)   The bank summary for the year shows payments for rent expenses of £1,600. The £1,600 paid was for rent from 1st March to 31st October 2009. Rent accrues evenly during the year.

Complete the ledger account below clearly showing the brought down and carried down figures as well as the rent for the year that needs to be taken to the statement of profit or loss.

Rent expenses

Date	Account name	£	Date	Account name	£

(b)   During the year £600 was paid out of the bank towards the Telephone expense account. On 31st January 2010, the business received a bill for £150 that related to the whole of November 2009, December 2009 and January 2010.

Complete the ledger account below clearly showing the brought down and carried down figures as well as the telephone expense for the year that needs to be taken to the statement of profit or loss.

Telephone expenses

Date	Account name	£	Date	Account name	£

(c) **Using the figures from your answers in (a) and (b) as well as balances given, complete the Trial Balance extract below as of 31st December 2009.**

Account	£	Dr	Cr
Revenue	9,690		
Discounts allowed	150		
SLCA	4,380		
Drawings	3,000		
Bank overdraft	350		
Accruals			
Prepayments			
Rent			
Telephone			
TOTALS			

Task 1.4

The following errors were identified when reconciling the sales ledger control account to the sales ledger.

(1)   A credit note for £100 was entered as an invoice in J Josie's individual account in the sales ledger.

(2)   A discount allowed of £10 to A Harman was omitted from his sales ledger.

(3)   An invoice for £453 in the sales ledger of G Shore was incorrectly posted as £435.

(4)   A bank receipt for £200 from a credit customer A Sloan was omitted from the sales ledger.

Use the following table to show the adjustments you need to make to the sales ledger.

Adjustment	Amount £	Debit	Credit
		(✓ as appropriate)	
(1)			
(2)			
(3)			
(4)			

Task 1.5

You are working on the preparation of a series of journal entries in preparation of a set of final accounts.

A trial balance has been prepared (and is included in task 1.6) and a suspense account has been opened with a credit balance of £4,485. You need to make some adjustments to eliminate the suspense account and other journals for adjustments are required.

(a) **A credit customer has gone into liquidation owing £2,500. This needs to be written off in the accounts. The management would also like an allowance for doubtful debts equal to 5% of the remaining receivables. The SLCA balance on the TB is £47,500.**

Journal	Dr	Cr

(b) **Cash sales of £3,600 including VAT were correctly entered into the bank account but no other entries were made.**

Journal	Dr	Cr

(c) The closing inventory has been valued at £4,577. Some of this inventory has been damaged. It originally cost £1,500 and can now only be sold on for £800. In order to sell the damaged goods, the business has also agreed to cover delivery costs of £50.

Journal	Dr	Cr

(d) Purchase information was transferred from the Purchase Day Book. There was a casting error in the total that went to the PLCA. This was undercast by £885.

Journal	Dr	Cr

You are now working on extending the trial balance for the adjustments you have dealt with in the journal entries prepared in Task 1.5.

Task 1.6

(a) Record these adjustments and extend the trial balance for each item dealt with in the journals.

(b) Extend the figures to the statement of profit or loss and statement of financial position.

ACCOUNT	Trial balance		Adjustments		SPL		SoFP	
	Dr	Cr	Dr	Cr	Dr	Cr	Dr	Cr
Capital		130,000						
Drawings	3,500							
Bank		574						
Motor Vehicles Cost	85,000							
Motor Vehicles Accumulated Depreciation		37,000						
Fixtures and Fittings Cost	129,000							
Fixtures and Fittings Accumulated Depreciation		54,000						
SLCA	47,500							
Allowance for Doubtful Debts		3,000						
PLCA		38,400						
Revenue		206,498						
Purchases	165,367							
Opening Inventory	3,205							
Rent	5,075							
Electricity	1,000							
Wages	43,900							
VAT		13,590						
Irrecoverable Debts	4,000							
Suspense		4,485						

(c) **Place a tick in the correct box(es)**

(i) **Which one of the following is NOT one of the Conceptual Framework's enhancing qualitative characteristics?**

Objective	Tick
Comparability	
Verifiability	
Relevance	
Understandability	

(ii) **Which one of these three would not require an adjustment in the cash book?**

Adjustment	Tick
Bank interest appears in the bank statement but has not been accounted for by the business	
The statement does not show a cheque that was paid into the bank yesterday	
A cheque received from a receivable has been placed on the debit side of the SLCA and the credit side of the cash book	

(iii) **Which of these can be capitalised as part of the cost of a new piece of machinery? (Please note, there could be more than one correct answer.)**

Adjustment	Tick
Delivery charges to get the machinery to the business' factory	
Insurance for the machinery	
Maintenance costs after machinery has been used by the business	
Essential repairs before the machinery can be used for the first time	

(iv) **Which of the following would appear on the credit side of the VAT account? (Please note, there could be more than one correct answer.)**

Adjustment	Tick
VAT on sales	
VAT on purchase returns	
VAT on van's part exchange value	
VAT on an irrecoverable debt	

1 Mock Assessment Answers

Task 1.1

Non-current assets register

Description	Acquisition date	Cost £	Depreciation £	Carrying value £	Funding method	Disposal proceeds	Disposal date
Computer Equipment							
Mainframe Server	17/07/06	14,000.00			Cash		
Year end 31/03/07			2,800.00	11,200.00			
Year end 31/03/08			2,800.00	8,400.00			
Year end 31/03/09			2,800.00	5,600.00			
HP Printer 571GS90	28/03/09	610.00			Credit		
Year end 31/03/09			122.00	488.00			
Motor Vehicles							
PQ09 NMH	14/09/07	9,000.00			Cash		
Year end 31/03/07			2,700.00	6,300.00			
Year end 31/03/08			1,890.00	4,410.00			
Year end 31/03/09						4600.00	20/03/09
EA55 SAR	12/02/08	10,000.00			Part-exchange		
Year end 31/03/08			3,000.00	7,000.00			
Year end 31/03/09			2,100.00	4,900.00			

Task 1.2

Fixtures and fittings cost

		£			£
Bal b/d		35,000	Disposals		1,700
Part exchange		900			
Bank		2,100	Bal c/d		36,300
		38,000			38,000
Bal b/d		36,300			

Fixtures and fittings accumulated depreciation

		£			£
Disposals		500	Bal b/d		4,700
Bal c/d		4,200			
		4,700			4,700
			Bal b/d		4,200

Disposals

		£			£
Fixtures and fittings		1,700	Accumulated depreciation		500
			Part exchange		900
			Loss on disposal		300
		1,700			1,700

Bank

		£			£
			Fixtures and fittings		2,100
Bal c/d		2,100			
		2,100			2,100
			Bal b/d		2,100

Task 1.3

(a)

Rent expenses

Date	Account name	£	Date	Account name	£
1/01/09	Bal b/d	400	31/12/09	Statement of profit or loss	2,400
31/12/09	Bank	1,600			
31/12/09	Bal c/d (W1)	400			
		2,400			2,400

(W1) Rent paid from 1 March to 31 October = £1,600 for 8 months.

Therefore monthly amount is £1,600/8 = £200.

Rent accrued November and December = £200 × 2 = £400

(b)

Telephone expenses

Date	Account name	£	Date	Account name	£
31/12/09	Bank	600	1/01/09	Bal b/d	90
31/12/09	Bal c/d (W1)	100	31/12/09	Statement of profit or loss	610
		700			700

(W1) Bill of £150 received after the year end on the 31 January

Telephone accrued November and December = £150 x 2/3 = £100

(c)

Account	£	Dr	Cr
Revenue	9,690		9,690
Discounts Allowed	150	150	
SLCA	4,380	4,380	
Drawings	3,000	3,000	
Bank Overdraft	350		350
Accruals			500
Prepayments			
Rent		2,400	
Telephone		610	
TOTALS		10,540	10,540

Task 1.4

Adjustment	Amount £	Debit	Credit
		(✓ as appropriate)	
(1)	200		✓
(2)	10		✓
(3)	18	✓	
(4)	200		✓

Task 1.5

(a)

Journal	Dr	Cr
Irrecoverable debt	2,500	
SLCA		2,500
Allowance for doubtful debts adjustment (SPL)	2,250	
Allowance for doubtful debt (SoFP)		2,250

(b)

Journal	Dr	Cr
Suspense	3,600	
Sales		3,000
VAT		600

(c)

Journal	Dr	Cr
Closing inventory – statement of financial position	3,827	
Closing inventory – statement of profit or loss		3,827

(d)

Journal	Dr	Cr
Suspense	885	
PLCA		885

Task 1.6 (a) – (b)

ACCOUNT	TRIAL BALANCE		ADJUSTMENTS		PROFITS + LOSS		BALANCE SHEET	
	Dr	Cr	Dr	Cr	Dr	Cr	Dr	Cr
Capital		130,000						130,000
Drawings	3,500						3,500	
Bank		574						574
Motor Vehicles Cost	85,000						85,000	
Motor Vehicles Accumulated Depreciation		37,000						37,000
Fixtures and Fittings Cost	129,000						129,000	
Fixtures and Fittings Accumulated Depreciation		54,000						54,000
SLCA	47,500			2,500			45,000	
Allowance for Doubtful Debts		3,000	750					2,250
PLCA		38,400		885				39,285
Revenue		206,498		3,000		209,498		
Purchases	165,367				165,367			
Opening Inventory	3,205				3,205			
Rent	5,075				5,075			
Electricity	1,000				1,000			
Wages	43,900				43,900			
VAT		13,590		600				14,190
Irrecoverable Debts	4,000		2,500		6,500			
Suspense		4,485	4,485					
Allowance for doubtful debt adjustments				750		750		
Closing inventory – Statement of financial position			3,827				3,827	
Closing inventory – Statement of profit or loss				3,827		3,827		
Loss for the year						10,972	10,972	
	487,547	487,547	11,562	11,562	225,047	225,047	277,299	277,299

(c)

(i)

Objective	Tick
Comparability	
Verifiability	
Relevance	✓
Understandability	

(ii)

Adjustment	Tick
Bank interest appears in the bank statement but has not been accounted for by the business	
The statement does not show a cheque that was paid into the bank yesterday	✓
A cheque received from a receivable has been placed on the debit side of the SLCA and the credit side of the cash book	

(iii)

Adjustment	Tick
Delivery charges to get the machinery to the business' factory	✓
Insurance for the machinery	
Maintenance costs after machinery has been used by the business	
Essential repairs before the machinery can be used for the first time	✓

(iv)

Adjustment	Tick
VAT on sales	✓
VAT on purchase returns	✓
VAT on Van's part exchange value	✓
VAT on an irrecoverable debt	

INDEX

KAPLAN PUBLISHING